T0071795

ON POETRY AND POETS

T. S. ELIOT

On Poetry and Poets

Farrar, Straus and Giroux

New York

Farrar, Straus and Giroux
18 West 18th Street, New York 10011

"The Fabulists" by Rudyard Kipling, quoted on pages 280–281, is from A *Diversity of Creatures*, copyright 1917 by Rudyard Kipling, reprinted by permission of Mrs. George Bambridge and Doubleday & Company, Inc.

Library of Congress Control Number: 2008944180
Paperback ISBN-13: 978-0-374-53197-3
Paperback ISBN-10: 0-374-53197-8

www.fsgbooks.com

P1

TO Valerie

Contents

ON POETRY AND POETS

Preface

WITH one exception [1] all the essays included in this book are subsequent to those included in my *Selected Essays*. Most of them were written within the last sixteen years. My *Selected Essays* was a miscellaneous collection; this book, as the title indicates, is limited to essays concerned with poets or with poetry.

The present collection differs from my *Selected Essays* in another respect. Only one essay in that book — the paper on Charles Whibley — was written for delivery to an audience; the rest were all written for publication in periodicals. Of the sixteen essays which make up the present book, ten were originally addressed directly to audiences; an eleventh essay, that on Virgil, was a broadcast talk. In publishing these addresses now, I have not attempted to transform them into what they might have been if originally designed for the eye instead of the ear; nor have I made alterations beyond omitting the prefatory remarks to *Poetry and Drama*, and also some of those preambular remarks and incidental pleasantries which, having been intended to seduce the listener, might merely irritate the reader. Nor did it seem to me right, in preparing for publication in one volume papers which were written at different times and for various occasions, either to remove passages which repeat statements made elsewhere, or to try to suppress inconsistencies and reconcile contradictions. Each item is substantially the same as on the date of its delivery or first publication.

[1] The paper on Sir John Davies which appeared in *The Times Literary Supplement* in 1926; it was rescued from oblivion, and recommended for inclusion here, by Mr. John Hayward.

Some papers or addresses, qualified by date and subject matter for inclusion, I have rejected, on re-reading after some lapse of time, as not good enough. I wish that I could have found worthy of inclusion two lectures delivered at Edinburgh University before the War, on *The Development of Shakespeare's Verse;* for what I was trying to say still seems to me worth saying. But the lectures struck me as badly written, and in need of thorough revision — a task to be deferred to some indefinite future. I regret the omission the less, however, as I had pillaged this set of lectures of one of its best passages — an analysis of the first scene of *Hamlet* — to incorporate in another address, *Poetry and Drama.* So, having already robbed one lecture for the benefit of another, I now append to *Poetry and Drama* another brief extract from the same Edinburgh lecture, a note on the balcony scene in *Romeo and Juliet.*

My acknowledgments appear in the form of footnotes to the several essays. They do not convey my grateful memories of hospitality in several cities — in Glasgow, Swansea, Minneapolis, Bangor [N. Wales] and Dublin. The debts of gratitude are too numerous to particularize; but as my essay on *Goethe as the Sage* was delivered on the occasion of my receiving the Hanseatic Goethe Prize, I should like to express my appreciation of the hospitality of the Stiftung F.V.S. [the foundation which awards the prize], the Rector of the University, and the Burgomaster and Senate of the City of Hamburg.

October 1956   T. S. E.

On Poetry

The Social Function of Poetry *

THE title of this essay is so likely to suggest different things to different people, that I may be excused for explaining first what I do not mean by it before going on to try to explain what I do mean. When we speak of the 'function' of anything we are likely to be thinking of what that thing *ought* to do rather than of what it does do or has done. That is an important distinction, because I do not intend to talk about what I think poetry *ought* to do. People who tell us what poetry ought to do, especially if they are poets themselves, usually have in mind the particular kind of poetry that they would like to write. It is always possible, of course, that poetry may have a different task in the future from what it has had in the past; but even if that is so, it is worth while to decide first what function it has had in the past, both at one time or another in one language or another, and universally. I could easily write about what I do with poetry myself, or what I should like to do, and then try to persuade you that this is exactly what all good poets have tried to do, or ought to have done, in the past — only they have not succeeded completely, but perhaps that is not their fault. But it seems to me probable that if poetry — and I mean *all* great poetry — has had no social function in the past, it is not likely to have any in the future.

When I say *all* great poetry I mean to avoid another way in

* An address delivered at the British-Norwegian Institute in 1943 and subsequently developed for delivery to an audience in Paris in 1945. It later appeared in *The Adelphi*.

which I might treat the subject. One might take up the various kinds of poetry, one after another, and discuss the social function of each kind in turn without reaching the general question of what is the function of poetry as poetry. I want to distinguish between the general and particular functions, so that we shall know what we are not talking about. Poetry may have a deliberate, conscious social purpose. In its more primitive forms this purpose is often quite clear. There are, for example, early runes and chants, some of which had very practical magical purposes — to avert the evil eye, to cure some disease, or to propitiate some demon. Poetry is early used in religious ritual, and when we sing a hymn we are still using poetry for a particular social purpose. The early forms of epic and saga may have transmitted what was held to be history before surviving for communal entertainment only; and before the use of written language a regular verse form must have been extremely helpful to the memory — and the memory of primitive bards, story-tellers and scholars must have been prodigious. In more advanced societies, such as that of ancient Greece, the recognized social functions of poetry are also very conspicuous. The Greek drama develops out of religious rites, and remains a formal public ceremony associated with traditional religious celebrations; the pindaric ode develops in relation to a particular social occasion. Certainly, these definite uses of poetry gave poetry a framework which made possible the attainment of perfection in particular kinds.

In more modern poetry some of these forms remain, such as that of the religious hymn which I have mentioned. The meaning of the term *didactic* poetry has undergone some change. *Didactic* may mean 'conveying information', or it may mean 'giving moral instruction', or it may mean something which comprehends both. Virgil's *Georgics*, for instance, are very beautiful poetry, and contain some very sound information about good farming. But it would seem impossible, at the present day, to write an up-to-date book about farming which should also be fine poetry: for one thing the subject itself has become much more complicated and scientific; and for another, it can be handled more readily in prose. Nor should we, as the Romans did, write astronomical and cosmological treatises in verse. The poem, the ostensible aim of which is to convey information, has been superseded by prose. Didactic poetry has gradually become limited to poetry of moral exhortation, or poetry which aims to *persuade* the reader to the author's point of view about something. It therefore includes a great deal of what can be called *satire*, though satire overlaps with burlesque and parody, the purpose of which is primarily to cause mirth. Some of Dryden's poems, in the seventeenth century, are satires in the sense that they aim to ridicule the objects against which they are directed, and also didactic in the aim to persuade the reader to a particular political or religious point of view; and in doing this they also make use of the allegorical method of disguising reality as fiction: *The Hind and the Panther*, which aims to persuade the reader that right was on the side of the Church of Rome against the Church of England, is his most remarkable poem in this kind. In the nineteenth century a good deal of the poetry of Shelley is inspired by a zeal for social and political reforms.

As for *dramatic* poetry, that has a social function of a kind now peculiar to itself. For whereas most poetry to-day is written to be read in solitude, or to be read aloud in a small company, dramatic verse alone has as its function the making an immediate, collective impression upon a large number of people gathered together to look at an imaginary episode acted upon a stage. Dramatic poetry is different from any other, but as its special laws are those of the drama its function is merged into that of the drama in general, and I am not here concerned with the special social function of the drama.

As for the special function of philosophical poetry, that would involve an analysis and an historical account of some length. I have, I think, already mentioned enough kinds of

poetry to make clear that the special function of each is related to some other function: of dramatic poetry to drama, of
didactic poetry of information to the function of its subject-
matter, of didactic poetry of philosophy or religion or politics
or morals to the function of these subjects. We might consider
the function of any of these kinds of poetry and still leave un-
touched the question of the function of *poetry*. For all these
things can be dealt with in prose.

But before proceeding I want to dismiss one objection that
may be raised. People sometimes are suspicious of any poetry
that has a particular purpose: poetry in which the poet is ad-
vocating social, moral, political or religious views. And they
are much more inclined to say that it isn't poetry when they
dislike the particular views; just as other people often think
that something is real poetry because it happens to express a
point of view which they like. I should say that the question
of whether the poet is using his poetry to advocate or attack a
social attitude does not matter. Bad verse may have a transient
vogue when the poet is reflecting a popular attitude of the moment; but real poetry survives not only a change of popular
opinion but the complete extinction of interest in the issues
with which the poet was passionately concerned. Lucretius'
poem remains a great poem, though his notions of physics and
astronomy are discredited; Dryden's, though the political quar-
rels of the seventeenth century no longer concern us; just as a
great poem of the past may still give great pleasure, though its
subject-matter is one which we should now treat in prose.

Now if we are to find the essential social function of poetry
we must look first at its more obvious functions, those which
it must perform if it is to perform any. The first, I think, that
we can be sure about is that poetry has to give pleasure. If you
ask what kind of pleasure then I can only answer, the kind of
pleasure that poetry gives: simply because any other answer
would take us far afield into aesthetics, and the general question of the nature of art.

I suppose it will be agreed that every good poet, whether he be a great poet or not, has something to give us besides pleasure: for if it were only pleasure, the pleasure itself could not be of the highest kind. Beyond any specific intention which poetry may have, such as I have already instanced in the various kinds of poetry, there is always the communication of some new experience, or some fresh understanding of the familiar, or the expression of something we have experienced but have no words for, which enlarges our consciousness or refines our sensibility. But it is not with such individual benefit from poetry, any more than it is with the quality of individual pleasure, that this paper is concerned. We all understand, I think, both the kind of pleasure which poetry can give, and the kind of difference, beyond the pleasure, which it makes to our lives. Without producing these two effects it simply is not poetry. We may acknowledge this, but at the same time overlook something which it does for us collectively, as a society. And I mean that in the widest sense. For I think it is important that every people should have its own poetry, not simply for those who enjoy poetry — such people could always learn other languages and enjoy their poetry — but because it actually makes a difference to the society as a whole, and that means to people who do not enjoy poetry. I include even those who do not know the names of their own national poets. That is the real subject of this paper.

We observe that poetry differs from every other art in having a value for the people of the poet's race and language, which it can have for no other. It is true that even music and painting have a local and racial character: but certainly the difficulties of appreciation in these arts, for a foreigner, are much less. It is true on the other hand that prose writings have significance in their own language which is lost in translation; but we all feel that we lose much less in reading a novel in translation than in reading a poem; and in a translation of some kinds of scientific work the loss may be virtually nil. That

poetry is much more local than prose can be seen in the history
of European languages. Through the Middle Ages to within a
few hundred years ago Latin remained the language for philosophy, theology, and science. The impulse towards the literary use of the languages of the peoples began with poetry.
And this appears perfectly natural when we realize that poetry
has primarily to do with the expression of feeling and emotion; and that feeling and emotion are particular, whereas
thought is general. It is easier to think in a foreign language
than it is to feel in it. Therefore no art is more stubbornly
national than poetry. A people may have its language taken
away from it, suppressed, and another language compelled
upon the schools; but unless you teach that people to *feel* in
a new language, you have not eradicated the old one, and it
will reappear in poetry, which is the vehicle of feeling. I have
just said 'feel in a new language', and I mean something more
than merely 'express their feelings in a new language'. A thought
expressed in a different language may be practically the same
thought, but a feeling or emotion expressed in a different language is not the same feeling or emotion. One of the reasons
for learning at least one foreign language well is that we acquire a kind of supplementary personality; one of the reasons
for not acquiring a new language *instead* of our own is that
most of us do not want to become a different person. A superior language can seldom be exterminated except by the ex-
termination of the people who speak it. When one language
supersedes another it is usually because that language has
advantages which commend it, and which offer not merely
a difference but a wider and more refined range, not only for
thinking but for feeling, than the more primitive language.

Emotion and feeling, then, are best expressed in the common language of the people — that is, in the language common to all classes: the structure, the rhythm, the sound, the
idiom of a language, express the personality of the people

which speaks it. When I say that it is poetry rather than prose that is concerned with the expression of emotion and feeling, I do not mean that poetry need have no intellectual content or meaning, or that great poetry does not contain more of such meaning than lesser poetry. But to develop this investigation would take me away from my immediate purpose. I will take it as agreed that people find the most conscious expression of their deepest feelings in the poetry of their own language rather than in any other art or in the poetry of other languages. This does not mean, of course, that true poetry is limited to feelings which everyone can recognize and understand; we must not limit poetry to *popular* poetry. It is enough that in a homogeneous people the feelings of the most refined and complex have something in common with those of the most crude and simple, which they have not in common with those of people of their own level speaking another language. And, when a civilization is healthy, the great poet will have something to say to his fellow countrymen at every level of education.

We may say that the duty of the poet, as poet, is only indirectly to his people: his direct duty is to his *language*, first to preserve, and second to extend and improve. In expressing what other people feel he is also changing the feeling by making it more conscious; he is making people more aware of what they feel already, and therefore teaching them something about themselves. But he is not merely a more conscious person than the others; he is also individually different from other people, and from other poets too, and can make his readers share consciously in new feelings which they had not experienced before. That is the difference between the writer who is merely eccentric or mad and the genuine poet. The former may have feelings which are unique but which cannot be shared, and are therefore useless; the latter discovers new variations of sensibility which can be appropriated by others. And in ex-

pressing them he is developing and enriching the language
which he speaks.

I have said quite enough about the impalpable differences of
feeling between one people and another, differences which are
affirmed in, and developed by, their different languages. But
people do not only experience the world differently in different
places, they experience it differently at different times. In fact,
our sensibility is constantly changing, as the world about us
changes: ours is not the same as that of the Chinese or the
Hindu, but also it is not the same as that of our ancestors
several hundred years ago. It is not the same as that of our
fathers; and finally, we ourselves are not quite the same persons that we were a year ago. This is obvious; but what is not
so obvious is that this is the reason why we cannot afford to
stop writing poetry. Most educated people take a certain pride
in the great authors of their language, though they may never
read them, just as they are proud of any other distinction of
their country: a few authors even become celebrated enough to
be mentioned occasionally in political speeches. But most people do not realize that this is not enough; that unless they go
on producing great authors, and especially great poets, their
language will deteriorate, their culture will deteriorate and
perhaps become absorbed in a stronger one.

One point is, of course, that if we have no living literature
we shall become more and more alienated from the literature
of the past; unless we keep up continuity, our literature of the
past will become more and more remote from us until it is as
strange to us as the literature of a foreign people. For our language goes on changing; our way of life changes, under the
pressure of material changes in our environment in all sorts of
ways; and unless we have those few men who combine an exceptional sensibility with an exceptional power over words, our
own ability, not merely to express, but even to feel any but the
crudest emotions, will degenerate.

It matters little whether a poet had a large audience in his own time. What matters is that there should always be at least a small audience for him in every generation. Yet what I have just said suggests that his importance is for his own time, or that dead poets cease to be of any use to us unless we have living poets as well. I would even press my first point and say that if a poet gets a large audience very quickly, that is a rather suspicious circumstance: for it leads us to fear that he is not really doing anything new, that he is only giving people what they are already used to, and therefore what they have already had from the poets of the previous generation. But that a poet should have the right, small audience in his own time *is* important. There should always be a small vanguard of people, appreciative of poetry, who are independent and somewhat in advance of their time or ready to assimilate novelty more quickly. The development of culture does not mean bringing everybody up to the front, which amounts to no more than making everyone keep step: it means the maintenance of such an *élite*, with the main, and more passive body of readers not lagging more than a generation or so behind. The changes and developments of sensibility which appear first in a few will work themselves into the language gradually, through their influence on other, and more readily popular authors; and by the time they have become well established, a new advance will be called for. It is, moreover, through the living authors that the dead remain alive. A poet like Shakespeare has influenced the English language very deeply, not only by his influence on his immediate successors. For the greatest poets have aspects which do not come to light at once; and by exercising a direct influence on other poets centuries later, they continue to affect the living language. Indeed, if an English poet is to learn how to use words in our time, he must devote close study to those who have used them best in *their* time; to those who, in their own day, have made the language new.

So far I have only suggested the final point to which I think the influence of poetry may be said to extend; and that can be put best by the assertion that, in the long run, it makes a difference to the speech, to the sensibility, to the lives of all the members of a society, to all the members of the community, to the whole people, whether they read and enjoy poetry or not: even, in fact, whether they know the names of their greatest poets or not. The influence of poetry, at the furthest periphery, is of course very diffused, very indirect, and very difficult to prove. It is like following the course of a bird or an aeroplane in a clear sky: if you have seen it when it was quite near, and kept your eye on it as it flew farther and farther away, you can still see it at a great distance, a distance at which the eye of another person, to whom you try to point it out, will be unable to find it. So, if you follow the influence of poetry, through those readers who are most affected by it, to those people who never read at all, you will find it present everywhere. At least you will find it if the national culture is living and healthy, for in a healthy society there is a continuous reciprocal influence and interaction of each part upon the others. And this is what I mean by the social function of poetry in its largest sense: that it does, in proportion to its excellence and vigour, affect the speech and the sensibility of the whole nation.

You must not imagine me to be saying that the language which we speak is determined exclusively by our poets. The structure of culture is much more complex than that. Indeed it will equally be true that the quality of our poetry is dependent upon the way in which the people use their language: for a poet must take as his material his own language as it is actually spoken around him. If it is improving, he will profit; if it is deteriorating, he must make the best of it. Poetry can to some extent preserve, and even restore, the beauty of a language; it can and should also help it to develop, to be just as subtle and precise in the more complicated conditions and for the changing purposes of modern life, as it was in and for a simpler age. But poetry, like every other single element in that mysterious social personality which we call our 'culture', must be dependent upon a great many circumstances which are beyond its control.

This leads me to a few after-thoughts of a more general nature. My emphasis to this point has been upon the national and local function of poetry; and this must be qualified. I do not wish to leave the impression that the function of poetry is to divide people from people, for I do not believe that the cultures of the several of Europe can flourish in isolation from each other. There have been, no doubt, in the past, high civilizations producing great art, thought and literature, which have developed in isolation. Of that I cannot speak with assurance, for some of them may not have been so isolated as at first appears. But in the history of Europe this has not been so. Even Ancient Greece owed much to Egypt, and something to the Asiatic frontiers; and in the relations of the Greek states to each other, with their different dialects and different manners, we may find a reciprocal influence and stimulus analogous to that of the countries of Europe upon each other. But the history of European literature will not show that any has been independent of the others; rather that there has been a constant give and take, and that each has in turn, from time to time, been revitalized by stimulation from outside. A general *autarky* in culture simply will not work: the hope of perpetuating the culture of any country lies in communication with others. But if separation of cultures within the unity of Europe is a danger, so also would be a unification which led to uniformity. The variety is as essential as the unity. For instance, there is much to be said, for certain limited purposes, for a universal *lingua franca* such as Esperanto or Basic English. But supposing that all communication between nations was carried on in such an artificial language, how imperfect it would be! Or rather, it would be wholly adequate in some respects, and there would be a complete lack of communication in others. Poetry is a constant reminder of all the things that can only be said in one language, and are untranslatable. The *spiritual* communication between people and people cannot be carried on without the individuals who take the trouble to learn at least one foreign language as well as one can learn any language but one's own, and who consequently are able, to a greater or less degree, to *feel* in another language as well as in their own. And one's understanding of another people, in this way, needs to be supplemented by the understanding of those individuals among that people who have gone to the pains to learn one's own language.

Incidentally, the study of another people's poetry is peculiarly instructive. I have said that there are qualities of the poetry of every language, which only those to whom the language is native can understand. But there is another side to this too. I have sometimes found, in trying to read a language which I did not know very well, that I did not understand a piece of prose until I understood it according to the standards of the school teacher: that is, I had to be sure of the meaning of every word, grasp the grammar and syntax, and then I could think the passage out in English. But I have also found sometimes that a piece of poetry, which I could not translate, containing many words unfamiliar to me, and sentences which I could not construe, conveyed something immediate and vivid, which was unique, different from anything in English — something which I could not put into words and yet felt that I understood. And on learning that language better I found that this impression was not an illusion, not something which I had imagined to be in the poetry, but something that was really there. So in poetry you can, now and then, penetrate into another country, so to speak, before your passport has been issued or your ticket taken.

The whole question of the relation of countries of different language but related culture, within the ambit of Europe, is therefore one into which we are led, perhaps unexpectedly, by inquiring into the social function of poetry. I certainly do not intend to pass from this point into purely political questions; but I could wish that those who are concerned with political questions would more often cross the frontier into these which I have been considering. For these give the spiritual aspect of problems the material aspect of which is the concern of politics. On my side of the line one is concerned with living things which have their own laws of growth, which are not always reasonable, but must just be accepted by the reason: things which cannot be neatly planned and put into order any more than the winds and the rains and the seasons can be disciplined.

If, finally, I am right in believing that poetry has a 'social function' for the whole of the people of the poet's language, whether they are aware of his existence or not, it follows that it matters to each people of Europe that the others should continue to have poetry. I cannot read Norwegian poetry, but if I were told that no more poetry was being written in the Norwegian language I should feel an alarm which would be much more than generous sympathy. I should regard it as a spot of malady which was likely to spread over the whole Continent; the beginning of a decline which would mean that people everywhere would cease to be able to express, and consequently be able to feel, the emotions of civilized beings. This of course might happen. Much has been said everywhere about the decline of religious belief; not so much notice has been taken of the decline of religious sensibility. The trouble of the modern age is not merely the inability to believe certain things about God and man which our forefathers believed, but the inability to *feel* towards God and man as they did. A belief in which you no longer believe is something which to some extent you can still understand; but when religious feeling disappears, the words in which men have struggled to express it become meaningless. It is true that religious feeling varies naturally from country to country, and from age to age, just as poetic feeling does; the feeling varies, even when the belief, the doctrine, remains the same. But this is a condition of human life, and what I am apprehensive of is death. It is equally possible that the feeling for poetry, and the feelings which are the material of poetry, may disappear everywhere: which might perhaps help to facilitate that unification of the world which some people consider desirable for its own sake.

The Music of Poetry *

THE poet, when he talks or writes about poetry, has peculiar qualifications and peculiar limitations: if we allow
for the latter we can better appreciate the former — a caution
which I recommend to poets themselves as well as to the
readers of what they say about poetry. I can never re-read any
of my own prose writings without acute embarrassment: I shirk
the task, and consequently may not take account of all the assertions to which I have at one time or another committed myself; I may often repeat what I have said before, and I may
often contradict myself. But I believe that the critical writings
of poets, of which in the past there have been some very distinguished examples, owe a great deal of their interest to the
fact that the poet, at the back of his mind, if not as his ostensible purpose, is always trying to defend the kind of poetry
he is writing, or to formulate the kind that he wants to write.
Especially when he is young, and actively engaged in battling
for the kind of poetry which he practises, he sees the poetry
of the past in relation to his own: and his gratitude to those
dead poets from whom he has learned, as well as his indifference to those whose aims have been alien to his own, may be
exaggerated. He is not so much a judge as an advocate. His
knowledge even is likely to be partial: for his studies will have
led him to concentrate on certain authors to the neglect of
others. When he theorizes about poetic creation, he is likely

* The third W. P. Ker Memorial Lecture, delivered at Glasgow University
in 1942, and published by Glasgow University Press in the same year.

to be generalizing one type of experience; when he ventures into aesthetics, he is likely to be less, rather than more competent than the philosopher; and he may do best merely to report, for the information of the philosopher, the data of his own introspection. What he writes about poetry, in short, must be assessed in relation to the poetry he writes. We must return to the scholar for ascertainment of facts, and to the more detached critic for impartial judgment. The critic, certainly, should be something of a scholar, and the scholar something of a critic. Ker, whose attention was devoted mainly to the literature of the past, and to problems of historical relationship, must be put in the category of scholars; but he had in a high degree the sense of value, the good taste, the understanding of critical canons and the ability to apply them, without which the scholar's contribution can be only indirect.

There is another, more particular respect in which the scholar's and the practitioner's acquaintance with versification differ. Here, perhaps, I should be prudent to speak only of myself. I have never been able to retain the names of feet and metres, or to pay the proper respect to the accepted rules of scansion. At school, I enjoyed very much reciting Homer or Virgil — in my own fashion. Perhaps I had some instinctive suspicion that nobody really knew how Greek ought to be pronounced, or what interweaving of Greek and native rhythms the Roman ear might appreciate in Virgil; perhaps I had only an instinct of protective laziness. But certainly, when it came to applying rules of scansion to English verse, with its very different stresses and variable syllabic values, I wanted to know why one line was good and another bad; and this, scansion could not tell me. The only way to learn to manipulate any kind of English verse seemed to be by assimilation and imitation, by becoming so engrossed in the work of a particular poet that one could produce a recognizable derivative. This is not to say that I consider the analytical study of metric, of the abstract forms which sound so extraordinarily different when handled by different poets, to be an utter waste of time. It is only that a study of anatomy will not teach you how to make a hen lay eggs. I do not recommend any other way of beginning the study of Greek and Latin verse than with the aid of those rules of scansion which were established by grammarians after most of the poetry had been written; but if we could revive those languages sufficiently to be able to speak and hear them as the authors did, we could regard the rules with indifference. We have to learn a dead language by an artificial method, and we have to approach its versification by an artificial method, and our methods of teaching have to be applied to pupils most of whom have only a moderate gift for language. Even in approaching the poetry of our own language, we may find the classification of metres, of lines with different numbers of syllables and stresses in different places, useful at a preliminary stage, as a simplified map of a complicated territory: but it is only the study, not of poetry but of poems, that can train our ear. It is not from rules, or by cold-blooded imitation of style, that we learn to write: we learn by imitation indeed, but by a deeper imitation than is achieved by analysis of style. When we imitated Shelley, it was not so much from a desire to write as he did, as from an invasion of the adolescent self by Shelley, which made Shelley's way, for the time, the only way in which to write.

The practice of English versification has, no doubt, been affected by awareness of the rules of prosody: it is a matter for the historical scholar to determine the influence of Latin upon the innovators Wyatt and Surrey. The great grammarian Otto Jespersen has maintained that the structure of English grammar has been misunderstood in our attempts to make it conform to the categories of Latin — as in the supposed 'subjunctive'. In the history of versification, the question whether poets have misunderstood the rhythms of the language in imitating foreign models does not arise: we must accept the practices of great poets of the past, because they are practices upon which our ear has been trained and must be trained. I believe that a number of foreign influences have gone to enrich the range and variety of English verse. Some classical scholars hold the view — this is a matter beyond my competence — that the native measure of Latin poetry was accentual rather than syllabic, that it was overlaid by the influence of a very different language — Greek — and that it reverted to something approximating to its early form, in poems such as the *Pervigilium Veneris* and the early Christian hymns. If so, I cannot help suspecting that to the cultivated audience of the age of Virgil, part of the pleasure in the poetry arose from the presence in it of two metrical schemes in a kind of counterpoint: even though the audience may not necessarily have been able to analyse the experience. Similarly, it may be possible that the beauty of some English poetry is due to the presence of more than one metrical structure in it. Deliberate attempts to devise English metres on Latin models are usually very frigid. Among the most successful are a few exercises by Campion, in his brief but too little read treatise on metrics; among the most eminent failures, in my opinion, are the experiments of Robert Bridges — I would give all his ingenious inventions for his earlier and more traditional lyrics. But when a poet has so thoroughly absorbed Latin poetry that its movement informs his verse without deliberate artifice — as with Milton and in some of Tennyson's poems — the result can be among the great triumphs of English versification.

What I think we have, in English poetry, is a kind of amalgam of systems of divers sources [though I do not like to use the word 'system', for it has a suggestion of conscious invention rather than growth]: an amalgam like the amalgam of races, and indeed partly due to racial origins. The rhythms of Anglo-Saxon, Celtic, Norman French, of Middle English and Scots, have all made their mark upon English poetry, together with the rhythms of Latin, and, at various periods, of French, Italian and Spanish. As with human beings in a composite race, different strains may be dominant in different individuals, even in members of the same family, so one or another element in the poetic compound may be more congenial to one or another poet or to one or another period. The kind of poetry we get is determined, from time to time, by the influence of one or another contemporary literature in a foreign language; or by circumstances which make one period of our own past more sympathetic than another; or by the prevailing emphasis in education. But there is one law of nature more powerful than any of these varying currents, or influences from abroad or from the past: the law that poetry must not stray too far from the ordinary everyday language which we use and hear. Whether poetry is accentual or syllabic, rhymed or rhymeless, formal or free, it cannot afford to lose its contact with the changing language of common intercourse.

It may appear strange, that when I profess to be talking about the 'music' of poetry, I put such emphasis upon conversation. But I would remind you, first, that the music of poetry is not something which exists apart from the meaning. Otherwise, we could have poetry of great musical beauty which made no sense, and I have never come across such poetry. The apparent exceptions only show a difference of degree: there are poems in which we are moved by the music and take the sense for granted, just as there are poems in which we attend to the sense and are moved by the music without noticing it. Take an apparently extreme example — the nonsense verse of Edward Lear. His non-sense is not vacuity of sense: it is a parody of sense, and that is the sense of it. The Jumblies is a poem of adventure, and of nostalgia for the romance of foreign voyage and exploration; The Yongy-Bongy Bo and The Dong with a Luminous Nose are poems of unrequited passion — 'blues' in fact. We enjoy the music, which is of a high order, and we enjoy the feeling of irresponsibility towards the sense. Or take a poem of another type, the Blue Closet of William Morris. It is a delightful poem, though I cannot explain what it means and I doubt whether the author could have explained it. It has an effect somewhat like that of a rune or charm, but runes and charms are very practical formulae designed to produce definite results, such as getting a cow out of a bog. But its obvious intention [and I think the author succeeds] is to produce the effect of a dream. It is not necessary, in order to enjoy the poem, to know what the dream means; but human beings have an unshakeable belief that dreams mean something: they used to believe — and many still believe — that dreams disclose the secrets of the future; the orthodox modern faith is that they reveal the secrets — or at least the more horrid secrets — of the past. It is a commonplace to observe that the meaning of a poem may wholly escape paraphrase. It is not quite so commonplace to observe that the meaning of a poem may be something larger than its author's conscious purpose, and something remote from its origins. One of the more obscure of modern poets was the French writer Stéphane Mallarmé, of whom the French sometimes say that his language is so peculiar that it can be understood only by foreigners. The late Roger Fry, and his friend Charles Mauron, published an English translation with notes to unriddle the meanings: when I learn that a difficult sonnet was inspired by seeing a painting on the ceiling reflected on the polished top of a table, or by seeing the light reflected from the foam on a glass of beer, I can only say that this may be a correct embryology, but it is not the meaning. If we are moved by a poem, it has meant something, perhaps something important, to us; if we are not moved, then it is, as poetry, meaningless. We can be deeply stirred by hearing the recitation of a poem in a language of which we understand no word; but if we are then told that the poem is gibberish and has no meaning, we shall consider that we have been deluded — this was no poem, it was merely an imitation of instrumental music. If, as we are aware, only a part of the meaning can be conveyed by paraphrase, that is because the poet is occupied with frontiers of consciousness beyond which words fail, though meanings still exist. A poem may appear to mean very different things to different readers, and all of these meanings may be different from what the author thought he meant. For instance, the author may have been writing some peculiar personal experience, which he saw quite unrelated to anything outside; yet for the reader the poem may become the expression of a general situation, as well as of some private experience of his own. The reader's interpretation may differ from the author's and be equally valid — it may even be better. There may be much more in a poem than the author was aware of. The different interpretations may all be partial formulations of one thing; the ambiguities may be due to the fact that the poem means more, not less, than ordinary speech can communicate.

So, while poetry attempts to convey something beyond what can be conveyed in prose rhythms, it remains, all the same, one person talking to another; and this is just as true if you sing it, for singing is another way of talking. The immediacy of poetry to conversation is not a matter on which we can lay down exact laws. Every revolution in poetry is apt to be, and sometimes to announce itself to be, a return to common speech. That is the revolution which Wordsworth announced in his prefaces, and he was right: but the same revolution had been carried out a century before by Oldham, Waller, Denham and Dryden; and the same revolution was due again something over a century later. The followers of a revolution develop the new poetic idiom in one direction or another; they polish or perfect it; meanwhile the spoken language goes on changing, and the poetic idiom goes out of date. Perhaps we do not realize how natural the speech of Dryden must have sounded to the most sensitive of his contemporaries. No poetry, of course, is ever exactly the same speech that the poet talks and hears: but it has to be in such a relation to the speech of his time that the listener or reader can say 'that is how I should

talk if I could talk poetry'. This is the reason why the best
contemporary poetry can give us a feeling of excitement and
a sense of fulfilment different from any sentiment aroused by
even very much greater poetry of a past age.

The music of poetry, then, must be a music latent in the
common speech of its time. And that means also that it must
be latent in the common speech of the poet's *place*. It would
not be to my present purpose to inveigh against the ubiquity
of standardized, or 'B.B.C.' English. If we all came to talk
alike there would no longer be any point in our not writing
alike: but until that time comes — and I hope it may be long
postponed — it is the poet's business to use the speech which
he finds about him, that with which he is most familiar. I
shall always remember the impression of W. B. Yeats reading
poetry aloud. To hear him read his own works was to be made
to recognize how much the Irish way of speech is needed to
bring out the beauties of Irish poetry: to hear Yeats reading
William Blake was an experience of a different kind, more
astonishing than satisfying. Of course, we do not want the
poet merely to reproduce exactly the conversational idiom of
himself, his family, his friends and his particular district: but
what he finds there is the material out of which he must make
his poetry. He must, like the sculptor, be faithful to the material in which he works; it is out of sounds that he has heard
that he must make his melody and harmony.

It would be a mistake, however, to assume that all poetry
ought to be melodious, or that melody is more than one of
the components of the music of words. Some poetry is meant
to be sung; most poetry, in modern times, is meant to be
spoken — and there are many other things to be spoken of
besides the murmur of innumerable bees or the moan of doves
in immemorial elms. Dissonance, even cacophony, has its
place: just as, in a poem of any length, there must be transitions between passages of greater and less intensity, to give a
rhythm of fluctuating emotion essential to the musical struc-

ture of the whole; and the passages of less intensity will be, in relation to the level on which the total poem operates, prosaic — so that, in the sense implied by that context, it may be said that no poet can write a poem of amplitude unless he is a master of the prosaic.[1]

What matters, in short, is the whole poem: and if the whole poem need not be, and often should not be, wholly melodious, it follows that a poem is not made only out of 'beautiful words'. I doubt whether, from the point of view of *sound* alone, any word is more or less beautiful than another — within its own language, for the question whether some languages are not more beautiful than others is quite another question. The ugly words are the words not fitted for the company in which they find themselves; there are words which are ugly because of rawness or because of antiquation; there are words which are ugly because of foreignness or ill-breeding [e.g. *television*]: but I do not believe that any word well-established in its own language is either beautiful or ugly. The music of a word is, so to speak, at a point of intersection: it arises from its relation first to the words immediately preceding and following it, and indefinitely to the rest of its context; and from another relation, that of its immediate meaning in that context to all the other meanings which it has had in other contexts, to its greater or less wealth of association. Not all words, obviously, are equally rich and well-connected: it is part of the business of the poet to dispose the richer among the poorer, at the right points, and we cannot afford to load a poem too heavily with the former — for it is only at certain moments that a word can be made to insinuate the whole history of a language and a civilization. This is an 'allusiveness' which is not the fashion or eccentricity of a peculiar type of poetry; but an allusiveness which is in the nature

[1] This is the complementary doctrine to that of the 'touchstone' line or passage of Matthew Arnold: this test of the greatness of a poet is the way he writes his less intense, but structurally vital, matter.

of words, and which is equally the concern of every kind of poet. My purpose here is to insist that a 'musical poem' is a poem which has a musical pattern of sound and a musical pattern of the secondary meanings of the words which compose it, and that these two patterns are indissoluble and one. And if you object that it is only the pure sound, apart from the sense, to which the adjective 'musical' can be rightly applied, I can only reaffirm my previous assertion that the sound of a poem is as much an abstraction from the poem as is the sense.

The history of blank verse illustrates two interesting and related points: the dependence upon speech and the striking difference, in what is prosodically the same form, between dramatic blank verse and blank verse employed for epical, philosophical, meditative and idyllic purposes. The dependence of verse upon speech is much more direct in dramatic poetry than in any other. In most kinds of poetry, the necessity for its reminding us of contemporary speech is reduced by the latitude allowed for personal idiosyncrasy: a poem by Gerard Hopkins, for instance, may sound pretty remote from the way in which you and I express ourselves — or rather, from the way in which our fathers and grandfathers expressed themselves: but Hopkins does give the impression that his poetry has the necessary fidelity to his way of thinking and talking to himself. But in dramatic verse the poet is speaking in one character after another, through the medium of a company of actors trained by a producer, and of different actors and different producers at different times: his idiom must be comprehensive of all the voices, but present at a deeper level than is necessary when the poet speaks only for himself. Some of Shakespeare's later verse is very elaborate and peculiar: but it remains the language, not of one person, but of a world of persons. It is based upon the speech of three hundred years ago, yet when we hear it well rendered we can forget the distance of time — as is brought home to us most patently in one of those plays, of which *Hamlet* is the chief, which can be fittingly produced in modern dress. By the time of Otway dramatic blank verse has become artificial and at best reminiscent; and when we get to the verse plays by nineteenth-century poets, of which the greatest is probably *The Cenci*, it is difficult to preserve any illusion of reality. Nearly all the greater poets of the last century tried their hands at verse plays. These plays, which few people read more than once, are treated with respect as fine poetry; and their insipidity is usually attributed to the fact that the authors, though great poets, were amateurs in the theatre. But even if the poets had had greater natural gifts for the theatre, or had toiled to acquire the craft, their plays would have been just as ineffective, unless their theatrical talent and experience had shown them the necessity for a different kind of versification. It is not primarily lack of plot, or lack of action and suspense, or imperfect realization of character, or lack of anything of what is called 'theatre', that makes these plays so lifeless: it is primarily that their rhythm of speech is something that we cannot associate with any human being except a poetry reciter.

Even under the powerful manipulation of Dryden dramatic blank verse shows a grave deterioration. There are splendid passages in *All for Love*: yet Dryden's characters talk more naturally at times in the heroic plays which he wrote in rhymed couplets, than they do in what would seem the more natural form of blank verse — though less naturally than do the characters of Corneille and Racine in French. The causes for the rise and decline of any form of art are always complex, and we can trace a number of contributory causes, while there seems to remain some deeper cause incapable of formulation: I should not care to advance any one reason why prose came to supersede verse in the theatre. But I feel sure that one reason why blank verse cannot be employed now in the drama is that so much non-dramatic poetry, and great non-dramatic poetry, has been written in it in the last three hundred years.

Our minds are saturated in these non-dramatic works in what is formally the same kind of verse. If we can imagine, as a flight of fancy, Milton coming before Shakespeare, Shakespeare would have had to discover quite a different medium from that which he used and perfected. Milton handled blank verse in a way which no one has ever approached or ever will approach: and in so doing did more than anyone or anything else to make it impossible for the drama: though we may also believe that dramatic blank verse had exhausted its resources, and had no future in any event. Indeed, Milton almost made blank verse impossible for any purpose for a couple of generations. It was the precursors of Wordsworth — Thompson, Young, Cowper — who made the first efforts to rescue it from the degradation to which the eighteenth-century imitators of Milton had reduced it. There is much, and varied, fine blank verse in the nineteenth century: the nearest to colloquial speech is that of Browning — but, significantly, in his monologues rather than in his plays.

To make a generalization like this is not to imply any judgment of the relative stature of poets. It merely calls attention to the profound difference between dramatic and all other kinds of verse: a difference in the music, which is a difference in the relation to the current spoken language. It leads to my next point: which is that the task of the poet will differ, not only according to his personal constitution, but according to the period in which he finds himself. At some periods, the task is to explore the musical possibilities of an established convention of the relation of the idiom of verse to that of speech; at other periods, the task is to catch up with the changes in colloquial speech, which are fundamentally changes in thought and sensibility. This cyclical movement also has a very great influence upon our critical judgment. At a time like ours, when a refreshment of poetic diction similar to that brought about by Wordsworth had been called for [whether it has been satisfactorily accomplished or not] we are inclined, in our judgments upon the past, to exaggerate the importance of the innovators at the expense of the reputation of the developers.

I have said enough, I think, to make clear that I do not believe that the task of the poet is primarily and always to effect a revolution in language. It would not be desirable, even if it were possible, to live in a state of perpetual revolution: the craving for continual novelty of diction and metric is as unwholesome as an obstinate adherence to the idiom of our grandfathers. There are times for exploration and times for the development of the territory acquired. The poet who did most for the English language is Shakespeare: and he carried out, in one short lifetime, the task of two poets. I can only say here, briefly, that the development of Shakespeare's verse can be roughly divided into two periods. During the first, he was slowly adapting his form to colloquial speech: so that by the time he wrote *Antony and Cleopatra* he had devised a medium in which everything that any dramatic character might have to say, whether high or low, 'poetical' or 'prosaic', could be said with naturalness and beauty. Having got to this point, he began to elaborate. The first period — of the poet who began with *Venus and Adonis*, but who had already, in *Love's Labour's Lost*, begun to see what he had to do — is from artificiality to simplicity, from stiffness to suppleness. The later plays move from simplicity towards elaboration. The late Shakespeare is occupied with the other task of the poet — that of experimenting to see how elaborate, how complicated, the music could be made without losing touch with colloquial speech altogether, and without his characters ceasing to be human beings. This is the poet of *Cymbeline*, *The Winter's Tale*, *Pericles*, and *The Tempest*. Of those whose exploration took them in this one direction only, Milton is the greatest master. We may think that Milton, in exploring the orchestral music of language, sometimes ceases to talk a social idiom at all; we may think that Wordsworth, in attempting to recover

the social idiom, sometimes oversteps the mark and becomes
pedestrian: but it is often true that only by going too far can
we find out how far we can go; though one has to be a very
great poet to justify such perilous adventures.

So far, I have spoken only of versification and not of poetic
structure; and it is time for a reminder that the music of verse
is not a line by line matter, but a question of the whole poem.
Only with this in mind can we approach the vexed question
of formal pattern and free verse. In the plays of Shakespeare
a musical design can be discovered in particular scenes, and in
his more perfect plays as wholes. It is a music of imagery as
well as sound: Mr. Wilson Knight has shown in his examination of several of the plays, how much the use of recurrent
imagery and dominant imagery, throughout one play, has to
do with the total effect. A play of Shakespeare is a very complex musical structure; the more easily grasped structure is that
of forms such as the sonnet, the formal ode, the ballade, the
villanelle, rondeau or sestina. It is sometimes assumed that
modern poetry has done away with forms like these. I have
seen signs of a return to them; and indeed I believe that the
tendency to return to set, and even elaborate patterns is permanent, as permanent as the need for a refrain or a chorus
to a popular song. Some forms are more appropriate to some
languages than to others, and any form may be more appropriate to some periods than to others. At one stage the stanza
is a right and natural formalization of speech into pattern. But
the stanza — and the more elaborate it is, the more rules to be
observed in its proper execution, the more surely this happens
— tends to become fixed to the idiom of the moment of its
perfection. It quickly loses contact with the changing colloquial speech, being possessed by the mental outlook of a past
generation; it becomes discredited when employed solely by
those writers who, having no impulse to form within them,
have recourse to pouring their liquid sentiment into a ready-
made mould in which they vainly hope that it will set. In a

perfect sonnet, what you admire is not so much the author's skill in adapting himself to the pattern as the skill and power with which he makes the pattern comply with what he has to say. Without this fitness, which is contingent upon period as well as individual genius, the rest is at best virtuosity: and where the musical element is the only element, that also vanishes. Elaborate forms return: but there have to be periods during which they are laid aside.

As for 'free verse', I expressed my view twenty-five years ago by saying that no verse is free for the man who wants to do a good job. No one has better cause to know than I, that a great deal of bad prose has been written under the name of free verse; though whether its authors wrote bad prose or bad verse, or bad verse in one style or in another, seems to me a matter of indifference. But only a bad poet could welcome free verse as a liberation from form. It was a revolt against dead form, and a preparation for new form or for the renewal of the old; it was an insistence upon the inner unity which is unique to every poem, against the outer unity which is typical. The poem comes before the form, in the sense that a form grows out of the attempt of somebody to say something; just as a system of prosody is only a formulation of the identities in the rhythms of a succession of poets influenced by each other.

Forms have to be broken and remade: but I believe that any language, so long as it remains the same language, imposes its laws and restrictions and permits its own licence, dictates its own speech rhythms and sound patterns. And a language is always changing; its developments in vocabulary, in syntax, pronunciation and intonation — even, in the long run, its deterioration — must be accepted by the poet and made the best of. He in turn has the privilege of contributing to the development and maintaining the quality, the capacity of the language to express a wide range, and subtle gradation, of feeling and emotion; his task is both to respond to change and make it conscious, and to battle against degradation below the standards which he has learnt from the past. The liberties that he may take are for the sake of order.

At what stage contemporary verse now finds itself, I must leave you to judge for yourselves. I suppose that it will be agreed that if the work of the last twenty years is worthy of being classified at all, it is as belonging to a period of search for a proper modern colloquial idiom. We have still a good way to go in the invention of a verse medium for the theatre, a medium in which we shall be able to hear the speech of contemporary human beings, in which dramatic characters can express the purest poetry without high-falutin and in which they can convey the most commonplace message without absurdity. But when we reach a point at which the poetic idiom can be stabilized, then a period of musical elaboration can follow. I think that a poet may gain much from the study of music: how much technical knowledge of musical form is desirable I do not know, for I have not that technical knowledge myself. But I believe that the properties in which music concerns the poet most nearly, are the sense of rhythm and the sense of structure. I think that it might be possible for a poet to work too closely to musical analogies: the result might be an effect of artificiality; but I know that a poem, or a passage of a poem, may tend to realize itself first as a particular rhythm before it reaches expression in words, and that this rhythm may bring to birth the idea and the image; and I do not believe that this is an experience peculiar to myself. The use of recurrent themes is as natural to poetry as to music. There are possibilities for verse which bear some analogy to the development of a theme by different groups of instruments; there are possibilities of transitions in a poem comparable to the different movements of a symphony or a quartet; there are possibilities of contrapuntal arrangement of subject-matter. It is in the concert room, rather than in the opera house, that the germ of a poem may be quickened. More than this I cannot say, but must leave the matter here to those who have had a musical education. But I would remind you again of the two tasks of poetry, the two directions in which language must at different times be worked: so that however far it may go in musical elaboration, we must expect a time to come when poetry will have again to be recalled to speech. The same problems arise, and always in new forms; and poetry has always before it, as F. S. Oliver said of politics, an 'endless adventure'.

What Is Minor Poetry? *

I DO not propose to offer, either at the beginning or at the end, a definition of 'minor poetry'. The danger of such a definition would be, that it might lead us to expect that we could settle, once for all, who are the 'major' and who are the 'minor' poets. Then, if we tried to make out two lists, one of major and one of minor poets in English literature, we should find that we agreed about a few poets for each list, that there would be more about whom we should differ, and that no two people would produce quite the same lists: and what then would be the use of our definition? What I think we can do, however, is to take notice of the fact that when we speak of a poet as 'minor', we mean different things at different times; we can make our minds a little clearer about what these different meanings are, and so avoid confusion and misunderstanding. We shall certainly go on meaning several different things by the term, so we must, as with many other words, make the best of it, and not attempt to squeeze everything into one definition. What I am concerned to dispel is any derogatory association connected with the term 'minor poetry', together with the suggestion that minor poetry is easier to read, or less worth while to read, than 'major poetry'. The question is simply, what kinds of minor poetry are there, and why should we read it?

* An address delivered before the Association of Bookmen of Swansea and West Wales at Swansea in September 1944. Subsequently published in *The Sewanee Review*.

The most direct approach, I think, is by considering the several kinds of anthologies of poetry: because one association of the term 'minor poetry' makes it mean 'the kind of poems that we only read in anthologies'. And, incidentally, I am glad of an opportunity to say something about the uses of anthologies, because, if we understand their uses, we can also be guarded against their dangers — for there are poetry-lovers who can be called anthology-addicts, and cannot read poetry in any other way. Of course the primary value of anthologies, as of all poetry, lies in their being able to give pleasure: but, beyond this, they should serve several purposes.

One kind of anthology, which stands by itself, is that which consists of poems by young poets, those who have not yet published volumes, or whose books are not yet widely known. Such collections have a particular value for both poets and readers, whether they represent the work of one group of poets, with certain principles in common, or whether the only unity of the contents is that given by the fact that all the poets belong to the same literary generation. For the young poet, it is generally desirable to have several stages of publicity, before he arrives at the point of having a small book all to himself. First, the periodicals: not the well-known ones with a national circulation — the only advantage, to the young poet, of appearing in these, is the possible guinea [or guineas] that he may receive on publication — but the small magazines, devoted to contemporary verse, and edited by young editors. These small magazines often appear to circulate only among contributors and would-be contributors; their condition is usually precarious, they appear at irregular intervals, and their existence is brief, yet their collective importance is out of all proportion to the obscurity in which they struggle. Apart from the value they may have in giving experience to future literary editors — and good literary editors have an important part to play in a healthy literature — they give the poet the advantage of seeing his work in print, of comparing it with that of his equally obscure, or slightly better known contemporaries, and of receiving the attention and criticism of those who are most likely to be in sympathy with his style of writing. For a poet must make a place for himself among other poets, and within his own generation, before he appeals to either a larger or an older public. To those people who are interested in publishing poetry, these small magazines also provide a means of keeping an eye on the beginners, and watching their progress. Next, a small group of young writers, with certain affinities or regional sympathies between them, may produce a volume together. Such groups frequently bind themselves together by formulating a set of principles or rules, to which usually nobody adheres; in course of time the group disintegrates, the feebler members vanish, and the stronger ones develop more individual styles. But the group, and the group anthology, serve a useful purpose: young poets do not ordinarily get, and indeed are better without, much attention from the general public, but they need the support and criticism of each other, and of a few other people. And, last, there are the more comprehensive anthologies of new verse, preferably compiled by more detached young editors. These have the value of giving the poetry reader a notion of what is going on, a chance of studying the changes in subject-matter and style, without going through a great number of periodicals or separate volumes; and they serve to direct his further attention to the progress of a few poets who may seem to him of promise. But even these collections do not reach the general reader, who as a rule will not have heard of any of the poets until they have produced several volumes and consequently found inclusion in other anthologies covering a greater span of time. When he looks at one of these books, he is apt to judge it by standards which should not be applied: to judge promise as if it were mature performance, and to judge the anthology, not by the few best poems in it, but at best by the average.

The anthologies which have the widest circulation are of

course those which, like the *Oxford Book of English Verse*, cover the whole of English literature up to the last generation; or those specializing in a particular period of the past; or those which cover the history of some part of poetry in English; or those which are limited to 'modern' poetry of the last two or three generations, including such living poets as have established some reputation. These last, of course, serve some of the purpose of the purely contemporary anthology as well. But, confining ourselves for convenience to those anthologies which include only the work of dead poets, let us ask what purposes they may be expected to serve their readers.

No doubt *The Golden Treasury*, or the *Oxford Book*, has given many people their introduction to Milton, to Wordsworth, or to Shelley [not to Shakespeare: but we don't expect to make our acquaintance with a dramatic poet through anthologies]. But I should not say that anyone who had read, and enjoyed, these poets, or half a dozen others, in an anthology, and yet had not the curiosity and appetite to tackle their complete works, and at least look to see what else they might like — I should not say that any such person was a real poetry lover. The value of anthologies in introducing us to the work of the greatest poets is soon over; and we do not go on reading anthologies for the selections from these poets, though they have to be there. The anthology also helps us to find out whether there are not some lesser poets of whose work we should like to know more — poets who do not figure so conspicuously in any history of literature, who may not have influenced the course of literature, poets whose work is not necessary for any abstract scheme of literary education, but who may have a strong *personal* appeal to certain readers. Indeed, I should be inclined to doubt the genuineness of the love of poetry of any reader who did not have one or more of these personal affections for the work of some poet of no great historical importance: I should suspect that the person who only liked the poets whom the history books agree to be the most important, was probably no more than a conscientious student, bringing very little of himself to his appreciations. This poet may not be very important, you should say defiantly, but his work is good for *me*. It is largely a matter of chance, whether and how one makes the acquaintance of such poetry. In a family library there may be a book which somebody bought at the time it was published, because it was highly spoken of, and which nobody read. It was in this way that I came across, as a boy, a poem for which I have preserved a warm affection: *The Light of Asia*, by Sir Edwin Arnold. It is a long epic poem on the life of Gautama Buddha: I must have had a latent sympathy for the subject-matter, for I read it through with gusto, and more than once. I have never had the curiosity to find out anything about the author but to this day it seems to me a good poem, and when I meet anyone else who has read and liked it, I feel drawn to that person. Now you don't, as a rule, come across extracts from forgotten epics in anthologies: nevertheless it is always possible that in an anthology you will be struck by some piece by an obscure author, which leads to a close acquaintance with the work of some poet whom nobody else seems to enjoy, or to have read.

Just as the anthology can introduce us to poets who are not very important, but whose work is what one happens to like, so a good anthology can give us useful knowledge of other poets who are very important, but whom we don't like. There are only two reasons for reading the whole of *The Faery Queen* or of Wordsworth's *Prelude*. One is that you enjoy reading it: and to enjoy either of the poems is a very good mark. But if you don't enjoy it, the only reason is that you are going to set up as a teacher of literature, or as a literary critic, and have *got* to know these poems. Yet Spenser and Wordsworth are both so important in the history of English literature because of all the other poetry which you understand better because of knowing them, that everybody ought to know something about them. There are not many anthologies which give substantial extracts from long poems — there is a very useful one, compiled by Charles Williams, who had the peculiar qualification of really enjoying all sorts of long poems which nobody else reads. But even a good anthology composed of short pieces can give one some knowledge, which is worth having, of those poets whom we do not enjoy. And just as everybody must have his personal tastes for some poetry which other people set no store by, so everybody, I suspect, has a blind spot towards the work of one or more poets who must be acknowledged to be great.

The next use of the anthology is one which can only be served if the compiler is not only very well read, but a man of very sensitive taste. There are many poets who have been generally dull, but who have occasional flashes. Most of us have not time to read through the works of competent and distinguished dull poets, specially those of another epoch, to find out the good bits for ourselves: and it would seldom be worth while even if we could afford the time. A century ago or more, every poetry lover devoured a new book by Tom Moore as soon as it came out: who to-day has read the whole even of *Lalla Rookh?* Southey was Poet Laureate, and accordingly wrote epics: I do know one person who had *Thalaba,* if not *The Curse of Kehama,* read to her as a child, and retains something of the same affection for it that I have for *The Light of Asia.* I wonder whether many people ever read *Gebir;* and yet Landor, the author of that dignified long poem, was a very able poet indeed. There are many long poems, however, which seem to have been very readable when they first appeared, but which no one now reads — though I suspect that nowadays, when prose fiction supplies the need that was filled, for most readers, by the verse romances of Scott and Byron and Moore, few people read a very long poem even when it is new from the press. So anthologies, and volumes of selections, are useful: because no one has time to read everything, and because there are poems only parts of which remain alive.

The anthology can have another use which, following the train of thought I have been pursuing, we might overlook. It lies in the interest of comparison, of being able to get, in a short space, a conspectus of the progress of poetry: and if there is much that we can only learn by reading one poet entire, there is much to learn by passing from one poet to another. To pass to and fro between a border ballad, an Elizabethan lyric, a lyric poem by Blake or Shelley, and a monologue by Browning, is to be able to get emotional experiences, as well as subjects for reflection, which concentration of attention on one poet cannot give. Just as in a well arranged dinner, what one enjoys is not a number of dishes by themselves but the combination of good things, so there are pleasures of poetry to be taken in the same way; and several very different poems, by authors of different temperaments and different ages, when read together, may each bring out the peculiar savour of each other, each having something that the others lack. To enjoy this pleasure we need a good anthology, and we need also some practice in the use of it.

I shall now return to the subject from which you may think that I have strayed. Though it is not only the minor poets who are represented in anthologies, we may think of the minor poets as those whom we only read in anthologies. I had to enter a *caveat* against this, in asserting that for every poetry reader there ought to be some minor poets whom it is worth while for *him* to read entire. But beyond this point we find more than one type of minor poet. There are of course poets who have written just one, or only a very few, good poems: so that there seems no reason for anybody going beyond the anthology. Such, for example, was Arthur O'Shaughnessy, whose poem beginning 'We are the music makers' is in any anthology which includes late nineteenth-century verse. Such, for some readers but not for all, will be Ernest Dowson, or John Davidson. But the number of poets of whom we can say that it holds true for all readers that they left only one or two particular

poems worth reading, is actually very small: the chances are
that if a poet has written one good poem, there will be something in the rest of his work which will be worth reading, for
at least a few persons. Leaving these few out of account, we
find that we often think of the minor poet as the poet who
has only written short poems. But we may at times also speak
of Southey, and Landor, and a host of writers in the seventeenth and eighteenth centuries, as minor poets also, although
they left poems of the most monumental size: and I think
that nowadays few, at least among younger readers, would
think of Donne as a minor poet, even if he had never written
satires and epistles, or of Blake as a minor poet, even if he had
never written his Prophetic Books. So we must count as minor
poets, in one sense, some poets whose reputation, such as it
is, rests upon very long poems; and as major poets, some who
wrote only short ones.

It might seem at first simpler to refer to the minor writers of
epics as *secondary*, or still more harshly as *failed great* poets.
They have failed, certainly, in the sense that no one reads their
long poems now: they are secondary, in the sense that we
judge long poems according to very high standards. We don't
feel that a long poem is worth the trouble unless it is, in its
kind, as good as *The Faery Queen*, or *Paradise Lost*, or *The
Prelude*, or *Don Juan*, or *Hyperion*, and the other long poems
which are in the first rank. Yet we have found that some of
these secondary poems are worth reading, for some people. We
notice further that we cannot simply divide long poems into a
small number of masterpieces and a large number of those we
needn't bother about. In between such poems as those I have
just mentioned, and an estimable minor work like *The Light
of Asia*, there are all sorts of long poems of different kinds and
of every degree of importance, so that we cannot draw any
definite line between the major and the minor. What about
Thomson's *Seasons* and Cowper's *Task?* — these are long poems
which, if one's interest lies in other directions, one may be con-

tent to know only by extracts; but I would not admit that they are minor poems, or that any part, of either of them, is as good as the whole. What about Mrs. Browning's *Aurora Leigh*, which I have never read, or that long poem by George Eliot of which I don't remember the name?

If we have difficulty in separating the writers of long poems into major and minor poets, we have no easier decision with writers of short poems. One very interesting case is George Herbert. We all know a few of his poems, which appear again and again in anthologies; but when we read through his collected poems, we are surprised to find how many of the poems strike us as just as good as those we have met within anthologies. But *The Temple* is something more than a number of religious poems by one author: it was, as the title is meant to imply, a book constructed according to a plan; and as we get to know Herbert's poems better, we come to find that there is something we get from the whole book, which is more than a sum of its parts. What has at first the appearance of a succession of beautiful but separate lyrics, comes to reveal itself as a continued religious meditation with an intellectual framework; and the book as a whole discloses to us the Anglican devotional spirit of the first half of the seventeenth century. What is more, we get to understand Herbert better, and feel rewarded for the trouble, if we know something about the English theological writers of his time; if we know something about the English mystical writers of the fourteenth century; and if we know something of certain other poets his contemporaries — Donne, Vaughan and Traherne, and come to perceive something in common between them in their Welsh origin and background; and finally, we learn something about Herbert by comparing the typical Anglican devotion which he expresses, with the more continental, and Roman, religious feeling of his contemporary Richard Crashaw. So in the end, I, for one, cannot admit that Herbert can be called a 'minor'

poet: for it is not of a few favourite poems that I am reminded
when I think of him, but of the whole work.

Now compare Herbert with two other poets, one a little
senior to him, and one of the previous generation, but both
very distinguished writers of lyrics. From the poems of Robert
Herrick, also an Anglican parson, but a man of very different
temperament, we also get the feeling of a unifying personality,
and we get to know this personality better by reading all of his
poems, and for having read all of his poems we enjoy still better the ones we like best. But first, there is no such continuous
conscious *purpose* about Herrick's poems; he is more the purely
natural and un-selfconscious man, writing his poems as the
fancy seizes him; and second, the personality expressed in them
is less unusual — in fact, it is its honest *ordinariness* which
gives the charm. Relatively, we get much more of him from
one poem than we do of Herbert from one poem: still, there
is *something* more in the whole than in the parts. Next, consider Thomas Campion, the Elizabethan writer of songs. I
should say that within his limits there was no more accomplished craftsman in the whole of English poetry than Campion. I admit that to understand his poems fully there are
some things one should know: Campion was a musician, and
he wrote his songs to be sung. We appreciate his poems better
if we have some acquaintance with Tudor music and with the
instruments for which it was written; we like them better if we
like this music; and we want not merely to read them, but to
hear some of them sung, and sung to Campion's own setting.
But we do not so much need to know any of the things that,
in the case of George Herbert, help us to understand him better and enjoy him more; we need not concern ourselves with
what he thought, or with what books he had read, or with his
racial background or his personality. All we need is the Elizabethan setting. What we get, when we proceed from those of
his poems which we read in anthologies, to read his entire collection, is a repeated pleasure, the enjoyment of new beauties

and new technical variations, but no such total impression. We cannot say, with him, that the whole is more than the sum of its parts.

I do not say that even this test — which, in any case, everyone must apply for himself, with various results — of whether the whole is more than the sum of its parts, is in itself a satisfactory criterion for distinguishing between a major and a minor poet. Nothing is so simple as that: and although we do not feel, after reading Campion, that we know the man Campion, as we do feel after reading Herrick, yet on other grounds, because he is so much the more remarkable craftsman, I should myself rate Campion as a more important poet than Herrick, though very much below Herbert. All I have affirmed is, that a work which consists of a number of short poems, even of poems which, taken individually, may appear rather slight, may, if it has a unity of underlying pattern, be the equivalent of a first-rate long poem in establishing an author's claim to be a 'major' poet. That claim may, of course, be established by one long poem, and when that long poem is good enough, when it has within itself the proper unity and variety, we do not need to know, or if we know we do not need to value highly, the poet's other works. I should myself regard Samuel Johnson as a major poet by the single testimony of *The Vanity of Human Wishes*, and Goldsmith by the testimony of *The Deserted Village*.

We seem, so far, to have arrived at the tentative conclusion that, whatever a minor poet may be, a major poet is one the whole of whose work we ought to read, in order fully to appreciate any part of it: but we have somewhat qualified this extreme assertion already by admitting any poet who has written even one long poem which combines enough variety in unity. But there are certainly very few poets in English of whose work one can say that the whole ought to be read. Shakespeare, certainly, and Milton: and as to Milton one can point out that his several long poems, *Paradise Lost, Paradise*

Regained, and *Samson Agonistes,* not only should each be read entire, for its own sake — we need to read them all, just as we need to read *all* of the plays of Shakespeare, in order fully to understand any one of them; and unless we read Shakespeare's sonnets as well, and the minor poems of Milton, there is something lacking to our appreciation of what we have read. But the poets for whom one can make such a claim are very few. One can get on very well in life without having read all the later poems of Browning or Swinburne; I would not affirm confidently that one ought to read everything by Dryden or Pope; and it is certainly not for *me* to say that there is no part of *The Prelude* or *The Excursion* which will not bear skipping. Very few people want to give much time to the early long poems of Shelley, *The Revolt of Islam* and *Queen Mab,* though the notes to the latter poem are certainly worth reading. So we shall have to say that a major poet is one of whose work we have to read a great deal, but not always the whole. And besides asking the question, 'Of which poets is it worth while to read the whole work?' we must also ask the question, 'Of which poets is it worth *my* while to read the whole?' The first question implies that we should always be trying to improve our taste. The second implies that we must be sincere about what taste we have. So, on the one hand, it is no use diligently going through even Shakespeare or Milton from cover to cover, unless you come across something there which you like at once: it is only this immediate pleasure which can give you either the motive power to read the whole, or the prospect of any benefit when you have done so. And there may be, indeed, there should be — as I have already said — some poets who mean enough to *you* to make you read the whole of their work, though they may not have that value for most other people. And this kind of liking does not only pertain to a stage in your development of taste which you will outgrow, but may indicate also some affinity between yourself and a particular author which will last a lifetime: it may even be that you are peculiarly qualified to appreciate a poet whom very few other people are able to enjoy.

I should say then that there is a kind of orthodoxy about the relative greatness and importance of our poets, though there are very few reputations which remain completely constant from one generation to another. No poetic reputation ever remains exactly in the same place: it is a stock market in constant fluctuation. There are the very great names which only fluctuate, so to speak, within a narrow range of points: whether Milton is up to 104 to-day, and down to 97¼ to-morrow, does not matter. There are other reputations like that of Donne, or Tennyson, which vary much more widely, so that one has to judge their value by an average taken over a long time; there are others again which are very steady a long way below par, and remain good investments at that price. And there are some poets who are good investments for *some* people, though no prices are quoted for them on the market, and the stock may be unsaleable — I am afraid that the comparison with the stock exchange rather fades out at this point. But I should say that although there is an objective ideal of orthodox taste in poetry, no one reader can be, or should try to be, quite orthodox. There are certainly some poets, whom so many generations of people of intelligence, sensibility and wide reading have liked, that [if we like any poetry] it is worth our while to try to find out why these people have liked them, and whether we cannot enjoy them too. Of the smaller poets, there are certainly some about whom, after sampling, we can pretty safely take the usual opinion that they are quite adequately represented by two or three poems: for, as I have said, nobody has time to find out everything for himself, and we must accept some things on the assurance of others.

The majority of smaller poets, however — of those who preserve any reputation at all — are poets of whom every reader of poetry should know something, but only a few of whom any one reader will come to know well. Some appeal to us because of a peculiar congeniality of personality; some because of their subject-matter, some because of a particular quality, of wit or pathos for example. When we talk about Poetry, with a capital P, we are apt to think only of the more intense emotion or the more magical phrase: nevertheless there are a great many casements in poetry which are not magic, and which do not open on the foam of perilous seas, but are perfectly good windows for all that. I think that George Crabbe was a very good poet, but you do not go to him for magic: if you like realistic accounts of village life in Suffolk a hundred and twenty years ago, in verse so well written that it convinces you that the same thing could not be said in prose, you will like Crabbe: Crabbe is a poet who has to be read in large chunks, if at all; so if you find him dull you must just glance and pass by. But it is worth while to know of his existence, in case he might be to your liking, and also because that will tell you something about the people who do like him.

The chief points which I have so far tried to make are, I think, these: The difference between major and minor poets has nothing to do with whether they wrote long poems, or only short poems — though the *very* greatest poets, who are few in number, have all had something to say which could only be said in a long poem. The important difference is whether a knowledge of the whole, or at least of a very large part, of a poet's work, makes one enjoy more, because it makes one understood better, any one of his poems. That implies a significant unity in his whole work. One can't put his increased understanding altogether into words: I could not say just why I think I understand and enjoy *Comus* better for having read *Paradise Lost*, or *Paradise Lost* better for having read *Samson Agonistes*, but I am convinced that this is so. I cannot always say why, through knowing a person in a number of different situations, and observing his behaviour in a variety of circumstances, I feel that I understand better his behaviour or demeanour on a particular occasion: but we do believe that that person is a unity, however inconsistent his conduct, and that acquaintance with him over a span of time makes him more intelligible. Finally, I have qualified this objective discrimination between major and minor poets by referring it back to the particular reader. For no two readers, perhaps, will any great poet have quite the same significance, however in accord they may be as to his eminence: all the more likely, then, that to no two people will the pattern of English poetry be quite the same. So that of two equally competent readers, a particular poet may be to one of major importance and to the other of minor.

There is a final reflection to be made, when we come to consider contemporary poetry. We sometimes find critics confidently asserting, on their first acquaintance with the work of a new poet, that this is 'major' or 'minor' poetry. Ignoring the possibility that what the critic is praising or placing may not be poetry at all [for sometimes one can say, '*If* this was poetry, it would be major poetry — but it isn't'] I don't think it is advisable to make up one's mind so quickly. The most that I should venture to commit myself to, about the work of any living poet when I met it for the first time, is whether this is *genuine* poetry or not. Has this poet something to say, a little different from what anyone has said before, and has he found, not only a different way of saying it, but *the* different way of saying it which expresses the difference in what he is saying? Even when I commit myself thus far, I know that I may be taking a speculative risk. I may be impressed by what he is *trying* to say, and overlook the fact that he hasn't found the new way of saying it; or the new idiom of speech which at first gives the impression that the author has something of his own to say, may turn out to be only a trick or mannerism which conceals a wholly conventional vision. For anyone who reads, like myself, a good many manuscripts, and manuscripts of writers no work by whom he may have seen before, the pitfalls are more dangerous still: for one lot of poems may be so much better than any of the others I have just been looking at, that I may mistake my momentary feeling of relief for an awareness of distinguished talent. Many people content themselves either with looking at anthologies — and even when they are struck by a poem, they may not realize the fact, or if they do, they may not notice the name of the author — or with waiting until it becomes apparent that some poet, after producing several volumes [and that in itself is some assurance], has been accepted by the reviewers [and it is not what reviewers say in writing about a poet, but their references to that poet when writing about some other poet, that impresses us most].

The first method does not get us very far; the second is not very safe. For one thing, we are all apt to be somewhat on the defensive about our own epoch. We like to feel that our own epoch can produce great art — all the more so because we may have a lurking suspicion that it can't: and we feel somehow that if we could believe that we had a great poet, that would in some way reassure us and give us self-confidence. This is a pathetic wish, but it also disturbs critical judgment, for we may jump to the conclusion that somebody is a great poet who is not; or we may quite unfairly depreciate a good poet because he isn't a great one. And with our contemporaries, we oughtn't to be so busy enquiring whether they are great or not; we ought to stick to the question: 'Are they *genuine?*' and leave the question whether they are great to the only tribunal which can decide: *time.*

In our own time there is, in fact, a considerable public for contemporary poetry: there is, perhaps, more curiosity, and more expectation, about contemporary poetry than there was a generation ago. There is the danger, on the one hand, of developing a reading public which will know nothing about any poet earlier than say Gerard Manley Hopkins, and which will not have the background necessary for critical appreciation. There is also the danger that people will wait to read a poet until his contemporary reputation is established; and the anx-

iety, for those of us who are in the business, that after another
generation has established its poets, we who are still contemporary will no longer be read. The danger for the reader is double:
that he will never get anything *quite* fresh, and that he will
never return to read what always remains fresh.

There is therefore a proportion to be observed between our
reading of old and modern poetry. I should not trust the taste
of anyone who never read any contemporary poetry, and I
should certainly not trust the taste of anyone who read nothing else. But even many people who read contemporary poetry
miss the pleasure, and the profit, of finding something out for
themselves. When you read *new* poetry, poetry by someone
whose name is not yet widely known, someone whom the reviewers have not yet passed, you are exercising, or should be
exercising, your *own* taste. There is nothing else to go by. The
problem is not, as it appears to many readers, that of trying to
like something you don't, but of leaving your sensibility free to
react naturally. I find this hard enough, myself: for when you
are reading a new poet with the deliberate purpose of coming
to a decision, that purpose may interfere and obscure your
awareness of what you feel. It is hard to ask the two questions,
'Is this good, whether I like it or not?' and 'Do I like this?' at
the same time: and I often find that the best test is when some
phrase, or image, or line out of a new poem, recurs to my mind
afterwards unsummoned. I find, too, that it is useful for me to
look at the new poems in the poetry magazines, and at the
selections from new poets in the contemporary anthologies:
because in reading these I am not bothered by the question,
'Ought I to see that these poems are published?' I think it is
similar to my experience, that when I go to hear a new piece
of music for the first time, or to see a new exhibition of pic-
tures, I prefer to go alone. For if I am alone, there is nobody
to whom I am obliged to express an immediate opinion. It
isn't that I need time to make up my mind: I need time in
order to know what I really felt at the moment. And that feel-

ing is not a judgment of greatness or importance: it is an awareness of *genuineness*. So, we are not really concerned, in reading a contemporary poet, with whether he is a 'major' or a 'minor' poet. But if we read one poem, and respond to it, we should want to read more by the same author; and when we have read enough, we ought to be able to answer the question, 'Is this merely more of the same thing?'— is it, in other words, merely the same, or different, without adding up to anything, or is there a relation between the poems which makes us see a little more in each of them? That is why, with the same reservation as about the work of dead poets, we must read not only separate poems, as we get them in anthologies, but the work of a poet.

What Is a Classic? *

T HE subject which I have taken is simply the question:
'What is a classic?' It is not a new question. There is, for
instance, a famous essay by Ste. Beuve with this title. The
pertinence of asking this question, with Virgil particularly in
mind, is obvious: whatever the definition we arrive at, it cannot be one which excludes Virgil — we may say confidently
that it must be one which will expressly reckon with him. But
before I go farther, I should like to dispose of certain prejudices and anticipate certain misunderstandings. I do not aim
to supersede, or to outlaw, any use of the word 'classic' which
precedent has made permissible. The word has, and will continue to have, several meanings in several contexts: I am concerned with one meaning in one context. In defining the term
in this way, I do not bind myself, for the future, not to use the
term in any of the other ways in which it has been used. If,
for instance, I am discovered on some future occasion, in writing, in public speech, or in conversation, to be using the word
'classic' merely to mean a 'standard author' in any language —
using it merely as an indication of the greatness, or of the
permanence and importance of a writer in his own field, as
when we speak of *The Fifth Form at St. Dominic's* as a classic
of schoolboy fiction, or *Handley Cross* as a classic of the hunting field — no one should expect one to apologize. And there

* The Presidential Address to the Virgil Society in 1944. Published by Faber
& Faber 1945.

is a very interesting book called *A Guide to the Classics*, which tells you how to pick the Derby winner. On other occasions, I permit myself to mean by 'the classics', either Latin and Greek literature *in toto*, or the greatest authors of those languages, as the context indicates. And, finally, I think that the account of the classic which I propose to give here should remove it from the area of the antithesis between 'classic' and 'romantic' — a pair of terms belonging to literary politics, and therefore arousing winds of passion which I ask Aeolus, on this occasion, to contain in the bag.

This leads me to my next point. By the terms of the classic-romantic controversy, to call any work of art 'classical', implies either the highest praise or the most contemptuous abuse, according to the party to which one belongs. It implies certain particular merits or faults: either the perfection of form, or the absolute zero of frigidity. But I want to define one kind of art, and am not concerned that it is absolutely and in every respect *better* or *worse* than another kind. I shall enumerate certain qualities which I should expect the classic to display. But I do not say that, if a literature is to be a great literature, it must have any one author, or any one period, in which all these qualities are manifested. If, as I think, they are all to be found in Virgil, that is not to assert that he is the greatest poet who ever wrote — such an assertion about any poet seems to me meaningless — and it is certainly not to assert that Latin literature is greater than any other literature. We need not consider it as a defect of any literature, if no one author, or no one period, is completely classical; or if, as is true of English literature, the period which most nearly fills the classical definition is not the greatest. I think that those literatures, of which English is one of the most eminent, in which the classical qualities are scattered between various authors and several periods, may well be the richer. Every language has its own resources, and its own limitations. The conditions of a language, and the conditions of the history of the people who speak it, may put out of question the expectation of a classical period, or a classical author. That is not in itself any more a matter for regret than it is for gratulation. It did happen that the history of Rome was such, the character of the Latin language was such, that at a certain moment a uniquely classical poet was possible: though we must remember that it needed that particular poet, and a lifetime of labour on the part of that poet, to make the classic out of his material. And, of course, Virgil couldn't know that *that* was what he was doing. He was, if any poet ever was, acutely aware of what he was trying to do: the one thing he couldn't aim at, or know that he was doing, was to compose a classic: for it is only by hindsight, and in historical perspective, that a classic can be known as such.

If there is one word on which we can fix, which will suggest the maximum of what I mean by the term 'a classic', it is the word *maturity*. I shall distinguish between the universal classic, like Virgil, and the classic which is only such in relation to the other literature in its own language, or according to the view of life of a particular period. A classic can only occur when a civilization is mature; when a language and a literature are mature; and it must be the work of a mature mind. It is the importance of that civilization and of that language, as well as the comprehensiveness of the mind of the individual poet, which gives the universality. To define *maturity* without assuming that the hearer already knows what it means, is almost impossible: let us say then, that if we are properly mature, as well as educated persons, we can recognize maturity in a civilization and in a literature, as we do in the other human beings whom we encounter. To make the meaning of maturity really apprehensible — indeed, even to make it acceptable — to the immature, is perhaps impossible. But if we are mature we either recognize maturity immediately, or come to know it on more intimate acquaintance. No reader of Shakespeare, for instance, can fail to recognize, increasingly as he himself grows up, the gradual ripening of Shakespeare's mind: even a less developed reader can perceive the rapid development of Elizabethan literature and drama as a whole, from early Tudor crudity to the plays of Shakespeare, and perceive a decline in the work of Shakespeare's successors. We can also observe, upon a little conversance, that the plays of Christopher Marlowe exhibit a greater maturity of mind and of style than the plays which Shakespeare wrote at the same age: it is interesting to speculate whether, if Marlowe had lived as long as Shakespeare, his development would have continued at the same pace. I doubt it: for we observe some minds maturing earlier than others, and we observe that those which mature very early do not always develop very far. I raise this point as a reminder, first that the value of maturity depends upon the value of that which matures, and second, that we should know when we are concerned with the maturity of individual writers, and when with the relative maturity of literary periods. A writer who individually has a more mature mind may belong to a less mature period than another, so that in that respect his work will be less mature. The maturity of a literature is the reflection of that of the society in which it is produced: an individual author — notably Shakespeare and Virgil — can do much to develop his language: but he cannot bring that language to maturity unless the work of his predecessors has prepared it for his final touch. A mature literature, therefore, has a history behind it: a history, that is not merely a chronicle, an accumulation of manuscripts and writings of this kind and that, but an ordered though unconscious progress of a language to realize its own potentialities within its own limitations.

It is to be observed, that a society, and a literature, like an individual human being, do not necessarily mature equally and concurrently in every respect. The precocious child is often, in some obvious ways, childish for his age in comparison with ordinary children. Is there any one period of English literature to which we can point as being fully mature, comprehensively and in equilibrium? I do not think so: and, as I shall repeat later, I hope it is not so. We cannot say that any individual poet in English has in the course of his life become a more mature man than Shakespeare: we cannot even say that any poet has done so much, to make the English language capable of expressing the most subtle thought or the most refined shades of feeling. Yet we cannot but feel that a play like Congreve's *Way of the World* is in some way more mature than any play of Shakespeare's: but only in this respect, that it reflects a more mature society — that is, it reflects a greater maturity of *manners*. The society for which Congreve wrote was, from our point of view, coarse and brutal enough: yet it is nearer to ours than the society of the Tudors: perhaps for that reason we judge it the more severely. Nevertheless, it was a society more polished and less provincial: its mind was shallower, its sensibility more restricted; it has lost some promise of maturity but realized another. So to maturity of *mind* we must add maturity of *manners*.

The progress towards maturity of language is, I think, more easily recognized and more readily acknowledged in the development of prose, than in that of poetry. In considering prose we are less distracted by individual differences in greatness, and more inclined to demand approximation towards a common standard, a common vocabulary and a common sentence structure: it is often, in fact, the prose which departs the farthest from these common standards, which is individual to the extreme, that we are apt to denominate 'poetic prose'. At a time when England had already accomplished miracles in poetry, her prose was relatively immature, developed sufficiently for certain purposes but not for others: at that same time, when the French language had given little promise of poetry as great as that in English, French prose was much more mature than English prose. You have only to compare any Tudor writer with Montaigne — and Montaigne himself, as a stylist, is only a precursor, his style not ripe enough to fulfil the French requirements for the classic. Our prose was ready for some tasks before it could cope with others: a Malory could come long before a Hooker, a Hooker before a Hobbes, and a Hobbes before an Addison. Whatever difficulties we have in applying this standard to poetry, it is possible to see that the development of a classic prose is the development towards a *common style*. By this I do not mean that the best writers are indistinguishable from each other. The essential and characteristic differences remain: it is not that the differences are less, but that they are more subtle and refined. To a sensitive palate the difference between the prose of Addison and that of Swift will be as marked as the difference between two vintage wines to a connoisseur. What we find, in a period of classic prose, is not a mere common convention of writing, like the common style of newspaper leader writers, but a community of taste. The age which precedes a classic age, may exhibit both eccentricity and monotony: monotony because the resources of the language have not yet been explored, and eccentricity because there is yet no generally accepted standard — if, indeed, that can be called eccentric where there is no centre. Its writing may be at the same time pedantic and licentious. The age following a classic age, may also exhibit eccentricity and monotony: monotony because the resources of the language have, for the time at least, been exhausted, and eccentricity because originality comes to be more valued than correctness. But the age in which we find a common style, will be an age when society has achieved a moment of order and stability, of equilibrium and harmony; as the age which manifests the greatest extremes of individual style will be an age of immaturity or an age of senility.

Maturity of language may naturally be expected to accompany maturity of mind and manners. We may expect the language to approach maturity at the moment when men have a critical sense of the past, a confidence in the present, and no conscious doubt of the future. In literature, this means that

the poet is aware of his predecessors, and that we are aware of
the predecessors behind his work, as we may be aware of an-
cestral traits in a person who is at the same time individual and
unique. The predecessors should be themselves great and honoured: but their accomplishment must be such as to suggest
still undeveloped resources of the language, and not such as to
oppress the younger writers with the fear that everything that
can be done has been done, in their language. The poet, certainly, in a mature age, may still obtain stimulus from the
hope of doing something that his predecessors have not done;
he may even be in revolt against them, as a promising adolescent may revolt against the beliefs, the habits and the manners of his parents; but, in retrospect, we can see that he is also
the continuer of their traditions, that he preserves essential
family characteristics, and that his difference of behaviour is a
difference in the circumstances of another age. And, on the
other hand, just as we sometimes observe men whose lives are
overshadowed by the fame of a father or grandfather, men of
whom any achievement of which they are capable appears
comparatively insignificant, so a late age of poetry may be consciously impotent to compete with its distinguished ancestry.
We meet poets of this kind at the end of any age, poets with
a sense of the past only, or alternatively, poets whose hope of
the future is founded upon the attempt to renounce the past.
The persistence of literary creativeness in any people, accordingly, consists in the maintenance of an unconscious balance
between tradition in the larger sense — the collective personality, so to speak, realized in the literature of the past — and
the originality of the living generation.

    We cannot call the literature of the Elizabethan period,
great as it is, wholly mature: we cannot call it classical. No
close parallel can be drawn between the development of Greek
and Latin literature, for Latin had Greek behind it; still less
can we draw a parallel between these and any modern literature, for modern literatures have both Latin and Greek behind

them. In the Renaissance there is an early semblance of maturity, which is borrowed from antiquity. We are aware of approaching nearer to maturity with Milton. Milton was in a better position to have a critical sense of the past — of a past in English literature — than his great predecessors. To read Milton is to be confirmed in respect for the genius of Spenser, and in gratitude to Spenser for having contributed towards making the verse of Milton possible. Yet the style of Milton is not a classic style: it is a style of a language still in formation, the style of a writer whose *masters* were not English, but Latin and to a less degree Greek. This, I think, is only saying what Johnson and in turn Landor said, when they complained of Milton's style not being quite English. Let us qualify this judgment by saying immediately that Milton did much to develop the language. One of the signs of approach towards a classic style is a development towards greater complexity of sentence and period structure. Such development is apparent in the single work of Shakespeare, when we trace his style from the early to the late plays: we can even say that in his late plays he goes as far in the direction of complexity as is possible within the limits of dramatic verse, which are narrower than those of other kinds. But complexity for its own sake is not a proper goal: its purpose must be, first, the precise expression of finer shades of feeling and thought; second, the introduction of greater refinement and variety of music. When an author appears, in his love of the elaborate structure, to have lost the ability to say anything simply; when his addiction to pattern becomes such that he says things elaborately which should properly be said simply, and thus limits his range of expression, the process of complexity ceases to be quite healthy, and the writer is losing touch with the spoken language. Nevertheless, as verse develops, in the hands of one poet after another, it tends from monotony to variety, from simplicity to complexity; as it declines, it tends towards monotony again, though it may perpetuate the formal structure to which genius gave life and meaning. You will judge for yourselves how far this generalization is applicable to the predecessors and followers of Virgil: we can all see this secondary monotony in the eighteenth-century imitators of Milton — who himself is never monotonous. There comes a time when a new simplicity, even a relative crudity, may be the only alternative.

You will have anticipated the conclusion towards which I have been drawing: that those qualities of the classic which I have so far mentioned — maturity of mind, maturity of manners, maturity of language and perfection of the common style — are most nearly to be illustrated, in English literature, in the eighteenth century; and, in poetry, most in the poetry of Pope. If that were all I had to say on the matter, it would certainly not be new, and it would not be worth saying. That would be merely proposing a choice between two errors at which men have arrived before: one, that the eighteenth century is the finest period of English literature; and the other, that the classical ideal should be wholly discredited. My own opinion is, that we have no classic age, and no classic poet, in English; that when we see why this is so, we have not the slightest reason for regret; but that, nevertheless, we must maintain the classic ideal before our eyes. Because we must maintain it, and because the English genius of language has had other things to do than to realize it, we cannot afford either to reject or to overrate the age of Pope; we cannot see English literature as a whole, or aim rightly in the future, without a critical appreciation of the degree to which the classical qualities are exemplified in the work of Pope: which means that unless we are able to enjoy the work of Pope, we cannot arrive at a full understanding of English poetry.

It is fairly obvious that the realization of classical qualities by Pope was obtained at a high price — to the exclusion of some greater potentialities of English verse. Now, to some extent, the sacrifice of some potentialities in order to realize others, is a condition of artistic creation, as it is a condition of

life in general. In life the man who refuses to sacrifice anything to gain anything else, ends in mediocrity or failure;
though, on the other hand, there is the specialist who has sacri-
ficed too much for too little, or who has been born too completely the specialist to have had anything to sacrifice. But in
the English eighteenth century, we have reason for feeling that
too much was excluded. There was the mature mind: but it
was a narrow one. English society and English letters were not
provincial, in the sense that they were not isolated from, and
not lingering behind, the best European society and letters.
Yet the age itself was, in a manner of speaking, a provincial
age. When one thinks of a Shakespeare, a Jeremy Taylor, a
Milton, in England — of a Racine, a Molière, a Pascal, in
France — in the seventeenth century, one is inclined to say
that the eighteenth century had perfected its formal garden,
only by restricting the area under cultivation. We feel that if
the classic is really a worthy ideal, it must be capable of ex-
hibiting an amplitude, a catholicity, to which the eighteenth
century cannot lay claim; qualities which are present in some
great authors, like Chaucer, who cannot be regarded in my
sense as classics of English literature; and which are fully present in the mediaeval mind of Dante. For in the Divine
Comedy, if anywhere, we find the classic in a modern European language. In the eighteenth century, we are oppressed
by the limited range of sensibility, and especially in the scale
of religious feeling. It is not that, in England at least, the
poetry is not Christian. It is not even that the poets were not
devout Christians; for a pattern of orthodoxy of principle, and
sincere piety of feeling, you may look long before you find a
poet more genuine than Samuel Johnson. Yet there are evidences of a deeper religious sensibility in the poetry of Shakespeare, whose belief and practice can be only a matter of
conjecture. And this restriction of religious sensibility itself
produces a kind of provinciality [though we must add that in
this sense the nineteenth century was more provincial still]:

the provinciality which indicates the disintegration of Chris-
tendom. the decay of a common belief and a common culture.
It would seem then, that our eighteenth century, in spite of its
classical achievement — an achievement, I believe, which still
has great importance as an example for the future — was lacking some condition which makes the creation of a true classic
possible. What this condition is, we must return to Virgil to
discover.

I should like first to rehearse the characteristics which I have
already attributed to the classic, with special application to
Virgil, to his language, his civilization, and the particular moment in the history of that language and civilization at which
he arrived. Maturity of mind: this needs history, and the consciousness of history. Consciousness of history cannot be fully
awake, except where there is other history than the history of
the poet's own people: we need this in order to see our own
place in history. There must be the knowledge of the history
of at least one other highly civilized people, and of a people
whose civilization is sufficiently cognate to have influenced and
entered into our own. This is a consciousness which the
Romans had, and which the Greeks, however much more
highly we may estimate their achievement — and indeed, we
may respect it all the more on this account — could not possess. It was a consciousness, certainly, which Virgil himself
did much to develop. From the beginning, Virgil, like his contemporaries and immediate predecessors, was constantly adapting and using the discoveries, traditions and inventions of
Greek poetry: to make use of a foreign literature in this way
marks a further stage of civilization beyond making use only
of the earlier stages of one's own — though I think we can say
that no poet has ever shown a finer sense of proportion than
Virgil, in the uses he made of Greek and of earlier Latin
poetry. It is this development of one literature, or one civilization, in relation to another, which gives a peculiar significance to the subject of Virgil's epic. In Homer, the conflict

between the Greeks and the Trojans is hardly larger in scope than a feud between one Greek city-state and a coalition of other city-states: behind the story of Aeneas is the conscious-ness of a more radical distinction, a distinction which is at the same time a statement of *relatedness*, between two great cul-tures, and, finally, of their reconciliation under an all-embrac-ing destiny.

Virgil's maturity of mind, and the maturity of his age, are exhibited in this awareness of history. With maturity of mind I have associated maturity of manners and absence of provinci-ality. I suppose that, to a modern European suddenly precipi-tated into the past, the social behaviour of the Romans and the Athenians would seem indifferently coarse, barbarous and offensive. But if the poet can portray something superior to contemporary practice, it is not in the way of anticipating some later, and quite different code of behaviour, but by an insight into what the conduct of his own people at his own time might be, at its best. House parties of the wealthy, in Edwardian England, were not exactly what we read of in the pages of Henry James: but Mr. James's society was an idealiza-tion, of a kind, of *that* society, and not an anticipation of any other. I think that we are conscious, in Virgil more than in any other Latin poet — for Catullus and Propertius seem ruffians, and Horace somewhat plebeian, by comparison — of a refine-ment of manner, springing from a delicate sensibility, and par-ticularly in that test of manners, private and public conduct between the sexes. It is not for me, in a gathering of people, all of whom may be better scholars than I, to review the story of Aeneas and Dido. But I have always thought the meeting of Aeneas with the shade of Dido, in Book VI, not only one of the most poignant, but one of the most civilized passages in poetry. It is complex in meaning and economical in expression, for it not only tells us about the attitude of Dido — still more important is what it tells us about the attitude of Aeneas. Dido's behaviour appears almost as a projection of Aeneas'

own conscience: this, we feel, is the way in which Aeneas' conscience would *expect* Dido to behave to him. The point, it
seems to me, is not that Dido is unforgiving — though it is
important that, instead of railing at him, she merely snubs him
— perhaps the most telling snub in all poetry: what matters
most is, that Aeneas does not forgive himself — and this, significantly, in spite of the fact of which he is well aware, that all
that he has done has been in compliance with destiny, or in
consequence of the machinations of gods who are themselves,
we feel, only instruments of a greater inscrutable power. Here,
what I chose as an instance of civilized manners, proceeds to
testify to civilized consciousness and conscience: but all of the
levels at which we may consider a particular episode, belong
to one whole. It will be observed, finally, that the behaviour
of Virgil's characters [I might except Turnus, the man without
a destiny] never appears to be according to some purely local
or tribal code of manners: it is in its time, both Roman and
European. Virgil certainly, on the plane of manners, is not
provincial.

To attempt to demonstrate the maturity of language and
style of Virgil is, for the present occasion, a superfluous task:
many of you could perform it better than I, and I think that
we should all be in accord. But it is worth repeating that Virgil's style would not have been possible without a literature
behind him, and without his having a very intimate knowledge
of this literature: so that he was, in a sense, re-writing Latin
poetry — as when he borrows a phrase or a device from a
predecessor and improves upon it. He was a learned author,
all of whose learning was relevant to his task; and he had, for
his use, just enough literature behind him and not too much.
As for maturity of style, I do not think that any poet has ever
developed a greater command of the complex structure, both
of sense and sound, without losing the resource of direct, brief
and startling simplicity when the occasion required it. On this
I need not dilate: but I think it is worth while to say a word

more about the *common style*, because this is something which
we cannot perfectly illustrate from English poetry, and to
which we are apt to pay less than deference. In modern European literature, the closest approximations to the ideal of a
common style, are probably to be found in Dante and Racine;
the nearest we have to it in English poetry is Pope, and Pope's
is a common style which, in comparison, is of a very narrow
range. A common style is one which makes us exclaim, not
'this is a man of genius using the language' but 'this realizes
the genius of the language'. We do not say this when we read
Pope, because we are too conscious of all the resources of the
English speech upon which Pope does not draw; we can at
most say 'this realizes the genius of the English language of a
particular epoch'. We do not say this when we read Shakespeare or Milton, because we are always conscious of the
greatness of the man, and of the miracles that *he* is perform-
ing with the language; we come nearer perhaps with Chaucer
— but that Chaucer is using a different, from our point of view
a cruder, speech. And Shakespeare and Milton, as later history
shows, left open many possibilities of other uses of English in
poetry: whereas, after Virgil, it is truer to say that no great
development was possible, until the Latin language became
something different.

At this point I should like to return to a question which I
have already suggested: the question whether the achievement
of a classic, in the sense in which I have been using the term
throughout, is, for the people and the language of its origin,
altogether an unmixed blessing — even though it is unquestionably a ground for pride. To have this question raised in
one's mind, it is almost enough simply to have contemplated
Latin poetry after Virgil, to have considered the extent to
which later poets lived and worked under the shadow of his
greatness: so that we praise or dispraise them, according to
standards which he set — admiring them, sometimes, for discovering some variation which was new, or even for merely

rearranging patterns of words so as to give a pleasing faint reminder of the remote original. But English poetry, and French poetry also, may be considered fortunate in this: that the greatest poets have exhausted only particular areas. We cannot say that, since the age of Shakespeare, and respectively since the time of Racine, there has been any really first-rate poetic drama in England or in France; since Milton, we have had no great epic poem, though there have been great long poems. It is true that every supreme poet, classic or not, tends to exhaust the ground he cultivates, so that it must, after yielding a diminishing crop, finally be left in fallow for some generations.

Here it may be objected that the effect on a literature which I am imputing to the classic, results not from the classic character of that work, but simply from its greatness: for I have denied to Shakespeare and to Milton the title of classics, in the sense in which I am employing the term throughout, and yet have admitted that no supremely great poetry of the same kind has been written since. That every great work of poetry tends to make impossible the production of equally great works of the same kind is indisputable. The reason may be stated partly in terms of conscious purpose: no first-rate poet would attempt to do again, what has already been done as well as it can be done in his language. It is only after the language — its cadence, still more than vocabulary and syntax — has, with time and social change, sufficiently altered, that another dramatic poet as great as Shakespeare, or another epic poet as great as Milton, can become possible. Not only every great poet, but every genuine, though lesser poet, fulfils once for all some possibility of the language, and so leaves one possibility less for his successors. The vein that he has exhausted may be a very small one; or may represent some major form of poetry, the epic or dramatic. But what the great poet has exhausted is merely one form, and not the whole language. When the great poet is also a great classic poet, he exhausts, not a form only, but the language of his time; and the lan-

guage of his time, as used by him, will be the language in its
perfection. So that it is not the poet alone of whom we have
to take account, but the language in which he writes: it is not
merely that a classic poet exhausts the language, but that an
exhaustible language is the kind which may produce a classic
poet.

We may be inclined to ask, then, whether we are not fortunate in possessing a language which, instead of having produced a classic, can boast a rich variety in the past, and the
possibility of further novelty in the future? Now while we are
inside a literature, while we speak the same language, and have
fundamentally the same culture as that which produced the
literature of the past, we want to maintain two things: a pride
in what our literature has already accomplished, and a belief
in what it may still accomplish in the future. If we cease to
believe in the future, the past would cease to be fully *our* past:
it would become the past of a dead civilization. And this consideration must operate with particular cogency upon the
minds of those who are engaged in the attempt to add to the
store of English literature. There is no classic in English:
therefore, any living poet can say, there is still hope that I —
and those after me, for no one can face with equanimity, once
he understands what is implied, the thought of being the *last*
poet — may be able to write something which will be worth
preserving. But from the aspect of eternity, such interest in the
future has no meaning: when two languages are both dead
languages, we cannot say that one is greater, because of the
number and variety of its poets, or the other because its genius
is more completely expressed in the work of one poet. What I
wish to affirm, at one and the same time, is this: that, because
English is a living language and the language in which we
live, we may be glad that it has never completely realized itself
in the work of one classic poet; but that, on the other hand,
the classic criterion is of vital importance to us. We need it
in order to judge our individual poets, though we refuse to

judge our literature as a whole in comparison with one which
has produced a classic. Whether a literature does culminate in
a classic, is a matter of fortune. It is largely, I suspect, a question of the degree of fusion of the elements within that language; so that the Latin languages can approximate more
closely to the classic, not simply because they are Latin, but
because they are more homogeneous than English, and therefore tend more naturally towards the *common style*: whereas
English, being the most various of great languages in its constituents, tends to variety rather than perfection, needs a longer
time to realize its potency, and still contains, perhaps, more
unexplored possibilities. It has, perhaps, the greatest capacity
for changing and yet remaining itself.

I am now approaching the distinction between the relative
and the absolute classic, the distinction between the literature
which can be called classic in relation to its own language, and
that which is classic in relation to a number of other languages.
But first I wish to record one more characteristic of the classic,
beyond those I have enumerated, which will help to establish
this distinction, and to mark the difference between such a
classic as Pope and such a classic as Virgil. It is convenient
to recapitulate certain assertions which I made earlier.

I suggested, at the beginning, that a frequent, if not universal feature of the maturing of individuals may be a process
of selection [not altogether conscious], of the development of
some potentialities to the exclusion of others; and that a
similarity may be found in the development of language and
literature. If this is so, we should expect to find that in a minor
classic literature, such as our own of the late seventeenth and
the eighteenth century, the elements excluded, to arrive at
maturity, will be more numerous or more serious; and that
satisfaction in the result, will always be qualified by our awareness of the possibilities of the language, revealed in the work
of earlier authors, which have been ignored. The classic age of
English literature is not representative of the total genius of

the race: as I have intimated, we cannot say that that genius is wholly realized in any one period — with the result that we can still, by referring to one or another period of the past, envisage possibilities for the future. The English language is one which offers wide scope for legitimate divergencies of style; it seems to be such that no one age, and certainly no one writer, can establish a norm. The French language has seemed to be much more closely tethered to a normal style; yet, even in French, though the language appeared to have established itself, once for all, in the seventeenth century, there is an *esprit gaulois*, an element of richness present in Rabelais and in Villon, the awareness of which may qualify our judgment of the *wholeness* of Racine or Molière, for we may feel that it is not only unrepresented but unreconciled. We may come to the conclusion, then, that the perfect classic must be one in which the whole genius of a people will be latent, if not all revealed; and that it can only appear in a language such that its whole genius can be present at once. We must accordingly add, to our list of characteristics of the classic, that of *comprehensiveness*. The classic must, within its formal limitations, express the maximum possible of the whole range of feeling which represents the character of the people who speak that language. It will represent this at its best, and it will also have the widest appeal: among the people to which it belongs, it will find its response among all classes and conditions of men.

When a work of literature has, beyond this comprehensiveness in relation to its own language, an equal significance in relation to a number of foreign literatures, we may say that it has also *universality*. We may for instance speak justly enough of the poetry of Goethe as constituting a classic, because of the place which it occupies in its own language and literature. Yet, because of its partiality, of the impermanence of some of its content, and the germanism of the sensibility; because Goethe appears, to a foreign eye, limited by his age, by his language, and by his culture, so that he is unrepresentative of the whole European tradition, and, like our own nineteenth-century authors, a little provincial, we cannot call him a *universal* classic. He is a universal author, in the sense that he is an author with whose works every European ought to be acquainted: but that is a different thing. Nor, on one count or another, can we expect to find the proximate approach to the classic in *any* modern language. It is necessary to go to the two dead languages: it is important that they are dead, because through their death we have come into our inheritance — the fact that they are dead would in itself give them no value, apart from the fact that all the peoples of Europe are their beneficiaries. And of all the great poets of Greece and Rome, I think that it is to Virgil that we owe the most for our standard of the classic: which, I will repeat, is not the same thing as pretending that he is the greatest, or the one to whom we are in every way the most indebted — it is of a particular debt that I speak. His comprehensiveness, his peculiar kind of comprehensiveness, is due to the unique position in our history of the Roman Empire and the Latin language: a position which may be said to conform to its *destiny*. This sense of destiny comes to consciousness in the *Aeneid*. Aeneas is himself, from first to last, a 'man in fate', a man who is neither an adventurer nor a schemer, neither a vagabond nor a careerist, a man fulfilling his destiny, not under compulsion or arbitrary decree, and certainly from no stimulus to glory, but by surrendering his will to a higher power behind the gods who would thwart or direct him. He would have preferred to stop in Troy, but he becomes an exile, and something greater and more significant than any exile; he is exiled for a purpose greater than he can know, but which he recognizes; and he is not, in a human sense, a happy or successful man. But he is the symbol of Rome; and, as Aeneas is to Rome, so is ancient Rome to Europe. Thus Virgil acquires the centrality of the unique classic; he is at the centre of European civilization, in a position which no other poet can share or usurp. The Roman Empire and the Latin lan-

guage were not any empire and any language, but an empire
and a language with a unique destiny in relation to ourselves;
and the poet in whom that Empire and that language came to
consciousness and expression is a poet of unique destiny.

If Virgil is thus the consciousness of Rome and the supreme
voice of her language, he must have a significance for us which
cannot be expressed wholly in terms of literary appreciation
and criticism. Yet, adhering to the problems of literature, or to
the terms of literature in dealing with life, we may be allowed
to imply more than we state. The value of Virgil to us, in
literary terms, is in providing us with a criterion. We may, as
I have said, have reasons to rejoice that this criterion is provided by a poet writing in a different language from our own:
but that is not a reason for rejecting the criterion. To preserve
the classical standard, and to measure every individual work of
literature by it, is to see that, while our literature as a whole
may contain everything, every single work in it may be defective in something. This may be a necessary defect, a defect
without which some quality present would be lacking: but we
must see it as a defect, at the same time that we see it as a
necessity. In the absence of this standard of which I speak, a
standard we cannot keep clearly before us if we rely on our
own literature alone, we tend, first to admire works of genius
for the wrong reasons — as we extol Blake for his *philosophy*,
and Hopkins for his *style*: and from this we proceed to greater
error, to giving the second-rate equal rank with the first-rate.
In short, without the constant application of the classical
measure, which we owe to Virgil more than to any other one
poet, we tend to become provincial.

By 'provincial' I mean here something more than I find in
the dictionary definitions. I mean more, for instance, than
'wanting the culture or polish of the capital', though, certainly,
Virgil was of the Capital, to a degree which makes any later
poet of equal stature look a little provincial; and I mean more
than 'narrow in thought, in culture, in creed' — a slippery defi-

nition this, for, from a modern liberal point of view, Dante was
'narrow in thought, in culture, in creed', yet it may be the
Broad Churchman, rather than the Narrow Churchman, who
is the more provincial. I mean also a distortion of values, the
exclusion of some, the exaggeration of others, which springs,
not from lack of wide geographical perambulation, but from
applying standards acquired within a limited area to the whole
of human experience; which confounds the contingent with
the essential, the ephemeral with the permanent. In our age,
when men seem more than ever prone to confuse wisdom
with knowledge, and knowledge with information, and to try
to solve problems of life in terms of engineering, there is coming into existence a new kind of provincialism which perhaps
deserves a new name. It is a provincialism, not of space, but
of time; one for which history is merely the chronicle of human
devices which have served their turn and been scrapped, one
for which the world is the property solely of the living, a property in which the dead hold no shares. The menace of this
kind of provincialism is, that we can all, all the peoples on the
globe, be provincials together; and those who are not content
to be provincials, can only become hermits. If this kind of provincialism led to greater tolerance, in the sense of forbearance,
there might be more to be said for it; but it seems more likely
to lead to our becoming indifferent, in matters where we
ought to maintain a distinctive dogma or standard, and to our
becoming intolerant, in matters which might be left to local or
personal preference. We may have as many varieties of religion as we like, provided we all send our children to the
same schools. But my concern here is only with the corrective
to provincialism in literature. We need to remind ourselves
that, as Europe is a whole [and still, in its progressive mutilation and disfigurement, the organism out of which any greater
world harmony must develop], so European literature is a
whole, the several members of which cannot flourish, if the
same blood-stream does not circulate throughout the whole

body. The blood-stream of European literature is Latin and Greek — not as two systems of circulation, but one, for it is through Rome that our parentage in Greece must be traced. What common measure of excellence have we in literature, among our several languages, which is not the classical measure? What mutual intelligibility can we hope to preserve, except in our common heritage of thought and feeling in those two languages, for the understanding of which, no European people is in any position of advantage over any other? No modern language could aspire to the universality of Latin, even though it came to be spoken by millions more than ever spoke Latin, and even though it came to be the universal means of communication between peoples of all tongues and cultures. No modern language can hope to produce a classic, in the sense in which I have called Virgil a classic. Our classic, the classic of all Europe, is Virgil.

In our several literatures, we have much wealth of which to boast, to which Latin has nothing to compare; but each literature has its greatness, not in isolation, but because of its place in a larger pattern, a pattern set in Rome. I have spoken of the new seriousness — *gravity* I might say — the new insight into history, illustrated by the dedication of Aeneas to Rome, to a future far beyond his living achievement. *His* reward was hardly more than a narrow beachhead and a political marriage in a weary middle age: his youth interred, its shadow moving with the shades the other side of Cumae. And so, I said, one envisages the destiny of ancient Rome. So we may think of Roman literature: at first sight, a literature of limited scope, with a poor muster of great names, yet universal as no other literature can be; a literature unconsciously sacrificing, in compliance to its destiny in Europe, the opulence and variety of later tongues, to produce, for us, the classic. It is sufficient that this standard should have been established once for all; the task does not have to be done again. But the maintenance of the standard is the price of our freedom, the defence of free-

dom against chaos. We may remind ourselves of this obligation, by our annual observance of piety towards the great ghost
who guided Dante's pilgrimage: who, as it was his function
to lead Dante towards a vision he could never himself enjoy,
led Europe towards the Christian culture which he could never
know; and who, speaking his final words in the new Italian
speech, said in farewell

> *il temporal foco e l'eterno*
> *veduto hai, figlio, e sei venuto in parte*
> *dov' io per me più oltre non discerno.*

> *Son, the temporal fire and the eternal, hast*
> *thou seen, and art come to a place where I,*
> *of myself discern no further.*

Poetry and Drama*

REVIEWING my critical output for the last thirty-odd years,
I am surprised to find how constantly I have returned
to the drama, whether by examining the work of the contemporaries of Shakespeare, or by reflecting on the possibilities of
the future. It may even be that people are weary of hearing me
on this subject. But, while I find that I have been composing
variations on this theme all my life, my views have been continually modified and renewed by increasing experience; so that
I am impelled to take stock of the situation afresh at every
stage of my own experimentation.

As I have gradually learned more about the problems of
poetic drama, and the conditions which it must fulfil if it is to
justify itself, I have made a little clearer to myself, not only
my own reasons for wanting to write in this form, but the
more general reasons for wanting to see it restored to its place.
And I think that if I say something about these problems and
conditions, it should make clearer to other people whether and
if so why poetic drama has anything potentially to offer the
playgoer, that prose drama cannot. For I start with the assumption that if poetry is merely a decoration, an added embellish-
ment, if it merely gives people of literary tastes the pleasure
of listening to poetry at the same time that they are witnessing
a play, then it is superfluous. It must justify itself dramatically,

* The first Theodore Spencer Memorial Lecture delivered at Harvard University and published by Faber & Faber and by the Harvard University Press in
1951.

and not merely be fine poetry shaped into a dramatic form.
From this it follows that no play should be written in verse
for which prose is *dramatically* adequate. And from this it follows, again, that the audience, its attention held by the dramatic action, its emotions stirred by the situation between the
characters, should be too intent upon the play to be wholly
conscious of the medium.

Whether we use prose or verse on the stage, they are both
but means to an end. The difference, from one point of view,
is not so great as we might think. In those prose plays which
survive, which are read and produced on the stage by later
generations, the prose in which the characters speak is as remote, for the best part, from the vocabulary, syntax, and
rhythm of our ordinary speech — with its fumbling for words,
its constant recourse to approximation, its disorder, and its
unfinished sentences — as verse is. Like verse, it has been written, and rewritten. Our two greatest prose stylists in the drama
— apart from Shakespeare and the other Elizabethans who
mixed prose and verse in the same play — are, I believe, Congreve and Bernard Shaw. A speech by a character of Congreve
or of Shaw has — however clearly the characters may be differ-
entiated — that unmistakable personal rhythm which is the
mark of a prose style, and of which only the most accomplished conversationalists — who are for that matter usually
monologuists — show any trace in their talk. We have all heard
[too often!] of Molière's character who expressed surprise when
told that he spoke prose. But it was M. Jourdain who was
right, and not his mentor or his creator: he did not speak
prose — he only talked. For I mean to draw a triple distinction:
between prose, and verse, and our ordinary speech which is
mostly below the level of either verse or prose. So if you look
at it in this way, it will appear that prose, on the stage, is as
artificial as verse: or alternatively, that verse can be as natural
as prose.

But while the sensitive member of the audience will appreciate, when he hears fine prose spoken in a play, that this is something better than ordinary conversation, he does not regard it as a wholly different language from that which he himself speaks, for that would interpose a barrier between himself and the imaginary characters on the stage. Too many people, on the other hand, approach a play which they know to be in verse, with the consciousness of the difference. It is unfortunate when they are repelled by verse, but can also be deplorable when they are attracted by it — if that means that they are prepared to enjoy the play and the language of the play as two separate things. The chief effect of style and rhythm in dramatic speech, whether in prose or verse, should be unconscious.

From this it follows that a mixture of prose and verse in the same play is generally to be avoided: each transition makes the auditor aware, with a jolt, of the medium. It is, we may say, justifiable when the author wishes to produce this jolt: when, that is, he wishes to transport the audience violently from one plane of reality to another. I suspect that this kind of transition was easily acceptable to an Elizabethan audience, to whose ears both prose and verse came naturally; who liked highfalutin and low comedy in the same play; and to whom it seemed perhaps proper that the more humble and rustic characters should speak in a homely language, and that those of more exalted rank should rant in verse. But even in the plays of Shakespeare some of the prose passages seem to be designed for an effect of contrast which, when achieved, is something that can never become old-fashioned. The knocking at the gate in *Macbeth* is an example that comes to everyone's mind; but it has long seemed to me that the alternation of scenes in prose with scenes in verse in *Henry IV* points an ironic contrast between the world of high politics and the world of common life. The audience probably thought they were getting their accustomed chronicle play garnished with amusing scenes of low life; yet the prose scenes of both Part I and Part II provide a sardonic comment upon the bustling ambitions of the chiefs of the parties in the insurrection of the Percys.

To-day, however, because of the handicap under which verse drama suffers, I believe that in verse drama prose should be used very sparingly indeed; that we should aim at a form of verse in which everything can be said that has to be said; and that when we find some situation which is intractable in verse, it is merely because our form of verse is inelastic. And if there prove to be scenes which we cannot put in verse, we must either develop our verse, or avoid having to introduce such scenes. For we have to accustom our audiences to verse to the point at which they will cease to be conscious of it; and to introduce prose dialogue would only be to distract their attention from the play itself to the medium of its expression. But if our verse is to have so wide a range that it can say anything that has to be said, it follows that it will not be 'poetry' all the time. It will only be 'poetry' when the dramatic situation has reached such a point of intensity that poetry becomes the natural utterance, because then it is the only language in which the emotions can be expressed at all.

It is indeed necessary for any long poem, if it is to escape monotony, to be able to say homely things without bathos, as well as to take the highest flights without sounding exaggerated. And it is still more important in a play, especially if it is concerned with contemporary life. The reason for writing even the more pedestrian parts of a verse play in verse instead of prose is, however, not only to avoid calling the audience's attention to the fact that it is at other moments listening to poetry. It is also that the verse rhythm should have its effect upon the hearers, without their being conscious of it. A brief analysis of one scene of Shakespeare's may illustrate this point. The opening scene of *Hamlet* — as well constructed an opening scene as that of any play ever written — has the advantage of being one that everybody knows.

What we do not notice, when we witness this scene in the theatre, is the great variation of style. Nothing is superfluous, and there is no line of poetry which is not justified by its dramatic value. The first twenty-two lines are built of the simplest words in the most homely idiom. Shakespeare had worked for a long time in the theatre, and written a good many plays, before reaching the point at which he could write those twenty-two lines. There is nothing quite so simplified and sure in his previous work. He first developed conversational, colloquial verse in the monologue of the character part — Faulconbridge in *King John*, and later the Nurse in *Romeo and Juliet*. It was a much further step to carry it unobtrusively into the dialogue of brief replies. No poet has begun to master dramatic verse until he can write lines which, like these in *Hamlet*, are *transparent*. You are consciously attending, not to the poetry, but to the meaning of the poetry. If you were hearing *Hamlet* for the first time, without knowing anything about the play, I do not think that it would occur to you to ask whether the speakers were speaking in verse or prose. The verse is having a different effect upon us from prose; but at the moment, what we are aware of is the frosty night, the officers keeping watch on the battlements, and the foreboding of a tragic action. I do not say that there is no place for the situation in which part of one's pleasure will be the enjoyment of hearing beautiful poetry — providing that the author gives it, in that place, dramatic inevitability. And of course, when we have both seen a play several times and read it between performances, we begin to analyse the means by which the author has produced his effects. But in the immediate impact of this scene we are unconscious of the medium of its expression.

From the short, brusque ejaculations at the beginning, suitable to the situation and to the character of the guards — but not expressing more character than is required for their function in the play — the verse glides into a slower movement with the appearance of the courtiers Horatio and Marcellus.

Horatio says 'tis but our fantasy, . . .

and the movement changes again on the appearance of Royalty, the ghost of the King, into the solemn and sonorous

What art thou, that usurp'st this time of night, . . .

[and note, by the way, this anticipation of the plot conveyed by the use of the verb *usurp*]; and majesty is suggested in a reference reminding us whose ghost this is:

> *So frown'd he once, when, in an angry parle,*
> *He smote the sledded Polacks on the ice.*

There is an abrupt change to staccato in Horatio's words to the Ghost on its second appearance; this rhythm changes again with the words

> *We do it wrong, being so majestical,*
> *To offer it the show of violence;*
> *For it is, as the air, invulnerable,*
> *And our vain blows malicious mockery.*

The scene reaches a resolution with the words of Marcellus:

> *It faded on the crowing of the cock.*
> *Some say that ever 'gainst that season comes*
> *Wherein our Saviour's birth is celebrated,*
> *The bird of dawning singeth all night long; . . .*

and Horatio's answer:

> *So have I heard and do in part believe it.*
> *But, look, the morn, in russet mantle clad,*
> *Walks o'er the dew of yon high eastern hill.*
> *Break we our watch up.*

This is great poetry, and it is dramatic; but besides being poetic and dramatic, it is something more. There emerges, when we analyse it, a kind of musical design also which reinforces and is

one with the dramatic movement. It has checked and accelerated the pulse of our emotion without our knowing it. Note
that in these last words of Marcellus there is a deliberate brief
emergence of the poetic into consciousness. When we hear
the lines

> But, look, the morn, in russet mantle clad,
> Walks o'er the dew of yon high eastern hill,

we are lifted for a moment beyond character, but with no
sense of unfitness of the words coming, and at this moment,
from the lips of Horatio. The transitions in the scene obey
laws of the music of dramatic poetry. Note that the two lines
of Horatio which I have quoted twice are preceded by a line
of the simplest speech which might be either verse or prose:

> So have I heard and do in part believe it,

and that he follows them abruptly with a half line which is
hardly more than a stage direction:

> Break we our watch up.

It would be interesting to pursue, by a similar analysis, this
problem of the double pattern in great poetic drama — the
pattern which may be examined from the point of view of
stagecraft or from that of the music. But I think that the examination of this one scene is enough to show us that verse is
not merely a formalization, or an added decoration, but that it
intensifies the drama. It should indicate also the importance
of the unconscious effect of the verse upon us. And lastly, I
do not think that this effect is felt only by those members of
an audience who 'like poetry' but also by those who go for the
play alone. By the people who do not like poetry, I mean those
who cannot sit down with a book of poetry and enjoy reading
it: these people also, when they go to a play in verse, should
be affected by the poetry. And these are the audiences whom
the writer of such a play ought to keep in mind.

At this point I might say a word about those plays which
we call *poetic*, though they are written in prose. The plays of
John Millington Synge form rather a special case, because they
are based upon the idiom of a rural people whose speech is
naturally poetic, both in imagery and in rhythm. I believe that
he even incorporated phrases which he had heard from these
country people of Ireland. The language of Synge is not available except for plays set among that same people. We can draw
more general conclusions from the plays in prose [so much
admired in my youth, and now hardly even read] by Maeterlinck. These plays are in a different way restricted in their subject matter; and to say that the characterization in them is dim
is an understatement. I do not deny that they have some
poetic quality. But in order to be poetic in prose, a dramatist
has to be so consistently poetic that his scope is very limited.
Synge wrote plays about characters whose originals in life
talked poetically, so he could make them talk poetry and remain real people. The poetic prose dramatist who has not this
advantage, has to be too poetic. The poetic drama in prose is
more limited by poetic convention or by our conventions as to
what subject matter is poetic, than is the poetic drama in verse.
A really dramatic verse can be employed, as Shakespeare employed it, to say the most matter-of-fact things.

Yeats is a very different case from Maeterlinck or Synge. A
study of his development as a dramatist would show, I think,
the great distance he went, and the triumph of his last plays.
In his first period, he wrote plays in verse about subjects con-
ventionally accepted as suitable for verse, in a metric which —
though even at that early stage having the personal Yeats
rhythm — is not really a form of speech quite suitable for anybody except mythical kings and queens. His middle-period
Plays for Dancers are very beautiful, but they do not solve any
problem for the dramatist in verse: they are poetic prose plays
with important interludes in verse. It was only in his last play

Purgatory that he solved his problem of speech in verse, and laid all his successors under obligation to him.

II

Now, I am going to venture to make some observations based on my own experience, which will lead me to comment on my intentions, failures, and partial successes, in my own plays. I do this in the belief that any explorer or experimenter in new territory may, by putting on record a kind of journal of his explorations, say something of use to those who follow him into the same regions and who will perhaps go farther.

The first thing of any importance that I discovered, was that a writer who has worked for years, and achieved some success, in writing other kinds of verse, has to approach the writing of a verse play in a different frame of mind from that to which he has been accustomed in his previous work. In writing other verse, I think that one is writing, so to speak, in terms of one's own voice: the way it sounds when you read it to yourself is the test. For it is yourself speaking. The question of communication, of what the reader will get from it, is not paramount: if your poem is right to you, you can only hope that the readers will eventually come to accept it. The poem can wait a little while; the approval of a few sympathetic and judicious critics is enough to begin with; and it is for future readers to meet the poet more than half way. But in the theatre, the problem of communication presents itself immediately. You are deliberately writing verse for other voices, not for your own, and you do not know whose voices they will be. You are aiming to write lines which will have an immediate effect upon an unknown and unprepared audience, to be interpreted to that audience by unknown actors rehearsed by an unknown producer. And the unknown audience cannot be expected to show any indulgence towards the poet. The poet cannot afford to write his play merely for his admirers, those who know his

non-dramatic work and are prepared to receive favourably anything he puts his name to. He must write with an audience in
view which knows nothing and cares nothing, about any previous success he may have had before he ventured into the theatre. Hence one finds out that many of the things one likes to
do, and knows how to do, are out of place; and that every line
must be judged by a new law, that of dramatic relevance.

When I wrote *Murder in the Cathedral* I had the advantage
for a beginner, of an occasion which called for a subject generally admitted to be suitable for verse. Verse plays, it has
been generally held, should either take their subject matter
from some mythology, or else should be about some remote
historical period, far enough away from the present for the
characters not to need to be recognizable as human beings,
and therefore for them to be licensed to talk in verse. Pic-
turesque period costume renders verse much more acceptable.
Furthermore, my play was to be produced for a rather special
kind of audience — an audience of those serious people who
go to 'festivals' and expect to have to put up with poetry —
though perhaps on this occasion some of them were not quite
prepared for what they got. And finally it was a religious play,
and people who go deliberately to a religious play at a religious
festival expect to be patiently bored and to satisfy themselves
with the feeling that they have done something meritorious.
So the path was made easy.

It was only when I put my mind to thinking what sort of
play I wanted to do next, that I realized that in *Murder in the
Cathedral* I had not solved any general problem; but that from
my point of view the play was a dead end. For one thing, the
problem of language which that play had presented to me was
a special problem. Fortunately, I did not have to write in the
idiom of the twelfth century, because that idiom, even if I
knew Norman French and Anglo-Saxon, would have been unintelligible. But the vocabulary and style could not be exactly
those of modern conversation — as in some modern French

plays using the plot and personages of Greek drama — because I had to take my audience back to an historical event; and they could not afford to be archaic, first because archaism would only have suggested the wrong period, and second because I wanted to bring home to the audience the contemporary relevance of the situation. The style therefore had to be *neutral*, committed neither to the present nor to the past. As for the versification, I was only aware at this stage that the essential was to avoid any echo of Shakespeare, for I was persuaded that the primary failure of nineteenth-century poets when they wrote for the theatre [and most of the greatest English poets had tried their hand at drama] was not in their theatrical technique, but in their dramatic language; and that this was due largely to their limitation to a strict blank verse which, after extensive use for non-dramatic poetry, had lost the flexibility which blank verse must have if it is to give the effect of conversation. The rhythm of regular blank verse had become too remote from the movement of modern speech. Therefore what I kept in mind was the versification of *Everyman*, hoping that anything unusual in the sound of it would be, on the whole, advantageous. An avoidance of too much iambic, some use of alliteration, and occasional unexpected rhyme, helped to distinguish the versification from that of the nineteenth century.

The versification of the dialogue in *Murder in the Cathedral* has therefore, in my opinion, only a *negative* merit: it succeeded in avoiding what had to be avoided, but it arrived at no positive novelty: in short, in so far as it solved the problem of speech in verse for writing to-day, it solved it for this play only, and provided me with no clue to the verse I should use in another kind of play. Here, then, were two problems left unsolved: that of the idiom and that of the metric [it is really one and the same problem], for general use in any play I might want to write in future. I next became aware of my reasons for depending, in that play, so heavily upon the assistance of the chorus. There were two reasons for this, which in the circumstances justified it. The first was that the essential action of the play — both the historical facts and the matter which I invented — was somewhat limited. A man comes home, foreseeing that he will be killed, and he is killed. I did not want to increase the number of characters, I did not want to write a chronicle of twelfth-century politics, nor did I want to tamper unscrupulously with the meagre records as Tennyson did [in introducing Fair Rosamund, and in suggesting that Becket had been crossed in love in early youth]. I wanted to concentrate on death and martyrdom. The introduction of a chorus of excited and sometimes hysterical women, reflecting in their emotion the significance of the action, helped wonderfully. The second reason was this: that a poet writing for the first time for the stage, is much more at home in choral verse than in dramatic dialogue. This, I felt sure, was something I could do, and perhaps the dramatic weaknesses would be somewhat covered up by the cries of the women. The use of a chorus strengthened the power, and concealed the defects of my theatrical technique. For this reason I decided that next time I would try to integrate the chorus more closely into the play.

I wanted to find out also, whether I could learn to dispense altogether with the use of prose. The two prose passages in *Murder in the Cathedral* could not have been written in verse. Certainly, with the kind of dialogue verse which I used in that play, the audience would have been uncomfortably aware that it was verse they were hearing. A sermon cast in verse is too unusual an experience for even the most regular churchgoers: nobody could have responded to it as a sermon at all. And in the speeches of the knights, who are quite aware that they are addressing an audience of people living eight hundred years after they themselves are dead, the use of platform prose is intended of course to have a special effect: to shock the audience out of their complacency. But this is a kind of trick. that is, a device tolerable only in one play and of no use for any other.

I may, for aught I know, have been slightly under the influence of *St. Joan.*

I do not wish to give you the impression that I would rule out of dramatic poetry these three things: historical or mythological subject matter, the chorus, and traditional blank verse. I do not wish to lay down any law that the only suitable characters and situations are those of modern life, or that a verse play should consist of dialogue only, or that a wholly new versification is necessary. I am only tracing out the route of exploration of one writer, and that one myself. If the poetic drama is to reconquer its place, it must, in my opinion, enter into overt competition with prose drama. As I have said, people are prepared to put up with verse from the lips of personages dressed in the fashion of some distant age: therefore they should be made to hear it from people dressed like ourselves, living in houses and apartments like ours, and using telephones and motor cars and radio sets. Audiences are prepared to accept poetry recited by a chorus, for that is a kind of poetry recital, which it does them credit to enjoy. And audiences [those who go to a verse play because it is in verse] expect poetry to be in rhythms which have lost touch with colloquial speech. What we have to do is to bring poetry into the world in which the audience lives and to which it returns when it leaves the theatre; not to transport the audience into some imaginary world totally unlike its own, an unreal world in which poetry is tolerated. What I should hope might be achieved, by a generation of dramatists having the benefit of our experience, is that the audience should find, at the moment of awareness that it is hearing poetry, that it is saying to itself: 'I could talk in poetry too!' Then we should not be transported into an artificial world; on the contrary, our own sordid, dreary daily world would be suddenly illuminated and transfigured.

I was determined, therefore, in my next play to take a theme of contemporary life, with characters of our own time living in our own world. *The Family Reunion* was the result. Here my first concern was the problem of the versification, to find a rhythm close to contemporary speech, in which the stresses could be made to come wherever we should naturally put them, in uttering the particular phrase on the particular occasion. What I worked out is substantially what I have continued to employ: a line of varying length and varying number of syllables, with a caesura and three stresses. The caesura and the stresses may come at different places, almost anywhere in the line; the stresses may be close together or well separated by light syllables; the only rule being that there must be one stress on one side of the caesura and two on the other. In retrospect, I soon saw that I had given my attention to versification, at the expense of plot and character. I had, indeed, made some progress in dispensing with the chorus; but the device of using four of the minor personages, representing the Family, sometimes as individual character parts and sometimes collectively as chorus, does not seem to me very satisfactory. For one thing, the immediate transition from individual, characterized part to membership of a chorus is asking too much of the actors: it is a very difficult transition to accomplish. For another thing, it seemed to me another trick, one which, even if successful, could not have been applicable in another play. Furthermore, I had in two passages used the device of a lyrical duet further isolated from the rest of the dialogue by being written in shorter lines with only two stresses. These passages are in a sense 'beyond character', the speakers have to be presented as falling into a kind of trance-like state in order to speak them. But they are so remote from the necessity of the action that they are hardly more than passages of poetry which might be spoken by anybody; they are too much like operatic arias. The member of the audience, if he enjoys this sort of thing, is putting up with a suspension of the action in order to enjoy a poetic fantasia: these passages are really less related to the action than are the choruses in *Murder in the Cathedral*.

I observed that when Shakespeare, in one of his mature

plays, introduces what might seem a purely poetic line or passage, it never interrupts the action, or is out of character, but on the contrary, in some mysterious way supports both action and character. When Macbeth speaks his so often quoted words beginning

To-morrow and to-morrow and to-morrow,

or when Othello, confronted at night with his angry father-in-law and friends, utters the beautiful line

Keep up your bright swords, for the dew will rust them,

we do not feel that Shakespeare has thought of lines which are beautiful poetry and wishes to fit them in somehow, or that he has for the moment come to the end of his dramatic inspiration and has turned to poetry to fill up with. The lines are surprising, and yet they fit in with the character; or else we are compelled to adjust our conception of the character in such a way that the lines will be appropriate to it. The lines spoken by Macbeth reveal the weariness of the weak man who had been forced by his wife to realize his own half-hearted desires and her ambitions, and who, with her death, is left without the motive to continue. The line of Othello expresses irony, dignity, and fearlessness; and incidentally reminds us of the time of night in which the scene takes place. Only poetry could do this; but it is *dramatic* poetry: that is, it does not interrupt but intensifies the dramatic situation.

It was not only because of the introduction of passages which called too much attention to themselves as poetry, and could not be dramatically justified, that I found *The Family Reunion* defective: there were two weaknesses which came to strike me as more serious still. The first was, that I had employed far too much of the strictly limited time allowed to a dramatist, in presenting a situation, and not left myself enough time, or provided myself with enough material, for developing it in action. I had written what was, on the whole, a good first

act; except that for a first act it was much too long. When the
curtain rises again, the audience is expecting, as it has a right
to expect, that something is going to happen. Instead, it finds
itself treated to a further exploration of the background: in
other words, to what ought to have been given much earlier if
at all. The beginning of the second act presents much of the
most difficult problem to producer and cast: for the audience's
attention is beginning to wander. And then, after what must
seem to the audience an interminable time of preparation, the
conclusion comes so abruptly that we are, after all, unready for
it. This was an elementary fault in mechanics.

But the deepest flaw of all, was in a failure of adjustment
between the Greek story and the modern situation. I should
either have stuck closer to Aeschylus or else taken a great deal
more liberty with his myth. One evidence of this is the appearance of those ill-fated figures, the Furies. They must, in future,
be omitted from the cast, and be understood to be visible only
to certain of my characters, and not to the audience. We tried
every possible manner of presenting them. We put them on
the stage, and they looked like uninvited guests who had
strayed in from a fancy dress ball. We concealed them behind
gauze, and they suggested a still out of a Walt Disney film.
We made them dimmer, and they looked like shrubbery just
outside the window. I have seen other expedients tried: I have
seen them signalling from across the garden, or swarming on to
the stage like a fooball team, and they are never right. They
never succeed in being either Greek goddesses or modern
spooks. But their failure is merely a symptom of the failure to
adjust the ancient with the modern.

A more serious evidence is that we are left in a divided
frame of mind, not knowing whether to consider the play the
tragedy of the mother or the salvation of the son. The two
situations are not reconciled. I find a confirmation of this in
the fact that my sympathies now have come to be all with the
mother, who seems to me, except perhaps for the chauffeur,

the only complete human being in the play; and my hero now strikes me as an insufferable prig.

Well, I had made some progress in learning how to write the first act of a play, and I had — the one thing of which I felt sure — made a good deal of progress in finding a form of versification and an idiom which would serve all my purposes, without recourse to prose, and be capable of unbroken transition between the most intense speech and the most relaxed dialogue. You will understand, after my making these criticisms of *The Family Reunion*, some of the errors that I endeavoured to avoid in designing *The Cocktail Party*. To begin with, no chorus, and no ghosts. I was still inclined to go to a Greek dramatist for my theme, but I was determined to do so merely as a point of departure, and to conceal the origins so well that nobody would identify them until I pointed them out myself. In this at least I have been successful; for no one of my acquaintance [and no dramatic critics] recognized the source of my story in the *Alcestis* of Euripides. In fact, I have had to go into detailed explanation to convince them — I mean, of course, those who were familiar with the plot of that play — of the genuineness of the inspiration. But those who were at first disturbed by the eccentric behaviour of my unknown guest, and his apparently intemperate habits and tendency to burst into song, have found some consolation in having their attention called to the behaviour of Heracles in Euripides' play.

In the second place, I laid down for myself the ascetic rule to avoid poetry which could not stand the test of strict dramatic utility: with such success, indeed, that it is perhaps an open question whether there is any poetry in the play at all. And finally, I tried to keep in mind that in a play, from time to time, something should happen; that the audience should be kept in the constant expectation that something is going to happen; and that, when it does happen, it should be different,

but not too different, from what the audience had been led to
expect.

I have not yet got to the end of my investigation of the
weaknesses of this play, but I hope and expect to find more
than those of which I am yet aware. I say 'hope' because while
one can never repeat a success, and therefore must always try
to find something different, even if less popular, to do, the desire to write something which will be free of the defects of
one's last work is a very powerful and useful incentive. I am
aware that the last act of my play only just escapes, if indeed
it does escape, the accusation of being not a last act but an epilogue; and I am determined to do something different, if I
can, in this respect. I also believe that while the self-education
of a poet trying to write for the theatre seems to require a long
period of disciplining his poetry, and putting it, so to speak, on
a very thin diet in order to adapt it to the needs of the stage,
he may find that later, when [and if] the understanding of
theatrical technique has become second nature, he can dare
to make more liberal use of poetry and take greater liberties
with ordinary colloquial speech. I base this belief on the evolution of Shakespeare, and on some study of the language in
his late plays.

In devoting so much time to an examination of my own
plays, I have, I believe, been animated by a better motive than
egotism. It seems to me that if we are to have a poetic drama,
it is more likely to come from poets learning how to write
plays, than from skilful prose dramatists learning to write
poetry. That some poets can learn how to write plays, and
write good ones, may be only a hope, but I believe a not un-
reasonable hope; but that a man who has started by writing
successful prose plays should then learn how to write good
poetry, seems to me extremely unlikely. And, under present-
day conditions, and until the verse play is recognized by the
larger public as a possible source of entertainment, the poet is
likely to get his first opportunity to work for the stage only

after making some sort of reputation for himself as the author of other kinds of verse. I have therefore wished to put on record, for what it may be worth to others, some account of the difficulties I have encountered, and the mistakes into which I have fallen, and the weaknesses I have had to try to overcome.

I should not like to close without attempting to set before you, though only a dim outline, the ideal towards which poetic drama should strive. It is an unattainable ideal: and that is why it interests me, for it provides an incentive towards further experiment and exploration, beyond any goal which there is prospect of attaining. It is a function of all art to give us some perception of an order in life, by imposing an order upon it. The painter works by selection, combination, and emphasis among the elements of the visible world; the musician in the world of sound. It seems to me that beyond the nameable, classifiable emotions and motives of our consicous life when directed towards action — the part of life which prose drama is wholly adequate to express — there is a fringe of indefinite extent, of feeling which we can only detect, so to speak, out of the corner of the eye and can never completely focus; of feeling of which we are only aware in a kind of temporary detachment from action. There are great prose dramatists — such as Ibsen and Chekhov — who have at times done things of which I would not otherwise have supposed prose to be capable, but who seem to me, in spite of their success, to have been hampered in expression by writing in prose. This peculiar range of sensibility can be expressed by dramatic poetry, at its moments of greatest intensity. At such moments, we touch the border of those feelings which only music can express. We can never emulate music, because to arrive at the condition of music would be the annihilation of poetry, and especially of dramatic poetry. Nevertheless, I have before my eyes a kind of mirage of the perfection of verse drama, which would be a design of human action and of words, such as to present at once the two aspects of dramatic and of musical order. It seems to me that

Shakespeare achieved this at least in certain scenes — even rather early, for there is the balcony scene of *Romeo and Juliet* — and that this was what he was striving towards in his late plays. To go as far in this direction as it is possible to go, without losing that contact with the ordinary everyday world with which drama must come to terms, seems to me the proper aim of dramatic poetry. For it is ultimately the function of art, in imposing a credible order upon ordinary reality, and thereby eliciting some perception of an order *in* reality, to bring us to a condition of serenity, stillness, and reconciliation; and then leave us, as Virgil left Dante, to proceed toward a region where that guide can avail us no farther.

NOTE TO 'POETRY AND DRAMA'

As I explained in my Preface, the passage in this essay analysing the first scene of *Hamlet* was taken from a lecture delivered some years previously at Edinburgh University. From the same Edinburgh lecture I have extracted the following note on the balcony scene in *Romeo and Juliet*:

In Romeo's beginning, there is still some artificiality:

> *Two of the fairest stars in all the heaven,*
> *Having some business, do intreat her eyes*
> *To twinkle in their spheres till they return.*

For it seems unlikely that a man standing below in the garden, even on a very bright moonlight night, would see the eyes of the lady above flashing so brilliantly as to justify such a comparison. Yet one is aware, from the beginning of this scene, that there is a musical pattern coming, as surprising in its kind as that in the early work of Beethoven. The arrangement of voices — Juliet has three single lines, followed by Romeo's three, four and five, followed by her longer speech — is very remarkable. In this pattern, one feels that it is Juliet's voice that has the leading part: to her voice is assigned the dominant phrase of the whole duet:

> *My bounty is as boundless as the sea,*
> *My love as deep: the more I give to thee*
> *The more I have, for both are infinite.*

And to Juliet is given the key-word 'lightning', which occurs again in the play, and is significant of the sudden and disastrous power of her passion, when she says

> *'Tis like the lightning, which doth cease to be*
> *Ere one can say 'it lightens'.*

In this scene, Shakespeare achieves a perfection of verse which, being perfection, neither he nor anyone else could excel — for this particular purpose. The stiffness, the artificiality, the poetic decoration, of his early verse has finally given place to a simplification to the language of natural speech, and this language of conversation again raised to great poetry, and to great poetry which is essentially dramatic: for the scene has a structure of which each line is an essential part.

The Three Voices of Poetry *

THE first voice is the voice of the poet talking to himself — or to nobody. The second is the voice of the poet addressing an audience, whether large or small. The third is the voice of the poet when he attempts to create a dramatic character speaking in verse; when he is saying, not what he would say in his own person, but only what he can say within the limits of one imaginary character addressing another imaginary character. The distinction between the first and the second voice, between the poet speaking to himself and the poet speaking to other people, points to the problem of poetic communication; the distinction between the poet addressing other people in either his own voice or an assumed voice, and the poet inventing speech in which imaginary characters address each other, points to the problem of the difference between dramatic, quasi-dramatic, and non-dramatic verse.

I wish to anticipate a question that some of you may well raise. Cannot a poem be written for the ear, or for the eye, of one person alone? You may say simply, 'Isn't love poetry at times a form of communication between one person and one other, with no thought of a further audience?'

There are at least two people who might have disagreed with me on this point: Mr. and Mrs. Robert Browning. In the poem 'One Word More', written as an epilogue to *Men and Women*,

* The eleventh Annual Lecture of the National Book League, delivered in 1953 and published for the N.B.L. by the Cambridge University Press.

and addressed to Mrs. Browning, the husband makes a striking
value judgment:

> Rafael made a century of sonnets,
> Made and wrote them in a certain volume,
> Dinted with the silver-pointed pencil
> Else he only used to draw Madonnas:
> These, the world might view — but one, the volume.
> Who that one, you ask? Your heart instructs you . . .
>
> You and I would rather read that volume . . .
> Would we not? than wonder at Madonnas . . .
>
> Dante once prepared to paint an angel:
> Whom to please? You whisper 'Beatrice' . . .
> You and I would rather see that angel,
> Painted by the tenderness of Dante,
> Would we not? — than read a fresh Inferno.

I agree that one *Inferno*, even by Dante, is enough; and perhaps we need not too much regret the fact that Rafael did not
multiply his Madonnas: but I can only say that I feel no curiosity whatever about Rafael's sonnets or Dante's angel. If
Rafael wrote, or Dante painted, for the eyes of one person
alone, let their privacy be respected. We know that Mr. and
Mrs. Browning liked to write poems to each other, because they
published them, and some of them are good poems. We know
that Rossetti thought that he was writing his 'House of Life'
sonnets for one person, and that he was only persuaded by his
friends to disinter them. Now, I do not deny that a poem may
be addressed to one person: there is a well-known form, not
always amatory in content, called The Epistle. We shall never
have conclusive evidence: for the testimony of poets as to what
they thought they were doing when they wrote a poem, cannot
be taken altogether at its face value. But my opinion is, that a
good love poem, though it may be addressed to one person, is
always meant to be overheard by other people. Surely, the

proper language of love — that is, of communication to the beloved and to no one else — is prose.

Having dismissed as an illusion the voice of the poet talking to one person only, I think that the best way for me to try to make my three voices audible, is to trace the genesis of the distinction in my own mind. The writer to whose mind the distinction is most likely to occur is probably the writer like myself, who has spent a good many years in writing poetry, before attempting to write for the stage at all. It may be, as I have read, that there is a dramatic element in much of my early work. It may be that from the beginning I aspired unconsciously to the theatre — or, unfriendly critics might say, to Shaftesbury Avenue and Broadway. I have, however, gradually come to the conclusion that in writing verse for the stage both the process and the outcome are very different from what they are in writing verse to be read or recited. Twenty years ago I was commissioned to write a pageant play to be called *The Rock*. The invitation to write the words for this spectacle — the occasion of which was an appeal for funds for church-building in new housing areas — came at a moment when I seemed to myself to have exhausted my meagre poetic gifts, and to have nothing more to say. To be, at such a moment, commissioned to write something which, good or bad, must be delivered by a certain date, may have the effect that vigorous cranking sometimes has upon a motor car when the battery is run down. The task was clearly laid out: I had only to write the words of prose dialogue for scenes of the usual historical pageant pattern, for which I had been given a scenario. I had also to provide a number of choral passages in verse, the content of which was left to my own devices: except for the reasonable stipulation that all the choruses were expected to have some relevance to the purpose of the pageant, and that each chorus was to occupy a precise number of minutes of stage time. But in carrying out this second part of my task, there was nothing to call my attention to the third, or dramatic voice: it

was the second voice, that of myself addressing — indeed ha-
ranguing — an audience, that was most distinctly audible. Apart
from the obvious fact that writing to order is not the same
thing as writing to please oneself, I learnt only that verse to be
spoken by a choir should be different from verse to be spoken
by one person; and that the more voices you have in your choir,
the simpler and more direct the vocabulary, the syntax, and
the content of your lines must be. This chorus of *The Rock*
was not a dramatic voice; though many lines were distributed,
the personages were unindividuated. Its members were speaking *for me*, not uttering words that really represented any supposed character of their own.

The chorus in *Murder in the Cathedral* does, I think, represent some advance in dramatic development: that is to say, I
set myself the task of writing lines, not for an anonymous
chorus, but for a chorus of women of Canterbury — one might
almost say, charwomen of Canterbury. I had to make some
effort to identify myself with these women, instead of merely
identifying them with myself. But as for the dialogue of the
play, the plot had the drawback [from the point of view of my
own dramatic education] of presenting only one dominant
character; and what dramatic conflict there is takes place within
the mind of that character. The third, or dramatic voice, did
not make itself audible to me until I first attacked the problem
of presenting two [or more] characters, in some sort of conflict, misunderstanding, or attempt to understand each other,
characters with each of whom I had to try to identify myself
while writing the words for him or her to speak. You may remember that Mrs. Cluppins, in the trial of the case of Bardell
v. Pickwick, testified that 'the voices was very loud, sir, and
forced themselves upon my ear'. 'Well, Mrs. Cluppins,' said
Sergeant Buzfuz, 'you were not listening, but you heard the
voices.' It was in 1938, then, that the third voice began to force
itself upon my ear.

At this point I can fancy the reader murmuring: 'I'm sure he

has said all this before.' I will assist memory by supplying the
reference. In a lecture on 'Poetry and Drama', delivered exactly
three years ago and subsequently published, I said:

'In writing other verse [i.e. non-dramatic verse] I think that
one is writing, so to speak, in terms of one's own voice: the way
it sounds when you read it to yourself is the test. For it is yourself speaking. The question of communication, of what the
reader will get from it, is not paramount. . . .'

There is some confusion of pronouns in this passage, but I
think that the meaning is clear; so clear, as to be a glimpse of
the obvious. At that stage, I noted only the difference between
speaking for oneself, and speaking for an imaginary character;
and I passed on to other considerations about the nature of
poetic drama. I was beginning to be aware of the difference
between the first and the third voice, but gave no attention to
the second voice, of which I shall say more presently. I am
now trying to penetrate a little further into the problem. So,
before going on to consider the other voices, I want to pursue
for a few moments the complexities of the third voice.

In a verse play, you will probably have to find words for several characters differing widely from each other in background,
temperament, education, and intelligence. You cannot afford
to identify one of these characters with yourself, and give him
[or her] all the 'poetry' to speak. The poetry [I mean, the language at those dramatic moments when it reaches intensity]
must be as widely distributed as characterization permits; and
each of your characters, when he has words to speak which are
poetry and not merely verse, must be given lines appropriate
to himself. When the poetry comes, the personage on the stage
must not give the impression of being merely a mouthpiece for
the author. Hence the author is limited by the kind of poetry,
and the degree of intensity in its kind, which can be plausibly
attributed to each character in his play. And these lines of
poetry must also justify themselves by their development of
the situation in which they are spoken. Even if a burst of mag-

nificent poetry is suitable enough for the character to which it is assigned, it must also convince us that it is necessary to the action; that it is helping to extract the utmost emotional intensity out of the situation. The poet writing for the theatre may, as I have found, make two mistakes: that of assigning to a personage lines of poetry not suitable to be spoken by that personage, and that of assigning lines which, however suitable to the personage, yet fail to forward the action of the play. There are, in some of the minor Elizabethan dramatists, passages of magnificent poetry which are in both respects out of place — fine enough to preserve the play for ever as literature, but yet so inappropriate as to prevent the play from being a dramatic masterpiece. The best-known instances occur in Marlowe's *Tamburlaine.*

How have the very great dramatic poets — Sophocles, or Shakespeare, or Racine — dealt with this difficulty? This is, of course, a problem which concerns all imaginative fiction — novels and prose plays — in which the characters may be said to live. I can't see, myself, any way to make a character live except to have a profound sympathy with that character. Ideally, a dramatist, who has usually far fewer characters to manipulate than a novelist, and who has only two hours or so of life to allow them, should sympathize profoundly with all of his characters: but that is a counsel of perfection, because the plot of a play with even a very small cast may require the presence of one or more characters in whose reality, apart from their contribution to the action, we are uninterested. I wonder, however, whether it is possible to make completely real a wholy villainous character — one toward whom neither the author nor anyone else can feel anything but antipathy. We need an admixture of *weakness* with either heroic virtue or satanic villainy, to make character plausible. Iago frightens me more than Richard III; I am not sure that Parolles, in *All's Well That Ends Well*, does not disturb me more than Iago. [And I am quite sure that Rosamund Vincy, in *Middle-*

march, frightens me far more than Goneril or Regan.] It seems
to me that what happens, when an author creates a vital character, is a sort of give-and-take. The author may put into that
character, besides its other attributes, some trait of his own,
some strength or weakness, some tendency to violence or to in-
decision, some eccentricity even, that he has found in himself.
Something perhaps never realized in his own life, something of
which those who know him best may be unaware, something
not restricted in transmission to characters of the same temperament, the same age, and, least of all, of the same sex. Some
bit of himself that the author gives to a character may be the
germ from which the life of that character starts. On the other
hand, a character which succeeds in interesting its author may
elicit from the author latent potentialities of his own being. I
believe that the author imparts something of himself to his
characters, but I also believe that he is influenced by the characters he creates. It would be only too easy to lose oneself in a
maze of speculation about the process by which an imaginary
character can become as real for us as people we have known.
I have penetrated into this maze so far only to indicate the difficulties, the limitations, the fascination, for a poet who is used
to writing poetry in his own person, of the problem of making
imaginary personages talk poetry. And the difference, the abyss,
between writing for the first and for the third voice.

The peculiarity of my third voice, the voice of poetic drama,
is brought out in another way by comparing it with the voice
of the poet in non-dramatic poetry which has a dramatic element in it — and conspicuously in the dramatic monologue.
Browning, in an uncritical moment, addressed himself as 'Robert Browning, you writer of plays'. How many of us have read
a play by Browning more than once; and, if we have read it
more than once, was our motive the expectation of enjoyment?
What personage, in a play by Browning, remains living in our
mind? On the other hand, who can forget Fra Lippo Lippi, or
Andrea del Sarto, or Bishop Blougram, or the other bishop who

ordered his tomb? It would seem without further examination, from Browning's mastery of the dramatic monologue, and his very moderate achievement in the drama, that the two forms must be essentially different. Is there, perhaps, another voice which I have failed to hear, the voice of the dramatic poet whose dramatic gifts are best exercised outside of the theatre? And certainly, if any poetry, not of the stage, deserves to be characterized as 'dramatic', it is Browning's.

In a play, as I have said, an author must have divided loyalties; he must sympathize with characters who may be in no way sympathetic to each other. And he must allocate the 'poetry' as widely as the limitations of each imaginary character permit. This necessity to divide the poetry implies some variation of the style of the poetry according to the character to whom it is given. The fact that a number of characters in a play have claims upon the author, for their allotment of poetic speech, compels him to try to extract the poetry from the character, rather than impose his poetry upon it. Now, in the dramatic monologue we have no such check. The author is just as likely to identify the character with himself, as himself with the character: for the check is missing that will prevent him from doing so — and that check is the necessity for identifying himself with some other character replying to the first. What we normally hear, in fact, in the dramatic monologue, is the voice of the poet, who has put on the costume and make-up either of some historical character, or of one out of fiction. His personage must be identified to us — as an individual, or at least as a type — before he begins to speak. If, as frequently with Browning, the poet is speaking in the role of an historical personage, like Lippo Lippi, or in the role of a known character of fiction, like Caliban, he has taken possession of that character. And the difference is most evident in his 'Caliban upon Setebos'. In *The Tempest*, it is Caliban who speaks; in 'Caliban upon Setebos', it is Browning's voice that we hear, Browning talking aloud through Caliban. It was Browning's greatest disciple, Mr. Ezra Pound, who adopted the term 'persona' to indicate the several historical characters through whom he spoke: and the term is just.

I risk the generalization also, which may indeed be far too sweeping, that dramatic monologue cannot create a character. For character is created and made real only in an action, a communication between imaginary people. It is not irrelevant that when the dramatic monologue is not put into the mouth of some character already known to the reader — from history or from fiction — we are likely to ask the question 'Who was the original?' About Bishop Blougram people have always been impelled to ask, how far was this intended to be a portrait of Cardinal Manning, or of some other ecclesiastic? The poet, speaking, as Browning does, in his own voice, cannot bring a character to life: he can only mimic a character otherwise known to us. And does not the point of mimicry lie in the recognition of the person mimicked, and in the incompleteness of the illusion? We have to be aware that the mimic and the person mimicked are different people: if we are actually deceived, mimicry becomes impersonation. When we listen to a play by Shakespeare, we listen not to Shakespeare but to his characters; when we read a dramatic monologue by Browning, we cannot suppose that we are listening to any other voice than that of Browning himself.

In the dramatic monologue, then, it is surely the second voice, the voice of the poet talking to other people, that is dominant. The mere fact that he is assuming a role, that he is speaking through a mask, implies the presence of an audience: why should a man put on fancy dress and a mask only to talk to himself? The second voice is, in fact, the voice most often and most clearly heard in poetry that is not of the theatre: in all poetry, certainly, that has a conscious social purpose — poetry intended to amuse or to instruct, poetry that tells a story, poetry that preaches or points a moral, or satire which is a form of preaching. For what is the point of a story without an audience, or of a sermon without a congregation? The voice of the poet addressing other people is the dominant voice of epic, though not the only voice. In Homer, for instance, there is heard also, from time to time, the dramatic voice: there are moments when we hear, not Homer telling us what a hero said, but the voice of the hero himself. *The Divine Comedy* is not in the exact sense an epic, but here also we hear men and women speaking to us. And we have no reason to suppose that Milton's sympathy with Satan was so exclusive as to seal him of the Devil's Party. But the epic is essentially a tale told to an audience, while drama is essentially an action exhibited to an audience.

Now, what about the poetry of the first voice — that which is not primarily an attempt to communicate with anyone at all?

I must make the point that this poetry is not necessarily what we call loosely 'lyric poetry'. The term 'lyric' itself is unsatisfactory. We think first of verse intended to be sung — from the songs of Campion and Shakespeare and Burns, to the arias of W. S. Gilbert, or the words of the latest 'musical number'. But we apply it also to poetry that was never intended for a musical setting, or which we dissociate from its music: we speak of the 'lyric verse' of the metaphysical poets, of Vaughan and Marvell as well as Donne and Herbert. The very definition of 'lyric', in the Oxford Dictionary, indicates that the word cannot be satisfactorily defined:

> Lyric: Now the name for short poems, usually divided into stanzas or strophes, and directly expressing the poet's own thoughts and sentiments.

How short does a poem have to be, to be called a 'lyric'? The emphasis on brevity, and the suggestion of division into stanzas, seem residual from the association of the voice with music. But there is no necessary relation between brevity and the expression of the poet's own thoughts and feelings. 'Come unto these

yellow sands' or 'Hark! hark! the lark' are lyrics — are they not?
— but what sense is there in saying that they express directly the
poet's own thoughts and sentiments? *London, The Vanity of
Human Wishes,* and *The Deserted Village* are all poems
which appear to express the poet's own thoughts and sentiments, but do we ever think of such poems as 'lyrical'? They
are certainly not short. Between them, all the poems I have
mentioned seem to fail to qualify as lyrics, just as Mr. Daddy
Longlegs and Mr. Floppy Fly failed to qualify as courtiers:

> *One never more can go to court,*
> *Because his legs have grown too short;*
> *The other cannot sing a song,*
> *Because his legs have grown too long!*

It is obviously the lyric in the sense of a poem 'directly expressing the poet's own thoughts and sentiments', not in the
quite unrelated sense of a short poem intended to be set to
music, that is relevant to my first voice — the voice of the poet
talking to himself — or to nobody. It is in this sense that the
German poet Gottfried Benn, in a very interesting lecture entitled *Probleme der Lyrik,* thinks of lyric as the poetry of the
first voice: he includes, I feel sure, such poems as Rilke's Duinese Elegies and Valéry's *La Jeune Parque.* Where he speaks
of 'lyric poetry', then, I should prefer to say 'meditative verse'.

What, asks Herr Benn in this lecture, does the writer of such
a poem, 'addressed to no one,' start with? There is first, he
says, an inert embryo or 'creative germ' [*ein dumpfer schöp-
ferischer Keim*] and, on the other hand, the Language, the resources of the words at the poet's command. He has something
germinating in him for which he must find words; but he cannot know what words he wants until he has found the words;
he cannot identify this embryo until it has been transformed
into an arrangement of the right words in the right order.
When you have the words for it, the 'thing' for which the
words had to be found has disappeared, replaced by a poem.

What you start from is nothing so definite as an emotion, in any ordinary sense; it is still more certainly not an idea; it is — to adapt two lines of Beddoes to a different meaning — a

> bodiless childful of life in the gloom
> Crying with frog voice, 'what shall I be?'

I agree with Gottfried Benn, and I would go a little further. In a poem which is neither didactic nor narrative, and not animated by any other social purpose, the poet may be concerned solely with expressing in verse — using all his resources of words, with their history, their connotations, their music — this obscure impulse. He does not know what he has to say until he has said it, and in the effort to say it he is not concerned with making other people understand anything. He is not concerned, at this stage, with other people at all: only with finding the right words or, anyhow, the least wrong words. He is not concerned whether anybody else will ever listen to them or not, or whether anybody else will ever understand them if he does. He is oppressed by a burden which he must bring to birth in order to obtain relief. Or, to change the figure of speech, he is haunted by a demon, a demon against which he feels powerless, because in its first manifestation it has no face, no name, nothing; and the words, the poem he makes, are a kind of form of exorcism of this demon. In other words again, he is going to all that trouble, not in order to communicate with anyone, but to gain relief from acute discomfort; and when the words are finally arranged in the right way — or in what he comes to accept as the best arrangement he can find — he may experience a moment of exhaustion, of appeasement, of absolution, and of something very near annihilation, which is in itself indescribable. And then he can say to the poem: 'Go away! Find a place for yourself in a book — and don't expect *me* to take any further interest in you.'

I don't believe that the relation of a poem to its origins is capable of being more clearly traced. You can read the essays

of Paul Valéry, who studied the workings of his own mind in
the composition of a poem more perseveringly than any other
poet has done. But if, either on the basis of what poets try to
tell you, or by biographical research, with or without the tools
of the psychologist, you attempt to explain a poem, you will
probably be getting further and further away from the poem
without arriving at any other destination. The attempt to explain the poem by tracing it back to its origins will distract
attention from the poem, to direct it on to something else
which, in the form in which it can be apprehended by the
critic and his readers, has no relation to the poem and throws
no light upon it. I should not like you to think that I am trying to make the writing of a poem more of a mystery than it
is. What I am maintaining is, that the first effort of the poet
should be to achieve clarity for himself, to assure himself that
the poem is the right outcome of the process that has taken
place. The most bungling form of obscurity is that of the poet
who has not been able to express himself to himself; the shod-
diest form is found when the poet is trying to persuade himself
that he has something to say when he hasn't.

So far I have been speaking, for the sake of simplicity, of
the three voices as if they were mutually exclusive: as if the
poet, in any particular poem, was speaking *either* to himself or
to others, and as if neither of the first two voices was audible
in good dramatic verse. And this indeed is the conclusion to
which Herr Benn's argument appears to lead him: he speaks
as if the poetry of the first voice — which he considers, moreover, to be on the whole a development of our own age — was
a totally different kind of poetry from that of the poet addressing an audience. But for me the voices are most often
found together — the first and second, I mean — in non-dramatic poetry; and together with the third in dramatic poetry too.
Even though, as I have maintained, the author of a poem may
have written it primarily without thought of an audience, he
will also want to know what the poem which has satisfied *him*

will have to say to other people. There are, first of all, those
few friends to whose criticism he may wish to submit it before
considering it completed. They can be very helpful, in suggesting a word or a phrase which the author has not been able
to find for himself; though their greatest service perhaps is to
say simply 'this passage won't do'— thus confirming a suspicion
which the author had been suppressing from his own consciousness. But I am not thinking primarily of the few judicious friends whose opinion the author prizes, but of the larger
and unknown audience — people to whom the author's name
means only his poem which they have read. The final handing
over, so to speak, of the poem to an unknown audience, for
what that audience will make of it, seems to me the consummation of the process begun in solitude and without thought
of the audience, the long process of gestation of the poem,
because it marks the final separation of the poem from the
author. Let the author, at this point, rest in peace.

So much for the poem which is primarily a poem of the first
voice. I think that in every poem, from the private meditation
to the epic or the drama, there is more than one voice to be
heard. If the author never spoke to himself, the result would
not be poetry, though it might be magnificent rhetoric; and
part of our enjoyment of great poetry is the enjoyment of over-
hearing words which are not addressed to us. But if the poem
were exclusively for the author, it would be a poem in a private
and unknown language; and a poem which was a poem only
for the author would not be a poem at all. And in poetic
drama, I am inclined to believe that all three voices are audible. First, the voice of each character — an individual voice
different from that of any other character: so that of each utterance we can say, that it could only have come from that
character. There may be from time to time, and perhaps when
we least notice it, the voices of the author and the character in
unison, saying something appropriate to the character, but
something which the author could say for himself also, though

the words may not have quite the same meaning for both.
That may be a very different thing from the ventriloquism
which makes the character only a mouthpiece for the author's
ideas or sentiments.

> To-morrow and to-morrow and to-morrow . . .

Is not the perpetual shock and surprise of these hackneyed
lines evidence that Shakespeare and Macbeth are uttering the
words in unison, though perhaps with somewhat different
meaning? And finally there are the lines, in plays by one of
the supreme poetic dramatists, in which we hear a more impersonal voice still than that of either the character or the
author.

> Ripeness is all

or

> Simply the thing I am
> Shall make me live.

And now I should like to return for a moment to Gottfried
Benn and his unknown, dark *psychic material* — we might say,
the octopus or angel with which the poet struggles. I suggest
that between the three kinds of poetry to which my three
voices correspond there is a certain difference of process. In the
poem in which the first voice, that of the poet talking to himself, dominates, the 'psychic material' tends to create its own
form — the eventual form will be to a greater or less degree
the form for that one poem and for no other. It is misleading,
or course, to speak of the material as creating or imposing its
own form: what happens is a simultaneous development of
form and material; for the form affects the material at every
stage; and perhaps all the material does is to repeat 'not that!
not that!' in the face of each unsuccessful attempt at formal
organization; and finally the material is identified with its
form. But in poetry of the second and in that of the third
voice, the form is already to some extent given. However much

it may be *trans*formed before the poem is finished, it can be represented from the start by an outline or scenario. If I choose to tell a story, I must have some notion of the plot of the story I propose to tell; if I undertake satire, moralizing, or invective, there is already something given which I can recognize and which exists for others as well as myself. And if I set out to write a play, I start by an act of choice: I settle upon a particular emotional situation, out of which characters and a plot will emerge, and I can make a plain prose outline of the play in advance — however much that outline may be altered before the play is finished, by the way in which the characters develop. It is likely, of course, that it is in the beginning the pressure of some rude unknown *psychic material* that directs the poet to tell that particular story, to develop that particular situation. And on the other hand, the frame, once chosen, within which the author has elected to work, may itself evoke other psychic material; and then, lines of poetry may come into being, not from the original impulse, but from a secondary stimulation of the unconscious mind. All that matters is, that in the end the voices should be heard in harmony; and, as I have said, I doubt whether in any real poem only one voice is audible.

The reader may well, by now, have been asking himself what I have been up to in all these speculations. Have I been toiling to weave a laboured web of useless ingenuity? Well, I have been trying to talk, not to myself — as you may have been tempted to think — but to the reader of poetry. I should like to think that it might interest the reader of poetry to test my assertions in his own reading. Can you distinguish these voices in the poetry you read, or hear recited, or hear in the theatre? If you complain that a poet is obscure, and apparently ignoring you, the reader, or that he is speaking only to a limited circle of initiates from which you are excluded — remember that what he may have been trying to do, was to put something into words which could not be said in any other way, and therefore in a language which may be worth the trouble of learning. If you complain that a poet is too rhetorical, and that he addresses you as if you were a public meeting, try to listen for the moments when he is not speaking to you, but merely allowing himself to be overheard: he may be a Dryden, a Pope, or a Byron. And if you have to listen to a verse play, take it first at its face value, as entertainment, for each character speaking for himself with whatever degree of reality his author has been able to endow him. Perhaps, if it is a great play, and you do not try too hard to hear them, you may discern the other voices too. For the work of a great poetic dramatist, like Shakespeare, constitutes a world. Each character speaks for himself, but no other poet could have found those words for him to speak. If you seek for Shakespeare, you will find him only in the characters he created; for the one thing in common between the characters is that no one but Shakespeare could have created any of them. The world of a great poetic dramatist is a world in which the creator is everywhere present, and everywhere hidden.

The Frontiers of Criticism*

T HE thesis of this paper is that there are limits, exceeding which in one direction literary criticism ceases to be literary, and exceeding which in another it ceases to be criticism.

In 1923 I wrote an article entitled *The Function of Criticism*. I must have thought well of this essay ten years later, as I included it in my *Selected Essays*, where it is still to be found. On re-reading this essay recently, I was rather bewildered, wondering what all the fuss had been about — though I was glad to find nothing positively to contradict my present opinions. For, leaving aside a wrangle with Mr. Middleton Murry about 'the inner voice' — a dispute in which I recognize the old *aporia* of Authority *v.* Individual Judgment — I found it impossible to recall to mind the background of my outburst. I had made a number of statements with assurance and considerable warmth; and it would seem that I must have had in mind one or more well-established critics senior to myself whose writings did not satisfy my requirements of what literary criticism should be. But I cannot recall a single book or essay, or the name of a single critic, as representative of the kind of impressionistic criticism which aroused my ire thirty-three years ago.

The only point in mentioning this essay now, is to call attention to the extent to which what I wrote on this subject in

* The Gideon Seymour Lecture delivered at the University of Minnesota in 1956 and published by the University.

1923 is 'dated'. Richards's *Principles of Literary Criticism* was
published in 1925. A great deal has happened in literary criticism since this influential book came out; and my paper was
written two years earlier. Criticism has developed and
branched out in several directions. The term 'The New Criticism' is often employed by people without realizing what a
variety it comprehends; but its currency does, I think, recognize the fact that the more distinguished critics of to-day, however widely they differ from each other, all differ in some significant way from the critics of a previous generation.

Many years ago I pointed out that every generation must
provide its own literary criticism; for, as I said, 'each generation
brings to the contemplation of art its own categories of appreciation, makes its own demands upon art, and has its own uses
for art.' When I made this statement I am sure that I had in
mind a good deal more than the changes of taste and fashion:
I had in mind at least the fact that each generation, looking
at masterpieces of the past in a different perspective, is affected in its attitude by a greater number of influences than
those which bore upon the generation previous. But I doubt
whether I had in mind the fact that an important work of
literary criticism can alter and expand the content of the term
'literary criticism' itself. Some years ago I drew attention to the
steady change in meaning of the word *education* from the sixteenth century to the present day, a change which had taken
place owing to the fact that education not only comprised
more and more subjects, but was being supplied for or imposed upon more and more of the population. If we could follow the evolution of the term *literary criticism* in the same
way, we would find something similar happening. Compare a
critical masterpiece like Johnson's *Lives of the Poets* with the
next great critical work to follow it, Coleridge's *Biographia
Literaria*. It is not merely that Johnson represents a literary
tradition to the end of which he himself belongs, while
Coleridge is defending the merits and criticizing the weak-

nesses of a new style. The difference more pertinent to what I have been saying, is due to the scope and variety of the interests which Coleridge brought to bear on his discussion of poetry. He established the relevance of philosophy, aesthetics and psychology; and once Coleridge had introduced these disciplines into literary criticism, future critics could ignore them only at their own risk. To appreciate Johnson an effort of historical imagination is needed; a modern critic can find much in common with Coleridge. The criticism of to-day, indeed, may be said to be in direct descent from Coleridge, who would, I am sure, were he alive now, take the same interest in the social sciences and in the study of language and semantics, that he took in the sciences available to him.

The consideration of literature in the light of one or more of these studies, is one of the two main causes of the transformation of literary criticism in our time. The other cause has not been so fully recognized. The increasing attention given to the study of English and American literature in our universities and indeed in our schools, has led to a situation in which many critics are teachers, and many teachers are critics. I am far from deploring the situation: most of the really interesting criticism to-day is the work of men of letters who have found their way into universities, and of scholars whose critical activity has been first exercised in the classroom. And nowadays, when serious literary journalism is an inadequate, as well as precarious means of support for all but a very few, this is as it must be. Only, it means that the critic to-day may have a somewhat different contact with the world, and be writing for a somewhat different audience from that of his predecessors. I have the impression that serious criticism now is being written for a different, a more limited though not necessarily a smaller public than was that of the nineteenth century.

I was struck not long ago by an observation of Mr. Aldous Huxley in a preface to the English translation of *The Supreme Wisdom*. a book by a French psychiatrist, Dr. Hubert Benoit, on the psychology of Zen Buddhism. Mr. Huxley's observation responded to the impression which I had myself received from that remarkable book when I read it in French. Huxley is comparing Western psychiatry with the discipline of the East as found in Tau and Zen:

'The aim of Western psychiatry [he says] is to help the troubled individual to adjust himself to the society of less troubled individuals — individuals who are observed to be well adjusted to one another and the local institutions, but about whose adjustment to the fundamental Order of Things no enquiry is made. . . . But there is another kind of normality — a normality of perfect functioning. . . . Even a man who is perfectly adjusted to a deranged society can prepare himself, if he so desires, to become adjusted to the Nature of Things.'

The applicability of this to my present matter is not immediately obvious. But just as Western psychiatry, from a Zen Buddhist point of view, is confused or mistaken as to what healing is for, and its attitude needs really to be reversed, so I wonder whether the weakness of modern criticism is not an uncertainty as to what criticism is for? As to what benefit it is to bring, and to whom? Its very richness and variety have perhaps obscured its ultimate purpose. Every critic may have his eye on a definite goal, may be engaged on a task which needs no justification, and yet criticism itself may be lost as to its aims. If so, this is not surprising: for is it not now a commonplace, that the sciences and even the humanities have reached a point in development at which there is so much to know about any specialty, that no student has the time to know much about anything else? And the search for a curriculum which shall combine specialized study with some general education has surely been one of the problems most discussed in our universities.

We cannot, of course, go back to the universe of Aristotle or of St. Thomas Aquinas; and we cannot go back to the state of literary criticism before Coleridge. But perhaps we can do

something to save ourselves from being overwhelmed by our
own critical activity, by continually asking such a question as:
when is criticism not literary criticism but something else?

I have been somewhat bewildered to find, from time to time,
that I am regarded as one of the ancestors of modern criticism,
if too old to be a modern critic myself. Thus in a book which
I read recently by an author who is certainly a modern critic, I
find a reference to 'The New Criticism', by which, he says,
'I mean not only the American critics, but the whole critical
movement that derives from T. S. Eliot.' I don't understand
why the author should isolate me so sharply from the American
critics; but on the other hand I fail to see any critical movement which can be said to derive from myself, though I hope
that as an editor I gave the New Criticism, or some of it,
encouragement and an exercise ground in *The Criterion*. However, I think that I should, to justify this apparent modesty,
indicate what I consider my own contribution to literary criticism to have been, and what are its limitations. The best of
my *literary* criticism — apart from a few notorious phrases
which have had a truly embarrassing success in the world —
consists of essays on poets and poetic dramatists who had influenced me. It is a by-product of my private poetry-workshop;
or a prolongation of the thinking that went into the formation
of my own verse. In retrospect, I see that I wrote best about
poets whose work had influenced my own, and with whose
poetry I had become thoroughly familiar, long before I desired
to write about them, or had found the occasion to do so. My
criticism has this in common with that of Ezra Pound, that
its merits and its limitations can be fully appreciated only
when it is considered in relation to the poetry I have written
myself. In Pound's criticism there is a more didactic motive:
the reader he had in mind, I think, was primarily the young
poet whose style was still unformed. But it is the love of certain poets who had influenced him, and [as I said of myself] a
prolongation of his thinking about his own work, that inspires

an early book which remains one of the best of Pound's literary essays, *The Spirit of Romance*.

This kind of criticism of poetry by a poet, or what I have called workshop criticism, has one obvious limitation. What has no relation to the poet's own work, or what is antipathetic to him, is outside of his competence. Another limitation of workshop criticism is that the critic's judgment may be unsound outside of his own art. My valuations of poets have remained pretty constant throughout my life; in particular, my opinions about a number of living poets have remained unchanged. It is, however, not only for this reason, that what I have in mind, in talking as I am to-day about criticism, is the criticism of poetry. Poetry, as a matter of fact, is what most critics in the past have had in mind when generalizing about literature. The criticism of prose fiction is of comparatively recent institution, and I am not qualified to discuss it; but it seems to me to require a somewhat different set of weights and measures from poetry. It might, indeed, provide an interesting subject for some critic of criticism — one who was neither poet nor novelist — to consider the differences between the ways in which the critic must approach the various *genres* of literature, and between the kinds of equipment needed. But poetry is the most convenient object of criticism to have in mind, when talking about criticism, simply for the reason that its formal qualities lend themselves most readily to generalization. In poetry, it might seem that style is everything. That is far from being true; but the illusion that in poetry we come nearer to a purely aesthetic experience makes poetry the most convenient *genre* of literature to keep in mind when we are discussing literary criticism itself.

A good deal of contemporary criticism, originating at that point at which criticism merges into scholarship, and at which scholarship merges into criticism, may be characterized as the criticism of explanation by origins. To make clear what I mean I shall mention two books which have had, in this connection, a rather bad influence. I do not mean that they are bad books. On the contrary: they are both books with which everyone should be acquainted. The first is John Livingston Lowes's *The Road to Xanadu* — a book which I recommend to every student of poetry who has not yet read it. The other is James Joyce's *Finnegans Wake* — a book which I recommend every student of poetry to read — at least some pages of. Livingston Lowes was a fine scholar, a good teacher, a lovable man and a man to whom I for one have private reasons to feel very grateful. James Joyce was a man of genius, a personal friend, and my citation here of *Finnegans Wake* is neither in praise nor dispraise of a book which is certainly in the category of works that can be called *monumental*. But the only obvious common characteristic of *The Road to Xanadu* and *Finnegans Wake* is that we may say of each: one book like this is enough.

For those who have never read *The Road to Xanadu*, I will explain that it is a fascinating piece of detection. Lowes ferreted out all the books which Coleridge had read [and Coleridge was an omnivorous and insatiable reader] and from which he had borrowed images or phrases to be found in *Kubla Khan* and *The Ancient Mariner*. The books that Coleridge read are many of them obscure and forgotten books — he read, for instance, every book of travels upon which he could lay his hands. And Lowes showed, once and for all, that poetic originality is largely an original way of assembling the most disparate and unlikely material to make a new whole. The demonstration is quite convincing, as evidence of how material is digested and transformed by the poetic genius. No one, after reading this book, could suppose that he understood *The Ancient Mariner* any better; nor was it in the least Dr. Lowes's intention to make the *poem* more intelligible as poetry. He was engaged on an investigation of process, an investigation which was, strictly speaking, beyond the frontier of literary criticism. How such material as those scraps of Coleridge's reading became transmuted into great poetry remains as much of a mys-

tery as ever. Yet a number of hopeful scholars have seized upon
the Lowes method as offering a clue to the understanding of
any poem by any poet who gives evidence of having read anything. 'I wonder,' a gentleman from Indiana wrote to me a
year or more ago, 'I wonder — it is possible that I am mad,
of course' [this was his interjection, not mine; of course he was
not in the least mad, merely slightly touched in one corner
of his head from having read *The Road to Xanadu*] 'whether
"the dead cats of civilization", "rotten hippo" and Mr. Kurtz
have some tenuous connection with "that corpse you planted
last year in your garden"?' This sounds like raving, unless you
recognize the allusions: it is merely an earnest seeker trying to
establish some connection between *The Waste Land* and
Joseph Conrad's *Heart of Darkness*.

Now while Dr. Lowes has fired such practitioners of herme-
neutics with emulative zeal, *Finnegans Wake* has provided
them with a model of what they would like all literary works
to be. I must hasten to explain that I am not deriding or den-
igrating the labours of those exegetists who have set themselves to unravel all the threads and follow all the clues in that
book. If *Finnegans Wake* is to be understood at all — and we
cannot judge it without such labour — that kind of detection
must be pursued; and Messrs. Campbell and Robinson [to
mention the authors of one such piece of work] have done an
admirable job. My grievance if any is against James Joyce, the
author of that monstrous masterpiece, for writing a book such
that large stretches of it are, without elaborate explanation,
merely beautiful nonsense [very beautiful indeed when recited
by an Irish voice as lovely as that of the author — would that
he had recorded more of it!]. Perhaps Joyce did not realize
how obscure his book is. Whatever the final judgment [and I
am not going to attempt a judgment] of the place of *Finnegans
Wake* may be, I do not think that most poetry [for it is a
kind of vast prose poem] is written in that way or requires that
sort of dissection for its enjoyment and understanding. But I

suspect that the enigmas provided by *Finnegans Wake* have given support to the error, prevalent nowadays, of mistaking explanation for understanding. After the production of my play *The Cocktail Party*, my mail was swollen for months with letters offering surprising solutions of what the writers believed to be the riddle of the play's meaning. And it was evident that the writers did not resent the puzzle they thought I had set them — they liked it. Indeed, though they were unconscious of the fact, they invented the puzzle for the pleasure of discovering the solution.

Here I must admit that I am, on one conspicuous occasion, not guiltless of having led critics into temptation. The notes to *The Waste Land*! I had at first intended only to put down all the references for my quotations, with a view to spiking the guns of critics of my earlier poems who had accused me of plagiarism. Then, when it came to print *The Waste Land* as a little book — for the poem on its first appearance in *The Dial* and in *The Criterion* had no notes whatever — it was discovered that the poem was inconveniently short, so I set to work to expand the notes, in order to provide a few more pages of printed matter, with the result that they became the remarkable exposition of bogus scholarship that is still on view to-day. I have sometimes thought of getting rid of these notes; but now they can never be unstuck. They have had almost greater popularity than the poem itself — anyone who bought my book of poems, and found that the notes to *The Waste Land* were not in it, would demand his money back. But I don't think that these notes did any harm to other poets: certainly I cannot think of any good contemporary poet who has abused this same practice. [As for Miss Marianne Moore, *her* notes to poems are always pertinent, curious, conclusive, delightful and give no encouragement whatever to the researcher of origins.] No, it is not because of my bad example to other poets that I am penitent: it is because my notes stimulated the wrong kind of interest among the seekers of sources.

It was just, no doubt, that I should pay my tribute to the
work of Miss Jessie Weston; but I regret having sent so many
enquirers off on a wild goose chase after Tarot cards and the
Holy Grail.

While I was pondering this question of the attempt to
understand a poem by explaining its origins, I came across a
quotation from C. C. Jung which struck me as having some
relevance. The passage was quoted by Fr. Victor White, O.P.
in his book *God and the Unconscious*. Fr. White quotes it in
the course of exposing a radical difference between the method
of Freud and the method of Jung.

'It is a generally recognised truth [says Jung] that physical
events can be looked at in two ways, that is from the mechanistic and from the energic standpoint. The mechanistic view
is purely causal; from this standpoint an event is conceived as
the result of a cause. . . . The energic viewpoint on the other
hand is in essence final; the event is traced from effect to cause
on the assumption that energy forms the essential basis of
changes in phenomena. . . .'

The quotation is from the first essay in the volume *Con-
tributions to Analytical Psychology*. I add another sentence,
not quoted by Fr. White, which opens the next paragraph:
'Both viewpoints are indispensable for the comprehension of
physical phenomena.'

I take this simply as a suggestive analogy. One can explain a
poem by investigating what it is made of and the causes that
brought it about; and explanation may be a necessary preparation for understanding. But to understand a poem it is also
necessary, and I should say in most instances still more necessary, that we should endeavour to grasp what the poetry is aiming to be; one might say — though it is long since I have
employed such terms with any assurance — endeavouring to
grasp its entelechy.

Perhaps the form of criticism in which the danger of excessive reliance upon causal explanation is greatest is the criti-

cal biography, especially when the biographer supplements his knowledge of external facts with psychological conjectures about inner experience. I do not suggest that the personality and the private life of a dead poet constitute sacred ground on which the psychologist must not tread. The scientist must be at liberty to study such material as his curiosity leads him to investigate — so long as the victim is dead and the laws of libel cannot be invoked to stop him. Nor is there any reason why biographies of poets should not be written. Furthermore, the biographer of an author should possess some critical ability; he should be a man of taste and judgment, appreciative of the work of the man whose biography he undertakes. And on the other hand any critic seriously concerned with a man's work should be expected to know something about the man's life. But a critical biography of a writer is a delicate task in itself; and the critic or the biographer who, without being a trained and practising psychologist, brings to bear on his subject such analytical skill as he has acquired by reading books written by psychologists, may confuse the issues still further.

The question of how far information about the poet helps us to understand the poetry is not so simple as one might think. Each reader must answer it for himself, and must answer it not generally but in particular instances, for it may be more important in the case of one poet and less important in the case of another. For the enjoyment of poetry can be a complex experience in which several forms of satisfaction are mingled; and they may be mingled in different proportions for different readers. I will give an illustration. It is generally agreed that the greatest part of Wordsworth's best poetry was written within a brief span of years — brief in itself, and brief in proportion to the whole span of Wordsworth's life. Various students of Wordsworth have propounded explanations to account for the mediocrity of his later output. Some years ago, Sir Herbert Read wrote a book on Wordsworth — an interesting book, though I think that his best appreciation of Wordsworth is found in a later essay in a volume entitled *A Coat of Many Colours* — in which he explained the rise and fall of Wordsworth's genius by the effects upon him of his affair with Annette Vallon, about which information had at that time come to light. More recently still, a Mr. Bateson has written a book about Wordsworth which is also of considerable interest [his chapter on 'The Two Voices' does help to understand Wordsworth's style]. In this book he maintains that Annette doesn't figure nearly so importantly as Sir Herbert Read had thought, and that the real secret was that Wordsworth fell in love with his sister Dorothy; that this explains, in particular, the Lucy poems, and explains why, after Wordsworth's marriage, his inspiration dried up. Well, he may be right: his argument is very plausible. But the real question, which every reader of Wordsworth must answer for himself, is: does it matter? does this account help me to understand the Lucy poems any better than I did before? For myself, I can only say that a knowledge of the springs which released a poem is not necessarily a help towards understanding the poem: too much information about the origins of the poem may even break my contact with it. I feel no need for any light upon the Lucy poems beyond the radiance shed by the poems themselves.

I am not maintaining that there is *no* context in which such information or conjecture as that of Sir Herbert Read and Mr. Bateson may be relevant. It is relevant if we want to understand Wordsworth; but it is not directly relevant to our understanding of his poetry. Or rather, it is not relevant to our understanding of *the poetry as poetry*. I am even prepared to suggest that there is, in all great poetry, something which must remain unaccountable however complete might be our knowledge of the poet, and that that is what matters most. When the poem has been made, something new has happened, something that cannot be wholly explained by *anything that went before*. That, I believe, is what we mean by 'creation'.

The explanation of poetry by examination of its sources is not the method of all contemporary criticism by any means; but it is a method which responds to the desire of a good many readers that poetry should be explained to them in terms of something else: the chief part of the letters I receive from persons unknown to me, concerning my own poems, consists of requests for a kind of explanation that I cannot possibly give. There are other tendencies such as that represented by Professor Richards's investigation of the problem of how the appreciation of poetry can be taught, or by the verbal subtleties of his distinguished pupil, Professor Empson. And I have recently noticed a development, which I suspect has its origin in the classroom methods of Professor Richards, which is, in its way, a healthy reaction against the diversion of attention from the poetry to the poet. It is found in a book published not long ago, entitled *Interpretations:* a series of essays by twelve of the younger English critics, each analysing one poem of his own choice. The method is to take a well-known poem — each of the poems analysed in this book is a good one of its kind — without reference to the author or to his other work, analyse it stanza by stanza and line by line, and extract, squeeze, tease, press every drop of meaning out of it that one can. It might be called the lemon-squeezer school of criticism. As the poems range from the sixteenth century to the present day, as they differ a good deal from one another — the book begins with 'The Phoenix and the Turtle' and ends with 'Prufrock' and Yeats's 'Among School Children', and as each critic has his own procedure, the result is interesting and a little confusing — and, it must be admitted, to study twelve poems each analysed so painstakingly is a very tiring way of passing the time. I imagine that some of the poets [they are all dead except myself] would be surprised at learning what their poems mean: I had one or two minor surprises myself, as on learning that the fog, mentioned early in 'Prufrock', had somehow got into the drawing-room. But the analysis of 'Prufrock'

was not an attempt to find origins, either in literature or in
the darker recesses of my private life; it was an attempt to find
out what the poem really meant — whether that was what I
had meant it to mean or not. And for that I was grateful.
There were several essays which struck me as good. But as
every method has its own limitations and dangers, it is only
reasonable to mention what seem to me the limitations and
dangers of this one, dangers against which, if it were practised
for what I suspect should be its chief use, that is, as an exercise
for pupils, it would be the business of the teacher to warn his
class.

The first danger is that of assuming that there must be just
one interpretation of the poem as a whole, that must be right.
There will be details of explanation, especially with poems
written in another age than our own, matters of fact, historical
allusions, the meaning of a certain word at a certain date,
which can be established, and the teacher can see that his
pupils get these right. But as for the meaning of the poem as
a whole, it is not exhausted by any explanation, for the meaning is what the poem means to different sensitive readers. The
second danger — a danger into which I do not think any of
the critics in the volume I have mentioned has fallen, but a
danger to which the reader is exposed — is that of assuming
that the interpretation of a poem, if valid, is necessarily an
account of what the author consciously or unconsciously was
trying to do. For the tendency is so general, to believe that we
understand a poem when we have identified its origins and
traced the process to which the poet submitted his materials,
that we may easily believe the converse — that any explanation
of the poem is also an account of how it was written. The
analysis of 'Prufrock' to which I have referred interested *me*
because it helped *me* to see the poem through the eyes of an
intelligent, sensitive and diligent reader. That is not at all to
say that *he* saw the poem through my eyes, or that his account
has anything to do with the experiences that led up to my

writing it, or with anything I experienced in the process of writing it. And my third comment is, that I should, as a test, like to see the method applied to some new poem, some very good poem, and one that was previously unknown to me: because I should like to find out whether, after perusing the analysis, I should be able to enjoy the poem. For nearly all the poems in the volume were poems that I had known and loved for many years; and after reading the analyses, I found I was slow to recover my previous feeling about the poems. It was as if someone had taken a machine to pieces and left me with the task of reassembling the parts. I suspect, in fact, that a good deal of the value of an interpretation is — that it should be my own interpretation. There are many things, perhaps, to know about this poem, or that, many facts about which scholars can instruct me which will help me to avoid definite *mis*understanding; but a valid interpretation, I believe, must be at the same time an interpretation of my own feelings when I read it.

It has been no part of my purpose to give a comprehensive view of all the types of literary criticism practised in our time. I wished first to call attention to the transformation of literary criticism which we may say began with Coleridge but which has proceeded with greater acceleration during the last twenty-five years. This acceleration I took to be prompted by the relevance of the social sciences to criticism, and by the teaching of literature [including *contemporary* literature] in colleges and universities. I do not deplore the transformation, for it seems to me to have been inevitable. In an age of uncertainty, an age in which men are bewildered by new sciences, an age in which so little can be taken for granted as common beliefs, assumptions and background of all readers, no explorable area can be forbidden ground. But, among all this variety, we may ask, what is there, if anything, that should be common to all literary criticism? Thirty years ago, I asserted that the essential function of literary criticism was 'the elucidation of works

of art and the correction of taste'. That phrase may sound
somewhat pompous to our ears in 1956. Perhaps I could put
it more simply, and more acceptably to the present age, by
saying to 'promote the understanding and enjoyment of literature'. I would add that there is implied here also the negative
task of pointing out what should *not* be enjoyed. For the critic
may on occasion be called upon to condemn the second-rate
and expose the fraudulent: though that duty is secondary to
the duty of discriminating praise of what is praiseworthy. And
I must stress the point that I do not think of *enjoyment* and
understanding as distinctive activities — one emotional and the
other intellectual. By *understanding* I do not mean *explanation*
though explanation of what can be explained may often be a
necessary preliminary to understanding. To offer a very simple
instance: to learn the unfamiliar words, and the unfamiliar
forms of words, is a necessary preliminary to the understanding of Chaucer; it is explanation: but one could master the
vocabulary, spelling, grammar and syntax of Chaucer — indeed,
to carry the instance a stage further, one could be very well
informed about the age of Chaucer, its social habits, its beliefs,
its learning and its ignorance — and yet not *understand the
poetry*. To understand a poem comes to the same thing as to
enjoy it for the right reasons. One might say that it means
getting from the poem such enjoyment as it is capable of giving: to enjoy a poem under a misunderstanding as to what it is,
is to enjoy what is merely a projection of our own mind. So
difficult a tool to handle, is language, that 'to enjoy' and 'to
get enjoyment from' do not seem to mean quite the same
thing: that to say that one 'gets enjoyment from' poetry does
not sound quite the same as to say that one 'enjoys poetry'.
And indeed, the very meaning of 'joy' varies with the object
inspiring joy; different poems, even, yield different satisfac-
tions. It is certain that we do not fully enjoy a poem unless
we understand it; and on the other hand, it is equally true
that we do not fully understand a poem unless we enjoy it.

And that means, enjoying it to the right degree and in the right way, relative to other poems [it is in the relation of our enjoyment of a poem to our enjoyment of other poems that *taste* is shown]. It should hardly be necessary to add that this implies that one *shouldn't* enjoy bad poems — unless their badness is of a sort that appeals to our sense of humour.

I have said that explanation may be a necessary preliminary to understanding. It seems to me, however, that I understand some poetry without explanation, for instance Shakespeare's

Full fathom five thy father lies

or Shelley's

Art thou pale for weariness
Of climbing heaven and gazing on the earth

for here, and in a great deal of poetry, I see nothing to be explained — nothing, that is, that would help me to understand it better and therefore enjoy it more. And sometimes explanation, as I have already hinted, can distract us altogether from *the poem as poetry*, instead of leading us in the direction of understanding. My best reason, perhaps, for believing that I am not deluded in thinking that I understand such poetry as the lyrics by Shakespeare and Shelley which I have just cited, is that these two poems give me as keen a thrill when I repeat them to-day as they did fifty years ago.

The difference, then, between the literary critic, and the critic who has passed beyond the frontier of literary criticism, is not that the literary critic is 'purely' literary, or that he has no other interests. A critic who was interested in nothing but 'literature' would have very little to say to us, for his literature would be a pure abstraction. Poets have other interests beside poetry — otherwise their poetry would be very empty: they are poets because their dominant interest has been in turning their experience and their thought [and to experience and to think means to have interests beyond poetry] — in turning their ex-

perience and their thinking into poetry. The critic accordingly
is a *literary* critic if his primary interest, in writing criticism, is
to help his readers to *understand and enjoy*. But he must have
other interests, just as much as the poet himself; for the literary critic is not merely a technical expert, who has learned the
rules to be observed by the writers he criticizes: the critic must
be the whole man, a man with convictions and principles, and
of knowledge and experience of life.

We can therefore ask, about any writing which is offered to
us as literary criticism, is it aimed towards understanding and
enjoyment? If it is not, it may still be a legitimate and useful
activity; but it is to be judged as a contribution to psychology,
or sociology, or logic, or pedagogy, or some other pursuit —
and is to be judged by specialists, not by men of letters. We
must not identify biography with criticism: biography is ordinarily useful in providing explanation which may open the
way to further understanding; but it may also, in directing our
attention on the poet, lead us away from the poetry. We must
not confuse knowledge — factual information — about a poet's
period, the conditions of the society in which he lived, the
ideas current in his time implicit in his writings, the state of
the language in his period — with understanding his poetry.
Such knowledge, as I have said, may be a necessary preparation for understanding the poetry; furthermore, it has a value
of its own, as history; but for the appreciation of the poetry, it
can only lead us to the door: we must find our own way in.
For the purpose of acquiring such knowledge, from the point
of view taken throughout this paper, is not primarily that we
should be able to project ourselves into a remote period, that
we should be able to think and feel, when reading the poetry,
as a contemporary of the poet might have thought and felt,
though such experience has its own value; it is rather to divest
ourselves of the limitations of our own age, and the poet,
whose work we are reading, of the limitations of *his* age, in
order to get the direct experience, the immediate contact with

his poetry. What matters most, let us say, in reading an ode of Sappho, is not that I should imagine myself to be an island Greek of twenty-five hundred years ago; what matters is the experience which is the same for all human beings of different centuries and languages capable of enjoying poetry, the spark which can leap across those 2,500 years. So the critic to whom I am most grateful is the one who can make me look at something I have never looked at before, or looked at only with eyes clouded by prejudice, set me face to face with it and then leave me alone with it. From that point, I must rely upon my own sensibility, intelligence, and capacity for wisdom.

If in literary criticism, we place all the emphasis upon *understanding*, we are in danger of slipping from understanding to mere explanation. We are in danger even of pursuing criticism as if it was a science, which it never can be. If, on the other hand, we over-emphasize *enjoyment*, we will tend to fall into the subjective and impressionistic, and our enjoyment will profit us no more than mere amusement and pastime. Thirty-three years ago, it seems to have been the latter type of criticism, the impressionistic, that had caused the annoyance I felt when I wrote on 'the function of criticism'. To-day it seems to me that we need to be more on guard against the purely explanatory. But I do not want to leave you with the impression that I wish to condemn the criticism of our time. These last thirty years have been, I think, a brilliant period in literary criticism in both Britain and America. It may even come to seem, in retrospect, too brilliant. Who knows?

On Poets

Virgil and the Christian World *

THE esteem in which Virgil has been held throughout Christian history may easily be made to appear, in a historical account of it, largely due to accidents, irrelevances, misunderstandings and superstitions. Such an account can tell you why Virgil's poems were prized so highly; but it may not give you any reason to infer that he deserved so high a place; still less might it persuade you that his work has any value for the world to-day or to-morrow or forever. What interests me here are those characteristics of Virgil which render him peculiarly sympathetic to the Christian mind. To assert this is not to accord him any exaggerated value as a poet, or even as a moralist, above that of all other poets Greek or Roman.

There is however one 'accident', or 'misunderstanding', which has played such a part in history that to ignore it would appear an evasion. This is of course the fourth *Eclogue*, in which Virgil, on the occasion of the birth or the expectation of a son to his friend Pollio, recently named consul, speaks in highflown language in what purports to be a mere letter of congratulation to the happy father.

> Now is come the last age of the song of Cumae; the great line of the centuries begins anew. Now the Virgin returns, the reign of Saturn returns. . . .

* Broadcast by the B.B.C. in 1951 and published in *The Listener*. The translation quoted is that of the Loeb Library. The translation of Dante quoted here and elsewhere is that of the Temple Classics.

> *He shall have the gift of divine life, shall see heroes
> mingled with gods, and shall himself be seen of them, and
> shall sway a world to which his father's virtues shall have
> brought peace. . . .*
>
> *The serpent shall perish, and the false poison plant shall
> perish; Assyrian spice shall spring up on every soil. . . .*

Such phrases have always seemed excessive, and the child who
was the subject of them never cut any great figure in the world.
It has even been suggested that Virgil was pulling his friend's
leg by this oriental hyperbole. Some scholars have thought that
he was imitating, or taking off, the style of the Sibylline oracles.
Some have conjectured that the poem is covertly addressed to
Octavius, or even that it concerns the offspring of Antony and
Cleopatra. A French scholar, Carcopino, gives good reason to
believe that the poem contains allusions to Pythagorean doctrine. The mystery of the poem does not seem to have attracted any particular attention until the Christian Fathers got
hold of it. The Virgin, the Golden Age, the Great Year, the
parallel with the prophecies of Isaiah; the child *cara deum
suboles* — 'dear offspring of the gods, great scion of Jupiter' —
could only be the Christ himself, whose coming was foreseen
by Virgil in the year 40 B.C. Lactantius and St. Augustine believed this; so did the entire mediaeval Church and Dante;
and even perhaps, in his own fashion, Victor Hugo.

It is possible that still other explanations may be found, and
we already know more about the probabilities than the Christian Fathers did. We also know that Virgil, who was a man
of great learning in his time, and, as Mr. Jackson Knight has
shown us, well informed in matters of folklore and antiquities,
had at least indirect acquaintance with the religions and with
the figurative language of the East. That would be sufficient
in itself to account for any suggestion of Hebrew prophecy.
Whether we consider the prediction of the Incarnation merely
a coincidence will depend on what we mean by coincidence;

whether we consider Virgil a Christian prophet will depend upon our interpretation of the word 'prophecy'. That Virgil himself was consciously concerned only with domestic affairs or with Roman politics I feel sure: I think that he would have been very much astonished by the career which his fourth *Eclogue* was to have. If a prophet were by definition a man who understood the full meaning of what he was saying, this would be for me the end of the matter. But if the word 'inspiration' is to have any meaning, it must mean just this, that the speaker or writer is uttering something which he does not wholly understand — or which he may even misinterpret when the inspiration has departed from him. This is certainly true of poetic inspiration: and there is more obvious reason for admiring Isaiah as a poet than for claiming Virgil as a prophet. A poet may believe that he is expressing only his private experience; his lines may be for him only a means of talking about himself without giving himself away; yet for his readers what he has written may come to be the expression both of their own secret feelings and of the exultation or despair of a generation. He need not know what his poetry will come to mean to others; and a prophet need not understand the meaning of his prophetic utterance.

We have a mental habit which makes it much easier for us to explain the miraculous in natural terms than to explain the natural in miraculous terms: yet the latter is as necessary as the former. A miracle which everybody accepted and believed in with no difficulty would be a strange miracle indeed; because what was miraculous for everybody would also seem natural to everybody. It seems to me that one can accept whatever explanation of the fourth *Eclogue*, by a scholar and historian, is the most plausible; because the scholars and historians can only be concerned with what Virgil *thought* he was doing. But, at the same time, if there is such a thing as inspiration — and we do go on using the word — then it is something which escapes historical research.

I have had to consider the fourth *Eclogue*, because it is so important in speaking of the history of Virgil's place in the Christian tradition that to avoid mention of it might lead to misunderstanding. And it is hardly possible to speak of it without indicating in what way one accepts, or rejects, the view that it prophesies the coming of Christ. I wanted only to make clear that the literal acceptance of this *Eclogue* as prophecy had much to do with the early admission of Virgil as suitable reading for Christians, and therefore opened the way for his influence in the Christian world. I do not regard this as simply an accident, or a mere curiosity of literature. But what really concerns me is the element in Virgil which gives him a significant, a unique place, at the end of the pre-Christian and at the beginning of the Christian world. He looks both ways; he makes a liaison between the old world and the new, and of his peculiar position we may take the fourth *Eclogue* as a symbol. In what respects, therefore, does the greatest of Roman poets anticipate the Christian world in a way in which the Greek poets do not? This question has been best answered by the late Theodor Haecker, in a book, published some years ago in an English translation under the title *Virgil the Father of the West*. I shall make use of Haecker's method.

Here I shall make a slight and perhaps trivial diversion. When I was a schoolboy, it was my lot to be introduced to the *Iliad* and to the *Aeneid* in the same year. I had, up to that point, found the Greek language a much more exciting study than Latin. I still think it a much greater language: a language which has never been surpassed as a vehicle for the fullest range and the finest shades of thought and feeling. Yet I found myself at ease with Virgil as I was not at ease with Homer. It might have been rather different if we had started with the *Odyssey* instead of the *Iliad*; for when we came to read certain selected books of the *Odyssey* — and I have never read more of the *Odyssey* in Greek than those selected books — I was much happier. My preference certainly did not, I am glad to say, mean that I thought Virgil the greater poet. That is the kind of error from which we are preserved in youth, simply because we are too natural to ask such an artificial question — artificial because, in whatever ways Virgil followed the procedure of Homer, he was not trying to do the same thing. One might just as reasonably try to rate the comparative 'greatness' of the *Odyssey* and James Joyce's *Ulysses*, simply because Joyce for quite different purposes used the framework of the *Odyssey*. The obstacle to my enjoyment of the *Iliad*, at that age, was the behaviour of the people Homer wrote about. The gods were as irresponsible, as much a prey to their passions, as devoid of public spirit and the sense of fair play, as the heroes. This was shocking. Furthermore, their sense of humour extended only to the crudest form of horseplay. Achilles was a ruffian; the only hero who could be commended for either conduct or judgment was Hector; and it seemed to me that this was Shakespeare's view also:

> If Helen then be wife to Sparta's king,
> As it is known she is, these moral laws
> Of nature and of nations speak aloud
> To have her back returned . . .

All this may seem to have been simply the caprice of a priggish little boy. I have modified my early opinions — the explanation I should now give is simply that I instinctively preferred the *world* of Virgil to the *world* of Homer — because it was a more civilized world of dignity, reason and order. When I say 'the world of Virgil', I mean what Virgil himself made of the world in which he lived. The Rome of the imperial era was coarse and beastly enough; in important respects far less civilized than Athens at its greatest. The Romans were less gifted than the Athenians for the arts, philosophy and pure science; and their language was more obdurate to the expression of either poetry or abstract thought. Virgil made of Roman civili-

zation in his poetry something better than it really was. His
sensibility is more nearly Christian than that of any other
Roman or Greek poet: not like that of an early Christian perhaps, but like that of Christianity from the time at which we
can say that a Christian civilization had come into being. We
cannot compare Homer and Virgil; but we can compare the
civilization which Homer accepted with the civilization of
Rome as refined by the sensibility of Virgil.

What, then, are the chief characteristics of Virgil which
make him sympathetic to the Christian mind? I think that the
most promising way of giving some indication briefly, is to follow the procedure of Haecker and try to develop the significance of certain key words. Such words are *labor*, *pietas*, and
fatum. The *Georgics* are, I think, essential to an understanding
of Virgil's philosophy — using the word with the distinction
that we do not mean quite the same thing when we speak of
the philosophy of a poet, as when we speak of the philosophy
of an abstract thinker. The *Georgics*, as a technical treatise on
farming, are both difficult and dull. Most of us have neither
the command of Latin necessary to read them with pleasure,
nor any desire to remind ourselves of schooltime agonies. I
shall only recommend them in the translation of Mr. Day
Lewis who has put them into modern verse. But they are a
work to which their author devoted time, toil and genius. Why
did he write them? It is not to be supposed that he was endeavouring to teach their business to the farmers of his native
soil; or that he aimed simply to provide a useful handbook for
townsmen eager to buy land and launch out as farmers. Nor is
it likely that he was merely anxious to compile records, for the
curiosity of later generations, of the methods of agriculture in
his time. It is more likely that he hoped to remind absentee
landowners, careless of their responsibilities and drawn by love
of pleasure or love of politics to the metropolis, of the fundamental duty to cherish the land. Whatever his conscious motive, it seems clear to me that Virgil desired to affirm the

dignity of agricultural labour, and the importance of good cultivation of the soil for the well-being of the state both materially and spiritually.

The fact that every major poetic form employed by Virgil has some precedent in Greek verse, must not be allowed to obscure the originality with which he recreated every form he used. There is I think no precedent for the *spirit* of the *Georgics*; and the attitude towards the soil, and the labour of the soil, which is there expressed, is something that we ought to find particularly intelligible now, when urban agglomeration, the flight from the land, the pillage of the earth and the squandering of natural resources are beginning to attract attention. It was the Greeks who taught us the dignity of leisure; it is from them that we inherit the perception that the highest life is the life of contemplation. But this respect for leisure, with the Greeks, was accompanied by a contempt for the banausic occupations. Virgil perceived that agriculture is fundamental to civilization, and he affirmed the dignity of manual labour. When the Christian monastic orders came into being, the contemplative life and the life of manual labour were first conjoined. These were no longer occupations for different classes of people, the one noble, the other inferior and suitable only for slaves or almost slaves. There was a great deal in the mediaeval world which was not Christian; and practice in the lay world was very different from that of the religious orders at their best: but at least Christianity did establish the principle that action and contemplation, labour and prayer, are both essential to the life of the complete man. It is possible that the insight of Virgil was recognized by monks who read his works in their religious houses.

Furthermore, we need to keep this affirmation of the *Georgics* in mind when we read the *Aeneid*. There, Virgil is concerned with the *imperium romanum*, with the extension and justification of imperial rule. He set an ideal for Rome, and for empire in general, which was never realized in history; but

the ideal of empire as Virgil sees it is a noble one. His devotion
to Rome was founded on devotion to the land; to the particular region, to the particular village, and to the family in the
village. To the reader of history this foundation of the general
on the particular may seem chimerical; just as the union of the
contemplative and the active life may seem to most people
chimerical. For mostly these aims are envisaged as alternatives:
we exalt the contemplative life, and disparage the active, or we
exalt the active, and regard the contemplative with amused
contempt if not with moral disapproval. And yet it may be the
man who affirms the apparently incompatible who is right.

We come to the second word. It is a commonplace that
the word *piety* is only a reduced, altered and specialized translation of *pietas*. We use it in two senses: in general, it suggests
devout church-going, or at least church-going with the appearance of devoutness. In another sense, it is always preceded by
the adjective 'filial', meaning correct behaviour toward a par-
ent. When Virgil speaks, as he does, of *pius Aeneas*, we are
apt to think of his care of his father, of his devotion to his
father's memory, and of his touching encounter with his father
on his descent into the nether regions. But the word *pietas*
with Virgil has much wider associations of meaning: it implies
an attitude towards the individual, towards the family, towards
the region, and towards the imperial destiny of Rome. And
finally Aeneas is 'pious' also in his respect towards the gods,
and in his punctilious observance of rites and offerings. It is an
attitude towards all these things, and therefore implies a unity
and an order among them: it is in fact an attitude towards life.

Aeneas is therefore not simply a man endowed with a number of virtues, each of which is a kind of piety — so that to call
him *pius* in general is merely to use a convenient collective
term. Piety is one. These are aspects of piety in different contexts, and they all imply each other. In his devotion to his
father he is not being just an admirable son. There is personal
affection, without which filial piety would be imperfect; but

personal affection is not piety. There is also devotion to his father as his father, as his progenitor: this is piety as the acceptance of a bond which one has not chosen. The quality of affection is altered, and its importance deepened, when it becomes love *due* to the object. But this filial piety is also the recognition of a further bond, that with the gods, to whom such an attitude is pleasing: to fail in it would be to be guilty of impiety also towards the gods. The gods must therefore be gods worthy of this respect; and without gods, or a god, regarded in this way, filial piety must perish. For then it becomes no longer a *duty*: your feeling towards your father will be due merely to the fortunate accident of congeniality, or will be reduced to a sentiment of gratitude for care and consideration. Aeneas is pious towards the gods, and in no way does his piety appear more clearly than when the gods afflict him. He had a good deal to put up with from Juno; and even his mother Venus, as the benevolent instrument of his destiny, put him into one very awkward position. There is in Aeneas a virtue — an essential ingredient in his piety — which is an analogue and foreshadow of Christian humility. Aeneas is the antithesis, in important respects, of either Achilles or Odysseus. In so far as he is heroic, he is heroic as the original Displaced Person, the fugitive from a ruined city and an obliterated society, of which the few other survivors except his own band languish as slaves of the Greeks. He was not to have, like Ulysses, marvellous and exciting adventures with such occasional erotic episodes as left no canker on the conscience of that wayfarer. He was not to return at last to the remembered hearth-fire, to find an exemplary wife awaiting him, to be reunited to his son, his dog and his servants. Aeneas' end is only a new beginning; and the whole point of the pilgrimage is something which will come to pass for future generations. His nearest likeness is Job, but his reward is not what Job's was, but is only in the accomplishment of his destiny. He suffers for himself, he acts only in obedience. He is, in fact, the prototype of a Christian hero.

For he is, humbly, a man with a mission; and the mission is everything.

The *pietas* is in this way explicable only in terms of *fatum*. This is a word which constantly recurs in the *Aeneid*; a word charged with meaning, and perhaps with more meaning than Virgil himself knew. Our nearest word is 'destiny', and that is a word which means more than we can find any definitions for. It is a word which can have no meaning in a mechanical universe: if that which is wound up must run down, what destiny is there in that? Destiny is not necessitarianism, and it is not caprice: it is something essentially meaningful. Each man has his destiny, though some men are undoubtedly 'men of destiny' in a sense in which most men are not; and Aeneas is egregiously a man of destiny, since upon him the future of the Western World depends. But this is an election which cannot be explained, a burden and responsibility rather than a reason for self-glorification. It merely happens to one man and not to others, to have the gifts necessary in some profound crisis, but he can take no credit to himself for the gifts and the responsibility assigned to him. Some men have had a deep conviction of their destiny, and in that conviction have prospered; but when they cease to act as an instrument, and think of themselves as the active source of what they do, their pride is punished by disaster. Aeneas is a man guided by the deepest conviction of destiny, but he is a humble man who knows that this destiny is something not to be desired and not to be avoided. Of what power is he the servant? Not of the gods, who are themselves merely instruments, and sometimes rebellious ones. The concept of destiny leaves us with a mystery, but it is a mystery not contrary to reason, for it implies that the world, and the course of human history, have meaning.

Nor does destiny relieve mankind of moral responsibility. Such, at least, is my reading of the episode of Dido. The love affair of Aeneas and Dido is arranged by Venus: neither of the lovers was free to abstain. Now Venus herself is not acting on a whim, or out of mischief. She is certainly proud of the destiny of her son, but her behaviour is not that of a doting mother: she is herself an instrument for the realization of her son's destiny. Aeneas and Dido had to be united, and had to be separated. Aeneas did not demur; he was obedient to his fate. But he was certainly very unhappy about it, and I think that he felt that he was behaving shamefully. For why else should Virgil have contrived his meeting with the Shade of Dido in Hades, and the snub that he receives? When he sees Dido he tries to excuse himself for his betrayal. *Sed me iussa deum* — but I was under orders from the gods; it was a very unpleasant decision to have imposed upon me, and I am sorry that you took it so hard. She avoids his gaze and turns away, with a face as immobile as if it had been carved from flint or Marpesian rock. I have no doubt that Virgil, when he wrote these lines, was assuming the role of Aeneas and feeling very decidedly a worm. No, destiny like that of Aeneas does not make the man's life any easier: it is a very heavy cross to bear. And I do not think of any hero of antiquity who found himself in quite this inevitable and deplorable position. I think that the poet who could best have emulated Virgil's treatment of this situation was Racine: certainly the Christian poet who gave the furious Roxane the blasting line 'Rentre dans le Néant d'où je t'ai fait sortir' could, if anyone, have found words for Dido on this occasion.

What then does this destiny, which no Homeric hero shares with Aeneas, mean? For Virgil's conscious mind, and for his contemporary readers, it means the *imperium romanum*. This in itself, as Virgil saw it, was a worthy justification of history. I think that he had few illusions and that he saw clearly both sides of every question — the case for the loser as well as the case for the winner. Nevertheless even those who have as little Latin as I must remember and thrill at the lines:

> *His ego nec metas rerum, nec tempora pono:*
> *Imperium sine fine dedi* . . .

Tu regere imperio populos, Romane, memento
[*hae tibi erunt artes*] *pacique imponere morem,*
parcere subiectis et debellare superbos . . .

I say that it was all the end of history that Virgil could be asked to find, and that it was a worthy end. And do you really think that Virgil was mistaken? You must remember that the Roman Empire was transformed into the Holy Roman Empire. What Virgil proposed to his contemporaries was the highest ideal even for an unholy Roman Empire, for any merely temporal empire. We are all, so far as we inherit the civilization of Europe, still citizens of the Roman Empire, and time has not yet proved Virgil wrong when he wrote *nec tempora pono: imperium sine fine dedi*. But, of course, the Roman Empire which Virgil imagined and for which Aeneas worked out his destiny was not exactly the same as the Roman Empire of the legionaries, the pro-consuls and governors, the business men and speculators, the demagogues and generals. It was something greater, but something which exists because Virgil imagined it. It remains an ideal, but one which Virgil passed on to Christianity to develop and to cherish.

In the end, it seems to me that the place which Dante assigned to Virgil in the future life, and the role of guide and teacher as far as the barrier which Virgil was not allowed to pass, was not capable of passing, is an exact statement of Virgil's relation to the Christian world. We find the world of Virgil, compared to the world of Homer, to approximate to a Christian world, in the choice, order and relationship of its values. I have said that this implies no comparison between Homer the poet and Virgil the poet. Neither do I think that it is exactly a comparison between the worlds in which they lived, considered apart from the interpretation of these worlds which the poets have given us. It may be merely that we know more about the world of Virgil, and understand it better; and therefore see more clearly how much, in the Roman ideal according to Virgil, is due to the shaping hand and the philosophical mind of Virgil himself. For, in the sense in which a poet is a philosopher [as distinct from the sense in which a great poet may embody a great philosophy in great poetry] Virgil is the greatest philosopher of ancient Rome. It is not, therefore, simply that the civilization in which Virgil lived is nearer to the civilization of Christianity than is that of Homer; we can say that Virgil, among classical Latin poets or prose writers, is uniquely near to Christianity. There is a phrase which I have been trying to avoid, but which I now find myself obliged to use: *anima naturaliter Christiana*. Whether we apply it to Virgil is a matter of personal choice; but I am inclined to think that he just falls short: and that is why I said just now that I think Dante has put Virgil in the right place. I will try to give the reason.

I think of another key word, besides *labor*, *pietas* and *fatum*, which I wish that I could illustrate from Virgil in the same way. What key word can one find in the *Divine Comedy* which is absent from the *Aeneid*? One word of course is *lume*, and all the words expressive of the spiritual significance of light. But this, I think, as used by Dante, has a meaning which belongs only to explicit Christianity, fused with a meaning which belongs to mystical experience. And Virgil is no mystic. The term which one can justifiably regret the lack of in Virgil is *amor*. It is, above all others, the key word for Dante. I do not mean that Virgil never uses it. *Amor* recurs in the *Eclogues* [*amor vincit omnia*]. But the loves of the shepherds represent hardly more than a poetic convention. The use of the word *amor* in the *Eclogues* is not illuminated by meanings of the word in the *Aeneid* in the way in which, for example, we return to Paolo and Francesca with greater understanding of their passion after we have been taken through the circles of love in the *Paradiso*. Certainly, the love of Aeneas and Dido has great tragic force. There is tenderness and pathos enough in the *Aeneid*. But Love is never given, to my mind, the same

significance as a principle of order in the human soul, in society and in the universe that *pietas* is given; and it is not Love
that causes *fatum*, or moves the sun and the stars. Even for intensity of physical passion, Virgil is more tepid than some
other Latin poets, and far below the rank of Catullus. If we
are not chilled we at least feel ourselves, with Virgil, to be
moving in a kind of emotional twilight. Virgil was, among all
authors of classical antiquity, one for whom the world made
sense, for whom it had order and dignity, and for whom, as for
no one before his time except the Hebrew prophets, history
had meaning. But he was denied the vision of the man who
could say:

'Within its depths I saw ingathered, bound by love in one
volume, the scattered leaves of all the universe.'

Legato con amor in un volume.

Sir John Davies*

C HIEF Justice John Davies died on December 7, 1626. He left a number of poems, a philosophical treatise, 'Reason's Academy,' some legal writings, and several long State Papers on Ireland. As a public servant he had a distinguished career; but very likely the poem which has preserved his memory, *Nosce Teipsum*, was what commended him to King James. Possibly James was more appreciative of learning than of poetical merit; but, in any case, he recognized merit in a poet who was, in some respects, as out of place in his own age as he is in ours.

Davies's shorter poems are usually graceful and occasionally lovely, but they are so completely eclipsed even by the modest reputation of *Nosce Teipsum* and *Orchestra* that they are never chosen as anthology pieces. *Nosce Teipsum*, by its gnomic utterance and its self-contained quatrains, lends itself to mutilation; but a stanza or two is all that has been anthologized. Probably all that most readers know of Davies is represented by the two stanzas in the *Oxford Book of English Verse*:

> *I know my soul hath power to know all things,*
> *Yet she is blind and ignorant in all:*
> *I know I'm one of Nature's little kings,*
> *Yet to the least and vilest things am thrall.*

* Published in *The Times Literary Supplement* in 1926.

> I know my life's a pain and but a span;
> I know my sense is mock'd in everything;
> And, to conclude, I know myself a Man —
> Which is a proud and yet a wretched thing.

Fine and complete as the two stanzas are they do not represent the poem, and no selection of stanzas can represent it.
Davies is a poet of fine lines, but he is more than that. He is
not one of that second rank of poets who, here and there, echo
the notes of the great. If there is, in *Orchestra*, a hint of the
influence of Spenser, it is no more than the debt which many
Elizabethans owe to that master of versification. And the plan,
the versification, and the content of *Nosce Teipsum* are, in
that age, highly original.

The poem of *Nosce Teipsum* is a long discussion in verse of
the nature of the soul and its relation to the body. Davies's
theories are not those of the later seventeenth-century philoso-
phers, nor are they very good Aristotelianism. Davies is more
concerned to prove that the soul is distinct from the body than
to explain how such distinct entities can be united. The soul is
a spirit, and, as such, has wit, will, reason and judgment. It
does not appear as the 'form' of the body, and the word 'form'
appears in the poem rather in the sense of 'representation'
[*similitudo*]. The soul is in the body as light is in the air —
which disposes of the scholastic question whether the soul is
more in one part of the body than another. Nor are the problems of sense perception difficult to resolve: Davies is not
troubled by the 'reception of forms without matter'. His contribution to the science of acoustics is the explanation that
sounds must pass through the 'turns and windings' of the ear:

> For should the voice directly strike the braine,
> It would astonish and confuse it much.

Whether or not Davies borrowed his theories — if they deserve
the name of theories — from Nemesius or from some other
Early Christian author, and whether he got them direct or

secondhand, it is evident that we cannot take them very seriously. But the end of the sixteenth century was not a period of philosophic refinement in England — where, indeed, philosophy had visibly languished for a hundred years and more. Considering the place and the time, this philosophical poem by an eminent jurist is by no means a despicable production. In an age when philosophy, apart from theology, meant usually [and especially in verse] a collection of Senecan commonplaces, Davies's is an independent mind.

The merit and curiosity of the poem, however, reside in the perfection of the instrument to the end. In a language of remarkable clarity and austerity Davies succeeds in maintaining the poem consistently on the level of poetry; he never flies to hyperbole or bombast, and he never descends, as he easily might, to the pedestrian and ludicrous. Certain odd lines and quatrains remain in the memory, as:

> But sith our life so fast away doth slide,
> As doth a hungry eagle through the wind,

[a simile which Alexander borrows for his *Julius Caesar*], or

> And if thou, like a child, didst feare before,
> Being in the darke, where thou didst nothing see;
> Now I have brought thee torch-light, fear no more;
> Now when thou diest, thou canst not hud-winkt be.

Davies has not had the credit for great felicity of phrase, but it may be observed that, when other poets have pilfered from him or have arrived independently at the same figure, it is usually Davies who has the best of it. Grosart compares the following two passages showing a simile used by Davies and by Pope:

> Much like a subtill spider, which doth sit
> In middle of her web, which spreadeth wide;
> If aught do touch the utmost thread of it,
> She feels it instantly on every side.

Pope:

> *The spider's touch, how exquisitely fine,*
> *Feels at each thread, and lives along the line.*

Davies's spider is the more alive, though he needs two more lines for her. Another instance is the well-known figure from the *Ancient Mariner*:

> *Still as a slave before his lord,*
> *The ocean hath no blast;*
> *His great bright eye most silently*
> *Up to the Moon is cast —*

where 'most' is a blemish. Davies has [in *Orchestra*]:

> *For loe the Sea that fleets about the Land,*
> *And like a girdle clips her solide waist,*
> *Musicke and measure both doth understand;*
> *For his great chrystall eye is always cast*
> *Up to the Moone, and on her fixèd fast;*
> *And as she daunceth in her pallid spheere*
> *So daunceth he about his center heere.*

But the mastery of workmanship of *Nosce Teipsum* and its beauty are not to be appreciated by means of scattered quotations. Its effect is cumulative. Davies chose a difficult stanza, one in which it is almost impossible to avoid monotony. He embellishes it with none of the flowers of conceit of his own age or the next, and he has none of the antitheses or verbal wit with which the Augustans sustain their periods. His vocabulary is clear, choice and precise. His thought is, for an Elizabethan poet, amazingly coherent; there is nothing that is irrelevant to his main argument, no excursions or flights. And, although every quatrain is complete in itself, the sequence is never a 'string of pearls' [such as was fashionable in the next age, as in Crashaw's *Weeper*]; the thought is continuous. Yet no stanza ever is identical in rhythm with another. The style appears plain, even bald, yet Davies's personal cadence is al-

ways there. Many critics have remarked the condensation of
thought, the economy of language, and the consistency of excellence; but some have fallen into the error of supposing that
Davies's merit is of prose. Hallam, after praising the poem, says:

'If it reaches the heart of all, it is through the reason. But
since strong argument in terse and correct style fails not to give
us pleasure in prose, it seems strange that it should lose its effect when it gains the aid of regular metre to gratify the ear
and assist the memory.'

Hallam's criticism is topsy-turvy. Hallam's heart must have
been peculiarly inaccessible, or his reason very easily touched.
The argument is not strong; had Davies entered the ring of
philosophical argument his contemporary, Cardinal Bellarmine,
could have knocked him out in the first round. Davies had not
a philosophical mind; he was primarily a poet, but with a gift
for philosophical exposition. His appeal is, indeed, to what
Hallam calls the heart, though we no longer employ that single
organ as the vehicle of all poetic feeling. The excellence of
the theory of body and soul which Davies expounded is, how
ever, irrelevant. If someone had provided him with a better
theory the poem might have been, in one aspect, a better one;
in another aspect it does not matter a fig. The wonder is that
Davies, in his place and time, could produce so coherent and
respectable a theory as he did. No one, not even Gray, has surpassed Davies in the use of the quatrain which he employed
for *Nosce Teipsum*; and no poem in any similar metre [com-
pare *The Witch of Atlas*] is metrically superior to *Orchestra*.
Even his little acrostic poems on the name of Queen Elizabeth
are admirable in grace and melody. And with this genius for
versification, with a taste in language remarkably pure for his
age, Davies had that strange gift, so rarely bestowed, for turning thought into feeling.

In the effort to 'place' Davies, who appears anomalous,
critics have compared him on the one hand to the Senecals,
to Chapman and Daniel and Greville, and on the other hand

to Donne and the metaphysicals. Neither classification is quite
exact. Davies's only direct debt as a poet seems to be to Spenser, the master of everybody. The type of his thought, and
consequently the tone of his expression, separates him from
the Senecals. His thought, as we have said, is inferior as philosophy, but it is coherent and free from eccentricity or pose.
He thinks like a scholastic, though the quality of his thought
would have shocked a scholastic. Chapman, Daniel and Greville, so far as they can be said to have thought at all, thought
like Latin rhetoricians. Like the other dramatists, they imbibed
from Seneca a philosophy which is essentially a theatrical pose.
Hence their language, even when pure and restrained — and
Daniel's is astonishingly pure and restrained — is always oro-
tund and oratorical; their verse is as if spoken in public, and
their feelings as if felt in public. Davies's is the language and
the tone of solitary meditation; he speaks like a man reasoning
with himself in solitiude, and he never raises his voice.

In the same way Davies may be said to have little in common with Donne. It is not merely Davies's restraint in the use
of simile and metaphor. The verbal conceit, as used by Donne,
implies a very different attitude towards ideas from that of
Davies, perhaps a much more conscious one. Donne was ready
to entertain almost any idea, to play with it, to follow it out of
curiosity, to explore all its possibilities of affecting his sensibility. Davies is much more mediaeval; his capacity for belief
is greater. He has but the one idea, which he pursues in all
seriousness — a kind of seriousness rare in his age. Thought is
not exploited for the sake of feeling, it is pursued for its own
sake; and the feeling is a kind of by-product, though a by-
product worth far more than the thought. The effect of the
sequence of the poem is not to diversify or embellish the feeling: it is wholly to intensify. The variation is in the metrics.

There is only one parallel to *Nosce Teipsum*, and, though it
is a daring one, it is not unfair to Davies. It is the several passages of exposition of the nature of the soul which occur in the

middle of the *Purgatorio*. To compare Davies with Dante may appear fantastic. But, after all, very few people read these parts of Dante, and fewer still get any pleasure out of them: in short, these passages are probably as little read or enjoyed as *Nosce Teipsum* itself. Of course they are vastly finer, for two quite different reasons — Dante was a vastly greater poet, and the philosophy which he expounds is infinitely more substantial and subtle:

> *Esce di mano a lui, che la vagheggia*
> *prima che sia, a guisa di fanciulla*
> *che piangendo e ridendo pargoleggia,*

> *l'anima semplicetta, che sa nulla,*
> *salvo che, mossa da lieto fattore,*
> *volentier torna a cio che la trastulla.*

> *Di picciol bene in pria sente sapore;*
> *quivi s'inganna, e retro ad esso corre,*
> *se guida o fren non torce suo amore.*

> *From his hands who fondly loves her ere she is*
> *in being, there issues, after the fashion of a little*
> *child that sports, now weeping, now laughing,*

> *the simple, tender soul, who knoweth naught save*
> *that, sprung from a joyous maker, willingly she*
> *turneth to that which delights her.*

> *First she tastes the savour of a trifling good; there*
> *she is beguiled and runneth after it, if guide or curb*
> *turn not her love aside.*

It is not in any way to put Davies on a level with Dante to say that anyone who can appreciate the beauty of such lines as these should be able to extract considerable pleasure from *Nosce Teipsum*.

Milton I*

W HILE it must be admitted that Milton is a very great
poet indeed, it is something of a puzzle to decide in
what his greatness consists. On analysis, the marks against him
appear both more numerous and more significant than the
marks to his credit. As a man, he is antipathetic. Either from
the moralist's point of view, or from the theologian's point of
view, or from the psychologist's point of view, or from that of
the political philosopher, or judging by the ordinary standards
of likeableness in human beings, Milton is unsatisfactory. The
doubts which I have to express about him are more serious
than these. His greatness as a poet has been sufficiently celebrated, though I think largely for the wrong reasons, and without the proper reservations. His misdeeds as a poet have been
called attention to, as by Mr. Ezra Pound, but usually in passing. What seems to me necessary is to assert at the same time
his greatness — in that what he could do well he did better
than anyone else has ever done — and the serious charges to
be made against him, in respect of the deterioration — the peculiar kind of deterioration — to which he subjected the language.

Many people will agree that a man may be a great artist, and
yet have a bad influence. There is more of Milton's influence
in the badness of the bad verse of the eighteenth century than
of anybody's else: he certainly did more harm than Dryden
and Pope, and perhaps a good deal of the obloquy which has

* Contributed to *Essays and Studies* of The English Association, Oxford University Press, 1936.

fallen on these two poets, especially the latter, because of their influence, ought to be transferred to Milton. But to put the matter simply in terms of 'bad influence' is not necessarily to bring a serious charge: because a good deal of the responsibility, when we state the problem in these terms, may devolve on the eighteenth-century poets themselves for being such bad poets that they were incapable of being influenced except for ill. There is a good deal more to the charge against Milton than this; and it appears a good deal more serious if we affirm that Milton's poetry could *only* be an influence for the worse, upon any poet whatever. It is more serious, also, if we affirm that Milton's bad influence may be traced much farther than the eighteenth century, and much farther than upon bad poets: if we say that it was an influence against which we still have to struggle.

There is a large class of persons, including some who appear in print as critics, who regard any censure upon a 'great' poet as a breach of the peace, as an act of wanton iconoclasm, or even hoodlumism. The kind of derogatory criticism that I have to make upon Milton is not intended for such persons, who cannot understand that it is more important, in some vital respects, to be a *good* poet than to be a *great* poet; and of what I have to say I consider that the only jury of judgment is that of the ablest poetical practitioners of my own time.

The most important fact about Milton, for my purpose, is his blindness. I do not mean that to go blind in middle life is itself enough to determine the whole nature of a man's poetry. Blindness must be considered in conjunction with Milton's personality and character, and the peculiar education which he received. It must also be considered in connexion with his devotion to, and expertness in, the art of music. Had Milton been a man of very keen senses — I mean of *all* the five senses — his blindness would not have mattered so much. But for a man whose sensuousness, such as it was, had been withered early by book-learning, and whose gifts were naturally aural, it

mattered a great deal. It would seem, indeed, to have helped
him to concentrate on what he could do best.

At no period is the visual imagination conspicuous in Milton's poetry. It would be as well to have a few illustrations of
what I mean by visual imagination. From *Macbeth*:

> *This guest of summer,*
> *The temple-haunting martlet, does approve*
> *By his loved mansionry that the heaven's breath*
> *Smells wooingly here: no jutty, frieze,*
> *Buttress, nor coign of vantage, but this bird*
> *Hath made his pendent bed and procreant cradle:*
> *Where they most breed and haunt, I have observed*
> *The air is delicate.*

It may be observed that such an image, as well as another
familiar quotation from a little later in the same play,

> *Light thickens, and the crow*
> *Makes wing to the rooky wood*

not only offer something to the eye, but, so to speak, to the
common sense. I mean that they convey the feeling of being in
a particular place at a particular time. The comparison with
Shakespeare offers another indication of the peculiarity of Milton. With Shakespeare, far more than with any other poet in
English, the combinations of words offer perpetual novelty;
they enlarge the meaning of the individual words joined: thus
'procreant cradle', 'rooky wood.' In comparison, Milton's
images do not give this sense of particularity, nor are the separate words developed in significance. His language is, if one
may use the term without disparagement, *artificial* and *conventional*.

> *O'er the smooth enamel'd green . . .*

> *. . . paths of this drear wood*
> *The nodding horror of whose shady brows*
> *Threats the forlorn and wandering passenger.*

['Shady brow' here is a diminution of the value of the two words from their use in the line from *Dr. Faustus*

> *Shadowing more beauty in their airy brows.*]

The imagery in *L'Allegro* and *Il Penseroso* is all general:

> *While the ploughman near at hand,*
> *Whistles o'er the furrowed land,*
> *And the milkmaid singeth blithe,*
> *And the mower whets his scythe,*
> *And every shepherd tells his tale,*
> *Under the hawthorn in the dale.*

It is not a particular ploughman, milkmaid, and shepherd that Milton sees [as Wordsworth might see them]; the sensuous effect of these verses is entirely on the ear, and is joined to the concepts of ploughman, milkmaid, and shepherd. Even in his most mature work, Milton does not infuse new life into the word, as Shakespeare does.

> *The sun to me is dark*
> *And silent as the moon,*
> *When she deserts the night*
> *Hid in her vacant interlunar cave.*

Here *interlunar* is certainly a stroke of genius, but is merely combined with 'vacant' and 'cave', rather than giving and receiving life from them. Thus it is not so unfair, as it might at first appear, to say that Milton writes English like a dead language. The criticism has been made with regard to his involved syntax. But a tortuous style, when its peculiarity is aimed at precision [as with Henry James], is not necessarily a dead one; only when the complication is dictated by a demand of verbal music, instead of by any demand of sense.

> *Thrones, dominations, princedoms, virtues, powers,*
> *If these magnific titles yet remain*
> *Not merely titular, since by decree*
> *Another now hath to himself engrossed*

All power, and us eclipsed under the name
Of King anointed, for whom all this haste
Of midnight march, and hurried meeting here,
This only to consult how we may best
With what may be devised of honours new
Receive him coming to receive from us
Knee-tribute yet unpaid, prostration vile,
Too much to one, but double how endured,
To one and to his image now proclaimed?

With which compare:

'However, he didn't mind thinking that if Cissy should prove all that was likely enough their having a subject in common couldn't but practically conduce; though the moral of it all amounted rather to a portent, the one that Haughty, by the same token, had done least to reassure him against, of the extent to which the native jungle harboured the female specimen and to which its ostensible cover, the vast level of mixed growths stirred wavingly in whatever breeze, was apt to be identifiable but as an agitation of the latest redundant thing in ladies' hats.'

This quotation, taken almost at random from *The Ivory Tower*, is not intended to represent Henry James at any hypothetical 'best', any more than the noble passage from *Paradise Lost* is meant to be Milton's hypothetical worst. The question is the difference of intention, in the elaboration of styles both of which depart so far from lucid simplicity. The sound, of course, is never irrelevant, and the style of James certainly depends for its effect a good deal on the sound of a voice, James's own, painfully explaining. But the complication, with James, is due to a determination not to simplify, and in that simplification lose any of the real intricacies and by-paths of mental movement; whereas the complication of a Miltonic sentence is an active complication, a complication deliberately introduced into what was a previously simplified and abstract thought. The dark angel here is not *thinking* or conversing, but making a speech carefully prepared for him; and the arrangement is for the sake of musical value, not for significance. A straightforward utterance, as of a Homeric or Dantesque character, would make the speaker very much more real to us; but reality is no part of the intention. We have in fact to read such a passage not analytically, to get the poetic impression. I am not suggesting that Milton has no idea to convey which he regards as important: only that the syntax is determined by the musical significance, by the auditory imagination, rather than by the attempt to follow actual speech or thought. It is at least more nearly possible to distinguish the pleasure which arises from the *noise*, from the pleasure due to other elements, than with the verse of Shakespeare, in which the auditory imagination and the imagination of the other senses are more nearly fused, and fused together with the thought. The result with Milton is, in one sense of the word, *rhetoric*. That term is not intended to be derogatory. This kind of 'rhetoric' is not necessarily bad in its influence; but it may be considered bad in relation to the historical life of a language as a whole. I have said elsewhere that the living English which was Shakespeare's became split up into two components one of which was exploited by Milton and the other by Dryden. Of the two, I still think Dryden's development the healthier, because it was Dryden who preserved, so far as it was preserved at all, the tradition of conversational language in poetry: and I might add that it seems to me easier to get back to healthy language from Dryden than it is to get back to it from Milton. For what such a generalization is worth, Milton's influence on the eighteenth century was much more deplorable than Dryden's.

If several very important reservations and exceptions are made, I think that it is not unprofitable to compare Milton's development with that of James Joyce. The initial similarities are musical taste and abilities, followed by musical training, wide and curious knowledge, gift for acquiring languages, and remarkable powers of memory perhaps fortified by defective vision. The important difference is that Joyce's imagination is not naturally of so purely auditory a type as Milton's. In his early work, and at least in part of *Ulysses*, there is visual and other imagination of the highest kind; and I may be mistaken in thinking that the later part of *Ulysses* shows a turning from the visible world to draw rather on the resources of phantasmagoria. In any case, one may suppose that the replenishment of visual imagery during later years has been insufficient; so that what I find in *Work in Progress* is an auditory imagination abnormally sharpened at the expense of the visual. There is still a little to be seen, and what there is to see is worth looking at. And I would repeat that with Joyce this development seems to me largely due to circumstances: whereas Milton may be said never to have seen anything. For Milton, therefore, the concentration on sound was wholly a benefit. Indeed, I find, in reading *Paradise Lost*, that I am happiest where there is least to visualize. The eye is not shocked in his twilit Hell as it is in the Garden of Eden, where I for one can get pleasure from the verse only by the deliberate effort not to visualize Adam and Eve and their surroundings.

I am not suggesting any close parallel between the 'rhetoric' of Milton and the later style of Joyce. It is a different music; and Joyce always maintains some contact with the conversational tone. But it may prove to be equally a blind alley for the future development of the language.

A disadvantage of the rhetorical style appears to be, that a dislocation takes place, through the hypertrophy of the auditory imagination at the expense of the visual and tactile, so that the inner meaning is separated from the surface, and tends to become something occult, or at least without effect upon the reader until fully understood. To extract everything possible from *Paradise Lost*, it would seem necessary to read it in two different ways, first solely for the sound, and second for the sense. The full beauty of his long periods can hardly be

enjoyed while we are wrestling with the meaning as well; and
for the pleasure of the ear the meaning is hardly necessary,
except in so far as certain key-words indicate the emotional
tone of the passage. Now Shakespeare, or Dante, will bear innumerable readings, but at each reading all the elements of
appreciation can be present. There is no interruption between
the surface that these poets present to you and the core. While
therefore, I cannot pretend to have penetrated to any 'secret'
of these poets, I feel that such appreciation of their work as I
am capable of points in the right direction; whereas I cannot
feel that my appreciation of Milton leads anywhere outside of
the mazes of sound. That, I feel, would be the matter for a
separate study, like that of Blake's prophetic books; it might be
well worth the trouble, but would have little to do with my
interest in the poetry. So far as I perceive anything, it is a
glimpse of a theology that I find in large part repellent, expressed through a mythology which would have better been
left in the Book of *Genesis*, upon which Milton has not improved. There seems to me to be a division, in Milton, between
the philosopher or theologian and the poet; and, for the latter,
I suspect also that this concentration upon the auditory imagination leads to at least an occasional levity. 1 can enjoy the
roll of

> . . . *Cambula, seat of Cathaian Can*
> *And Samarchand by Oxus, Temir's throne,*
> *To Paquin of Sinaean kings, and thence*
> *To Agra and Lahor of great Mogul*
> *Down to the golden Chersonese, or where*
> *The Persian in Ecbatan sate, or since*
> *In Hispahan, or where the Russian Ksar*
> *On Mosco, or the Sultan in Bizance,*
> *Turchestan-born . . . ,*

and the rest of it, but I feel that this is not serious poetry, not
poetry fully occupied about its business, but rather a solemn
game. More often, admittedly, Milton uses proper names in

moderation, to obtain the same effect of magnificence with them as does Marlowe — nowhere perhaps better than in the passage from *Lycidas*:

> *Whether beyond the stormy Hebrides,*
> *Where thou perhaps under the whelming tide*
> *Visit'st the bottom of the monstrous world;*
> *Or whether thou to our moist vows deny'd*
> *Sleep'st by the fable of Bellerus old,*
> *Where the great vision of the guarded Mount*
> *Looks toward Namancos and Bayona's hold . . .*

than which for the single effect of grandeur of sound, there is nothing finer in poetry.

I make no attempt to appraise the 'greatness' of Milton in relation to poets who seem to me more comprehensive and better balanced; it has seemed to me more fruitful for the present to press the parallel between *Paradise Lost* and *Work in Progress*; and both Milton and Joyce are so exalted in their own kinds, in the whole of literature, that the only writers with whom to compare them are writers who have attempted something very different. Our views about Joyce, in any case, must remain at the present time tentative. But there are two attitudes both of which are necessary and right to adopt in considering the work of any poet. One is when we isolate him, when we try to understand the rules of his own game, adopt his own point of view: the other, perhaps less usual, is when we measure him by outside standards, most pertinently by the standards of language and of something called Poetry, in our own language and in the whole history of European literature. It is from the second point of view that my objections to Milton are made: it is from this point of view that we can go so far as to say that, although his work realizes superbly one important element in poetry, he may still be considered as having done damage to the English language from which it has not wholly recovered.

Milton II*

SAMUEL Johnson, addressing himself to examine Milton's versification, in the *Rambler* of Saturday, January 12, 1751, thought it necessary to excuse his temerity in writing upon a subject already so fully discussed. In justification of his essay this great critic and poet remarked: 'There are, in every age, new errors to be rectified, and new prejudices to be opposed.' I am obliged to phrase my own apology rather differently. The errors of our own times have been rectified by vigorous hands, and the prejudices opposed by commanding voices. Some of the errors and prejudices have been associated with my own name, and of these in particular I shall find myself impelled to speak; it will, I hope, be attributed to me for modesty rather than for conceit if I maintain that no one can correct an error with better authority than the person who has been held responsible for it. And there is, I think, another justification for my speaking about Milton, besides the singular one which I have just given. The champions of Milton in our time, with one notable exception, have been scholars and teachers. I have no claim to be either: I am aware that my only claim upon your attention, in speaking of Milton or of any other great poet, is by appeal to your curiosity, in the hope that you may care to know what a contemporary writer of verse thinks of one of his predecessors.

I believe that the scholar and the practitioner in the field of

* The Henrietta Hertz Lecture, delivered to the British Academy, 1947 and subsequently at the Frick Museum, New York.

literary criticism should supplement each other's work. The criticism of the practitioner will be all the better, certainly, if he is not wholly destitute of scholarship; and the criticism of the scholar will be all the better if he has some experience of the difficulties of writing verse. But the orientation of the two critics is different. The scholar is more concerned with the understanding of the masterpiece in the environment of its author: with the world in which that author lived, the temper of his age, his intellectual formation, the books which he had read, and the influences which had moulded him. The practitioner is concerned less with the author than with the poem; and with the poem in relation to his own age. He asks: Of what *use* is the poetry of this poet to poets writing to-day? Is it, or can it become, a living force in English poetry still unwritten? So we may say that the scholar's interest is in the permanent, the practitioner's in the immediate. The scholar can teach us where we should bestow our *admiration* and *respect:* the practitioner should be able, when he is the right poet talking about the right poet, to make an old masterpiece actual, give it contemporary importance, and persuade his audience that it is interesting, exciting, enjoyable, and *active.* I can give only one example of contemporary criticism of Milton, by a critic of the type to which I belong if I have any critical pretensions at all: that is the Introduction to Milton's *English Poems* in the 'World Classics' series, by the late Charles Williams. It is not a comprehensive essay; it is notable primarily because it provides the best prolegomenon to *Comus* which any modern reader could have; but what distinguishes it throughout [and the same is true of most of Williams's critical writing] is the author's warmth of feeling and his success in communicating it to the reader. In this, so far as I am aware, the essay of Williams is a solitary example.

I think it is useful, in such an examination as I propose to make, to keep in mind some critic of the past, of one's own type, by whom to measure one's opinions: a critic sufficiently remote in time, for his local errors and prejudices to be not identical with one's own. That is why I began by quoting Samuel Johnson. It will hardly be contested that as a critic of poetry Johnson wrote as a practitioner and not as a scholar. Because he was a poet himself, and a good poet, what he wrote about poetry must be read with respect. And unless we know and appreciate Johnson's poetry we cannot judge either the merits or the limitations of his criticism. It is a pity that what the common reader to-day has read, or has remembered, or has seen quoted, are mostly those few statements of Johnson's from which later critics have vehemently dissented. But when Johnson held an opinion which seems to us wrong, we are never safe in dismissing it without inquiring why he was wrong; he had his own 'errors and prejudices', certainly, but for lack of examining them sympathetically we are always in danger of merely countering error with error and prejudice with prejudice. Now Johnson was, in his day, very much a modern: he was concerned with how poetry should be written in his own time. The fact that he came towards the end, rather than the beginning of a style, the fact that his time was rapidly passing away, and that the canons of taste which he observed were about to fall into desuetude, does not diminish the interest of his criticism. Nor does the likelihood that the development of poetry in the next fifty years will take quite different directions from those which to me seem desirable to explore, deter me from asking the questions that Johnson implied: How should poetry be written now? and what place does the answer to this question give to Milton? And I think that the answers to these questions may be different now from the answers that were correct twenty-five years ago.

There is one prejudice against Milton, apparent on almost every page of Johnson's *Life of Milton*, which I imagine is still general: we, however, with a longer historical perspective, are in a better position than was Johnson to recognize it and to make allowance for it. This is a prejudice which I share my-

self: an antipathy towards Milton the man. Of this in itself
I have nothing further to say: all that is necessary is to record
one's awareness of it. But this prejudice is often involved with
another, more obscure: and I do not think that Johnson had
disengaged the two in his own mind. The fact is simply that
the Civil War of the seventeenth century, in which Milton is
a symbolic figure, has never been concluded. The Civil War is
not ended: I question whether any serious civil war ever does
end. Throughout that period English society was so convulsed
and divided that the effects are still felt. Reading Johnson's
essay one is always aware that Johnson was obstinately and
passionately of another party. No other English poet, not
Wordsworth, or Shelley, lived through or took sides in such
momentous events as did Milton; of no other poet is it so difficult to consider the poetry simply as poetry, without our theological and political dispositions, conscious and unconscious,
inherited or acquired, making an unlawful entry. And the
danger is all the greater because these emotions now take
different vestures. It is now considered grotesque, on political
grounds, to be of the party of King Charles; it is now, I believe, considered equally grotesque, on moral grounds, to be
of the party of the Puritans; and to most persons to-day the
religious views of both parties may seem equally remote.
Nevertheless, the passions are unquenched, and if we are not
very wide awake their smoke will obscure the glass through
which we examine Milton's poetry. Something has been done,
certainly, to persuade us that Milton was never really of any
party, but disagreed with everyone. Mr. Wilson Knight, in
Chariot of Wrath, has argued that Milton was more a mon-
archist than a republican, and not in any modern sense a
'democrat', and Professor Saurat has produced evidence to
show that Milton's theology was highly eccentric, and as scan-
dalous to Protestants as to Catholics — that he was, in fact,
a sort of Christadelphian, and perhaps not a very orthodox
Christadelphian at that; while on the other hand Mr. C. S.

Lewis has opposed Professor Saurat by skilfully arguing that
Milton, at least in *Paradise Lost*, can be acquitted of heresy
even from a point of view so orthodox as that of Mr. Lewis
himself. On these questions I hold no opinion: it is probably
beneficial to question the assumption that Milton was a sound
Free Churchman and member of the Liberal Party; but I think
that we still have to be on guard against an unconscious par-
tisanship if we aim to attend to the poetry for the poetry's sake.

So much for our prejudices. I come next to the positive objection to Milton which has been raised in our own time, that
is to say, the charge that he is an unwholesome influence. And
from this I shall proceed to the permanent strictures of reproof [to employ a phrase of Johnson's] and, finally, to the
grounds on which I consider him a great poet and one whom
poets to-day might study with profit.

For a statement of the *generalized* belief in the unwhole-
someness of Milton's influence I turn to Mr. Middleton Murry's
critique of Milton in his *Heaven and Earth* — a book which
contains chapters of profound insight, interrupted by passages
which seem to me intemperate. Mr. Murry approaches Milton
after his long and patient study of Keats; and it is through the
eyes of Keats that he sees Milton.

'Keats [*Mr. Murry writes*] as a poetic artist, second to none
since Shakespeare, and Blake, as a prophet of spiritual values
unique in our history, both passed substantially the same
judgement on Milton: "Life to him would be death to me."
And whatever may be our verdict on the development of
English poetry since Milton, we must admit the justice of
Keats's opinion that Milton's magnificence led nowhere. "English must be kept up," said Keats. To be influenced beyond a
certain point by Milton's art, he felt, dammed the creative
flow of the English genius in and through itself. In saying this,
I think, Keats voiced the very inmost of the English genius.
To pass under the spell of Milton is to be condemned to
imitate him. It is quite different with Shakespeare. Shake-

speare baffles and liberates; Milton is perspicuous and con-
stricts.'

This is a very confident affirmation, and I criticize it with
some diffidence because I cannot pretend to have devoted as
much study to Keats, or to have as intimate an understanding
of his difficulties, as Mr. Murry. But Mr. Murry seems to me
here to be trying to transform the predicament of a particular
poet with a particular aim at a particular moment in time into
a censure of timeless validity. He appears to assert that the
liberative function of Shakespeare and the constrictive menace
of Milton are permanent characteristics of these two poets. 'To
be influenced beyond a certain point' by any one master is
bad for any poet; and it does not matter whether that influence is Milton's or another's; and as we cannot anticipate
where that point will come, we might be better advised to call
it an *uncertain* point. If it is not good to remain under the
spell of Milton, is it good to remain under the spell of Shakespeare? It depends partly upon what *genre* of poetry you are
trying to develop. Keats wanted to write an epic, and he found,
as might be expected, that the time had not arrived at which
another English epic, comparable in grandeur to *Paradise Lost*,
could be written. He also tried his hand at writing plays: and
one might argue that *King Stephen* was more blighted by
Shakespeare than *Hyperion* by Milton. Certainly, *Hyperion*
remains a magnificent fragment which one re-reads; and *King
Stephen* is a play which we may have read once, but to which
we never return for enjoyment. Milton made a great epic impossible for succeeding generations; Shakespeare made a great
poetic drama impossible; such a situation is inevitable, and it
persists until the language has so altered that there is no
danger, because no possibility, of imitation. Anyone who tries
to write poetic drama, even to-day, should know that half of
his energy must be exhausted in the effort to escape from the
constricting toils of Shakespeare: the moment his attention is
relaxed, or his mind fatigued, he will lapse into bad Shake-

spearian verse. For a long time after an epic poet like Milton, or a dramatic poet like Shakespeare, nothing can be done. Yet the effort must be repeatedly made; for we can never know in advance when the moment is approaching at which a new epic, or a new drama, will be possible; and when the moment does draw near it may be that the genius of an individual poet will perform the last mutation of idiom and versification which will bring that new poetry into being.

I have referred to Mr. Murry's view of the bad influence of Milton as generalized, because it is implicitly the whole personality of Milton that is in question: not specifically his beliefs, or his language or versification, but the beliefs as realized in that particular personality, and his poetry as the expression of it. By the *particular* view of Milton's influence as bad, I mean that view which attends to the language, the syntax, the versification, the imagery. I do not suggest that there is here a complete difference of subject matter: it is the difference of approach, the difference of the focus of interest, between the philosophical critic and the literary critic. An incapacity for the abstruse, and an interest in poetry which is primarily a technical interest, dispose my mind towards the more limited and perhaps more superficial task. Let us proceed to look at Milton's influence from this point of view, that of the writer of poetry in our own time.

The reproach against Milton, that his technical influence has been bad, appears to have been made by no one more positively than by myself. I find myself saying, as recently as 1936, that this charge against Milton 'appears a good deal more serious if we affirm that Milton's poetry could *only* be an influence for the worse, upon any poet whatever. It is more serious, also, if we affirm that Milton's bad influence may be traced much farther than the eighteenth century, and much farther than upon bad poets: if we say that it was an influence against which we still have to struggle.'

In writing these sentences I failed to draw a threefold dis-

tinction, which now seems to me of some importance. There
are three separate assertions implied. The first is, that an influence has been bad in the past: this is to assert that good
poets, in the eighteenth or nineteenth century, would have
written better if they had not submitted themselves to the
influence of Milton. The second assertion is, that the contemporary situation is such that Milton is a master whom we
should avoid. The third is, that the influence of Milton, or of
any particular poet, can be *always* bad, and that we can predict
that wherever it is found at any time in the future, however
remote, it will be a bad influence. Now, the first and third of
these assertions I am no longer prepared to make, because,
detached from the second, they do not appear to me to have
any meaning.

For the first, when we consider one great poet of the past,
and one or more other poets, upon whom we say he has exerted
a bad influence, we must admit that the responsibility, if there
be any, is rather with the poets who were influenced than with
the poet whose work exerted the influence. We can, of course,
show that certain tricks or mannerisms which the imitators
display are due to conscious or unconscious imitation and
emulation, but that is a reproach against their injudicious
choice of a model and not against their model itself. And we
can never prove that any particular poet would have written
better poetry if he had escaped that influence. Even if we
assert, what can only be a matter of faith, that Keats would
have written a very great epic poem if Milton had not preceded him, is it sensible to pine for an unwritten masterpiece,
in exchange for one which we possess and acknowledge? And
as for the remote future, what can we affirm about the poetry
that will be written then, except that we should probably be
unable to understand or to enjoy it, and that therefore we can
hold no opinion as to what 'good' and 'bad' influences will
mean in that future? The only relation in which the question
of influence, good and bad, is significant, is the relation to the

immediate future. With that question I shall engage at the end. I wish first to mention another reproach against Milton, that represented by the phrase 'dissociation of sensibility'.

I remarked many years ago, in an essay on Dryden, that:

'In the seventeenth century a dissociation of sensibility set in, from which we have never recovered; and this dissociation, as is natural, was due to the influence of the two most powerful poets of the century, Milton and Dryden.'

The longer passage from which this sentence is taken is quoted by Dr. Tillyard in his *Milton*. Dr. Tillyard makes the following comment:

'Speaking only of what in this passage concerns Milton, I would say that there is here a mixture of truth and falsehood. Some sort of dissociation of sensibility in Milton, not necessarily undesirable, has to be admitted; but that he was responsible for any such dissociation in others [at least till this general dissociation had inevitably set in] is untrue.'

I believe that the general affirmation represented by the phrase 'dissociation of sensibility' [one of the two or three phrases of my coinage — like 'objective correlative' — which have had a success in the world astonishing to their author] retains some validity; but I now incline to agree with Dr. Tillyard that to lay the burden on the shoulders of Milton and Dryden was a mistake. If such a dissociation did take place, I suspect that the causes are too complex and too profound to justify our accounting for the change in terms of literary criticism. All we can say is, that something like this did happen; that it had something to do with the Civil War; that it would even be unwise to say it was caused by the Civil War, but that it is a consequence of the same causes which brought about the Civil War; that we must seek the causes in Europe, not in England alone; and for what these causes were, we may dig and dig until we get to a depth at which words and concepts fail us.

Before proceeding to take up the case against Milton, as it

stood for poets twenty-five years ago — the second, and only
significant meaning of 'bad influence' — I think it would be
best to consider what permanent strictures of reproof may be
drawn: those censures which, when we make them, we must
assume to be made by enduring laws of taste. The essence of
the permanent censure of Milton is, I believe, to be found in
Johnson's essay. This is not the place in which to examine
certain particular and erroneous judgments of Johnson; to explain his condemnation of *Comus* and *Samson* as the application of dramatic canons which to us seem inapplicable; or to
condone his dismissal of the versification of *Lycidas* by the
specialization, rather than the absence, of his sense of rhythm.
Johnson's most important censure of Milton is contained in
three paragraphs, which I must ask leave to quote in full.

'Throughout all his greater works [*says Johnson*] there pre-
vails an uniform peculiarity of *diction*, a mode and cast of
expression which bears little resemblance to that of any former
writer; and which is so far removed from common use, that an
unlearned reader, when he first opens the book, finds himself
surprised by a new language.

'This novelty has been, by those who can find nothing wrong
with Milton, imputed to his laborious endeavours after words
suited to the grandeur of his ideas. *Our language*, says Addison,
sunk under him. But the truth is, that both in prose and in
verse, he had formed his style by a perverse and pedantic principle. He was desirous to use English words with a foreign
idiom. This in all his prose is discovered and condemned; for
there judgment operates freely, neither softened by the beauty,
nor awed by the dignity of his thoughts; but such is the power
of his poetry, that his call is obeyed without resistance, the
reader feels himself in captivity to a higher and nobler mind,
and criticism sinks in admiration.

'Milton's style was not modified by his subject; what is
shown with greater extent in *Paradise Lost* may be found in
Comus. One source of his peculiarity was his familiarity with

the Tuscan poets; the disposition of his words is, I think, frequently Italian; perhaps sometimes combined with other tongues. Of him at last, may be said what Jonson said of Spenser, that he *wrote no language*, but has formed what Butler called a *Babylonish dialect*, in itself harsh and barbarous, but made by exalted genius and extensive learning the vehicle of so much instruction and so much pleasure, that, like other lovers, we find grace in its deformity.'

This criticism seems to me substantially true: indeed, unless we accept it, I do not think we are in the way to appreciate the peculiar greatness of Milton. His style is not a *classic* style, in that it is not the elevation of a *common* style, by the final touch of genius, to greatness. It is, from the foundation, and in every particular, a personal style, not based upon common speech, or common prose, or direct communication of meaning. Of some great poetry one has difficulty in pronouncing just what it is, what infinitesimal touch, that has made all the difference from a plain statement which anyone could make; the slight transformation which, while it leaves a plain statement a plain statement, has always the maximal, never the minimal, alteration of ordinary language. Every distortion of construction, the foreign idiom, the use of a word in a foreign way or with the meaning of the foreign word from which it is derived rather than the accepted meaning in English, every idiosyncrasy is a particular act of violence which Milton has been the first to commit. There is no cliché, no poetic diction in the derogatory sense, but a perpetual sequence of original acts of lawlessness. Of all modern writers of verse, the nearest analogy seems to me to be Mallarmé, a much smaller poet, though still a great one. The personalities, the poetic theories of the two men could not have been more different; but in respect of the violence which they could do to language, and justify, there is a remote similarity. Milton's poetry is poetry as the farthest possible remove from prose; his prose seems to me too near to half-formed poetry to be a good prose.

To say that the work of a poet is at the farthest possible remove from prose would once have struck me as condemnatory: it now seems to me simply, when we have to do with a Milton, the precision of its peculiar greatness. As a poet, Milton seems to me probably the greatest of all eccentrics. His work illustrates no general principles of good writing; the only principles of writing that it illustrates are such as are valid only for Milton himself to observe. There are two kinds of poet who can ordinarily be of use to other poets. There are those who suggest, to one or another of their successors, something which they have not done themselves, or who provoke a different way of doing the same thing: these are likely to be not the greatest, but smaller, imperfect poets with whom later poets discover an affinity. And there are the great poets from whom we can learn negative rules: no poet can teach another to write well, but some great poets can teach others some of the things to avoid. They teach us what to avoid, by showing us what great poetry can do without — how *bare* it can be. Of these are Dante and Racine. But if we are ever to make use of Milton we must do so in quite a different way. Even a small poet can learn something from the study of Dante, or from the study of Chaucer: we must perhaps wait for a great poet before we find one who can profit from the study of Milton.

I repeat that the remoteness of Milton's verse from ordinary speech, his invention of his own poetic language, seems to me one of the marks of his greatness. Other marks are his sense of structure, both in the general design of *Paradise Lost* and *Samson*, and in his syntax; and finally, and not least, his inerrancy, conscious or unconscious, in writing so as to make the best display of his talents, and the best concealment of his weaknesses.

The appropriateness of the subject of *Samson* is too obvious to expatiate upon: it was probably the one dramatic story out of which Milton could have made a masterpiece. But the complete suitability of *Paradise Lost* has not, I think, been so often remarked. It was surely an intuitive perception of what he could not do, that arrested Milton's project of an epic on King Arthur. For one thing, he had little interest in, or understanding of, individual human beings. In *Paradise Lost* he was not called upon for any of that understanding which comes from an affectionate observation of men and women. But such an interest in human beings was not required — indeed its *absence* was a necessary condition — for the creation of his figures of Adam and Eve. These are not a man and woman such as any we know: if they were, they would not be Adam and Eve. They are the original *Man* and *Woman*, not types, but prototypes. They have the general characteristics of men and women, such that we can recognize, in the temptation and the fall, the first motions of the faults and virtues, the abjection and the nobility, of all their descendants. They have ordinary humanity to the right degree, and yet are not, and should not be, ordinary mortals. Were they more particularized they would be false, and if Milton had been more interested in humanity, he could not have created them. Other critics have remarked upon the exactness, without defect or exaggeration, with which Moloch, Belial, and Mammon, in the second book, speak according to the particular sin which each represents. It would not be suitable that the infernal powers should have, in the human sense, characters, for a character is always mixed; but in the hands of an inferior manipulator, they might easily have been reduced to *humours*.

The appropriateness of the material of *Paradise Lost* to the genius and the limitations of Milton is still more evident when we consider the visual imagery. I have already remarked, in a paper written some years ago, on Milton's weakness of visual observation, a weakness which I think was always present — the effect of his blindness may have been rather to strengthen the compensatory qualities than to increase a fault which was already present. Mr. Wilson Knight, who has devoted close study to recurrent imagery in poetry, has called attention to

Milton's propensity towards images of engineering and mechanics; to me it seems that Milton is at his best in imagery
suggestive of vast size, limitless space, abysmal depth, and
light and darkness. No theme and no setting, other than that
which he chose in *Paradise Lost*, could have given him such
scope for the kind of imagery in which he excelled, or made
less demand upon those powers of visual imagination which
were in him defective.

Most of the absurdities and inconsistencies to which Johnson calls attention, and which, so far as they can justly be isolated in this way, he properly condemns, will I think appear
in a more correct proportion if we consider them in relation
to this general judgment. I do not think that we should attempt to *see* very clearly any scene that Milton depicts: it
should be accepted as a shifting phantasmagory. To complain,
because we first find the arch-fiend 'chain'd on the burning
lake', and in a minute or two see him making his way to the
shore, is to expect a kind of consistency which the world to
which Milton has introduced us does not require.

This limitation of visual power, like Milton's limited interest in human beings, turns out to be not merely a negligible
defect, but a positive virtue, when we visit Adam and Eve in
Eden. Just as a higher degree of characterization of Adam and
Eve would have been unsuitable, so a more vivid picture of the
earthly Paradise would have been less paradisiacal. For a
greater definiteness, a more detailed account of flora and
fauna, could only have assimilated Eden to the landscapes of
earth with which we are familiar. As it is, the impression of
Eden which we retain, is the most suitable, and is that which
Milton was most qualified to give: the impression of *light* — a
daylight and a starlight, a light of dawn and of dusk, the light
which, remembered by a man in his blindness, has a supernatural glory unexperienced by men of normal vision.

We must, then, in reading *Paradise Lost*, not expect to see
clearly; our sense of sight must be blurred, so that our *hearing*

may become more acute. *Paradise Lost*, like *Finnegans Wake* [for I can think of no work which provides a more interesting parallel: two books by great blind musicians, each writing a language of his own based upon English] makes this peculiar demand for a readjustment of the reader's mode of apprehension. The emphasis is on the sound, not the vision, upon the word, not the idea; and in the end it is the unique versification that is the most certain sign of Milton's intellectual mastership.

On the subject of Milton's versification, so far as I am aware, little enough has been written. We have Johnson's essay in the *Rambler*, which deserves more study than it has received, and we have a short treatise by Robert Bridges on *Milton's Prosody*. I speak of Bridges with respect, for no poet of our time has given such close attention to prosody as he. Bridges catalogues the systematic irregularities which give perpetual variety to Milton's verse, and I can find no fault with his analysis. But however interesting these analyses are, I do not think that it is by such means that we gain an appreciation of the peculiar rhythm of a poet. It seems to me also that Milton's verse is especially refractory to yielding up its secrets to examination of the single line. For his verse is not formed in this way. It is the period, the sentence and still more the paragraph, that is the unit of Milton's verse; and emphasis on the line structure is the minimum necessary to provide a counter-pattern to the period structure. It is only in the period that the wave-length of Milton's verse is to be found: it is his ability to give a perfect and unique pattern to every paragraph, such that the full beauty of the line is found in its context, and his ability to work in larger musical units than any other poet — that is to me the most conclusive evidence of Milton's supreme mastery. The peculiar feeling, almost a physical sensation of a breathless leap, communicated by Milton's long periods, and by his alone, is impossible to procure from rhymed verse. In deed, this mastery is more conclusive evidence of his intellectual power, than is his grasp of any *ideas* that he borrowed or invented. To be able to control so many words at once is the token of a mind of most exceptional energy.

It is interesting at this point to recall the general observations upon blank verse, which a consideration of *Paradise Lost* prompted Johnson to make towards the end of his essay.

'The music of the English heroic lines strikes the ear so faintly, that it is easily lost, unless all the syllables of every line co-operate together; this co-operation can only be obtained by the preservation of every verse unmingled with another as a distinct system of sounds; and this distinctness is obtained and preserved by the artifice of rhyme. The variety of pauses, so much boasted by the lovers of blank verse, changes the measures of an English poet to the periods of a declaimer; and there are only a few skilful and happy readers of Milton, who enable their audience to perceive where the lines end or begin. *Blank verse*, said an ingenious critic, *seems to be verse only to the eye.*'

Some of my audience may recall that this last remark, in almost the same words, was often made, a literary generation ago, about the 'free verse' of the period: and even without this encouragement from Johnson it would have occurred to my mind to declare Milton to be the greatest master of free verse in our language. What is interesting about Johnson's paragraph, however, is that it represents the judgment of a man who had by no means a deaf ear, but simply a *specialized* ear, for verbal music. Within the limits of the poetry of his own period, Johnson is a very good judge of the relative merits of several poets as writers of blank verse. But on the whole, the blank verse of his age might more properly be called unrhymed verse; and nowhere is this difference more evident than in the verse of his own tragedy *Irene:* the phrasing is admirable, the style elevated and correct, but each line cries out for a companion to rhyme with it. Indeed, it is only with labour, or by occasional inspiration, or by submission to the influence of the older dramatists, that the blank verse of the nineteenth century succeeds in making the absence of rhyme inevitable and right, with the rightness of Milton. Even Johnson admitted that he could not wish that Milton had been a rhymer. Nor did the nineteenth century succeed in giving to blank verse the flexibility which it needs if the tone of common speech, talking of the topics of common intercourse, is to be employed; so that when our more modern practitioners of blank verse do not touch the sublime, they frequently sink to the ridiculous. Milton perfected non-dramatic blank verse and at the same time imposed limitations, very hard to break, upon the use to which it may be put if its greatest musical possibilities are to be exploited.

I come at last to compare my own attitude, as that of a poetical practitioner perhaps typical of a generation twenty-five years ago, with my attitude to-day. I have thought it well to take matters in the order in which I have taken them to discuss first the censures and detractions which I believe to have permanent validity, and which were best made by Johnson, in order to make clearer the causes, and the justification, for hostility to Milton on the part of poets at a particular juncture. And I wished to make clear those excellences of Milton which particularly impress me, before explaining why I think that the study of his verse might at last be of benefit to poets.

I have on several occasions suggested, that the important changes in the idiom of English verse which are represented by the names of Dryden and Wordsworth, may be characterized as successful attempts to escape from a poetic idiom which had ceased to have a relation to contemporary speech. This is the sense of Wordsworth's Prefaces. By the beginning of the present century another revolution in idiom — and such revolutions bring with them an alteration of metric, a new appeal to the ear — was due. It inevitably happens that the young poets engaged in such a revolution will exalt the merits of those poets of the past who offer them example and stimulation, and cry

down the merits of poets who do not stand for the qualities
which they are zealous to realize. This is not only inevitable,
it is right. It is even right, and certainly inevitable, that their
practice, still more influential than their critical pronouncements, should attract their own readers to the poets by whose
work they have been influenced. Such influence has certainly
contributed to the taste [if we can distinguish the *taste* from
the *fashion*] for Donne. I do not think that any modern poet,
unless in a fit of irresponsible peevishness, has ever denied
Milton's consummate powers. And it must be said that Milton's diction is not a poetic diction in the sense of being a de-
based currency: when he violates the English language he is
imitating nobody, and he is inimitable. But Milton does, as I
have said, represent poetry at the extreme limit from prose;
and it was one of our tenets that verse should have the virtues
of prose, that diction should become assimilated to cultivated
contemporary speech, before aspiring to the elevation of poetry. Another tenet was that the subject-matter and the
imagery of poetry should be extended to topics and objects
related to the life of a modern man or woman; that we were
to seek the non-poetic, to seek even material refractory to
transmutation into poetry, and words and phrases which had
not been used in poetry before. And the study of Milton could
be of no help here: it was only a hindrance.

We cannot, in literature, any more than in the rest of life,
live in a perpetual state of revolution. If every generation of
poets made it their task to bring poetic diction up to date with
the spoken language, poetry would fail in one of its most important obligations. For poetry should help, not only to refine
the language of the time, but to prevent it from changing too
rapidly: a development of language at too great a speed would
be a development in the sense of a progressive deterioration,
and that is our danger to-day. If the poetry of the rest of this
century takes the line of development which seems to me, reviewing the progress of poetry through the last three centuries,

the right course, it will discover new and more elaborate patterns of a diction now established. In this search it might have much to learn from Milton's extended verse structure; it might also avoid the danger of a *servitude* to colloquial speech and to current jargon. It might also learn that the music of verse is strongest in poetry which has a definite meaning expressed in the properest words. Poets might be led to admit that a knowledge of the literature of their own language, with a knowledge of the literature and the grammatical construction of other languages, is a very valuable part of the poet's equipment. And they might, as I have already hinted, devote some study to Milton as, outside the theatre, the greatest master in our language of freedom within form. A study of *Samson* should sharpen anyone's appreciation of the justified irregularity, and put him on guard against the pointless irregularity. In studying *Paradise Lost* we come to perceive that the verse is continuously animated by the departure from, and return to, the regular measure; and that, in comparison with Milton, hardly any subsequent writer of blank verse appears to exercise any freedom at all. We can also be led to the reflection that a monotony of unscannable verse fatigues the attention even more quickly than a monotony of exact feet. In short, it now seems to me that poets are sufficiently liberated from Milton's reputation, to approach the study of his work without danger, and with profit to their poetry and to the English language.

Johnson as Critic and Poet*

IT IS primarily with Johnson as a critic, as the author of *The Lives of the Poets*, that I am here concerned. But I shall have something to say of his poetry also; because I think that in studying the criticism of poetry, by a critic who is also a poet, we can only appreciate his criticism — its standards, its merits, and its limitations, in the light of the kind of poetry that he wrote himself. I consider Johnson one of the three greatest critics of poetry in English literature: the other two being Dryden and Coleridge. All of these men were poets, and with all of them, a study of their poetry is highly relevant to the study of their criticism, because each of them was interested in a particular kind of poetry.

If this relevance is less apparent in the case of Johnson, than with Dryden and Coleridge, it is for trivial reasons. A great deal of bibliography has accumulated about Johnson, yet relatively little has been written about his writings; his two long poems have been neglected; and as for *The Lives of the Poets*, few educated persons have read more than half a dozen of them, and of these half-dozen, what is remembered is chiefly the passages with which everyone disagrees. One reason for indifference to his criticism, is that he was not the initiator of any poetic movement: he was a secondary poet at the end of a movement which had been initiated by greater poets than he, and his poems represent a personal variation of a style which

* The Ballard Matthews Lectures, delivered at University College, North Wales in 1944.

was well established. Dryden, and Coleridge in partnership
with Wordsworth, represent for us something *new* in poetry
in their time. What Dryden wrote about poetry is therefore
more exciting than what Johnson wrote. In his critical essays,
he was outlining laws of writing for two generations to come:
Johnson's view is retrospective. Dryden, concerned with defending his own way of writing, proceeds from the general to
the particular: he affirms principles, and criticizes particular
poets only in illustration of his argument; Johnson, in the
course of criticizing the work of particular poets — and of poets
whose work was ended — is led to generalizations. Their historical situations were quite different. It is not, in the long run,
relevant to our judgment of an author's greatness, whether he
comes at the beginning of an age or at the end; but we are inclined to favour unduly the former. Of Johnson's influence
there is nothing to say; and we are always impressed by a reputation for influence, as influence is a form of power. But when the
tide of influence, which a writer may set in motion for a generation or two, has come to its full, and another force has
drawn the waters in a different direction, and when several
tides have risen and fallen, great writers remain of equal po-
tentiality of influence in the future. It remains to be seen
whether the literary influence of Johnson, as, in political
thought, the influence of his friend of the other party, Ed-
mund Burke, does not merely await a generation which has not
yet been born to receive it.

An obvious obstacle to our enjoyment in reading *The Lives
of the Poets* as a whole — and we must read it as a whole if
we are to appreciate the magnitude of Johnson's achievement
— is that we have not read the works of many of the poets included, and no inducement of pleasure or profit can be offered
us to do so. Some of his minor eighteenth-century poets I have
read in order to understand why Johnson approved of them;
some I have only glanced at; and there are a number, of whom
Johnson's commendation is so mild or his treatment so per-

functory, that I have not bothered even to look them up. Nobody wants to read the verses of Stepney or Walsh; I hardly think that any Ph.D. candidate would be encouraged by his advisers to devote his thesis to a study of the work of Christopher Pitt. Johnson's assertion that Yalden's poems 'deserve perusal' is no more convincing than a letter of introduction written for an importunate visitor whom the writer wants to get rid of. The student of the history of literary taste may be struck by Johnson's remark that 'perhaps no composition in our language has been oftener perused than Pomfret's *Choice*' and want to find out why. But the common reader will probably be more discontented by Johnson's omissions, than made curious by all his inclusions. Everyone knows that the collection represented the choice of a group of booksellers, or publishers, who presumably thought that the works of all these authors were saleable, and who certainly thought, with more evident reason, that prefaces by Dr. Johnson would go far to compensate for the want of copyright, in commending their edition to the public. We may be pretty sure that Johnson himself, though he did his best by everybody, would not have thought all of his authors worth including. Yet we know that Johnson had some liberty to add to the collection, for we are told that he suggested three of the poets, of one of whom, Sir Richard Blackmore, I shall have something more to say.

That the predecessors and contemporaries of Shakespeare, and the metaphysical poets before Cowley, were at that time unsaleable, would have been justification for the booksellers' vetoing any proposal by Johnson for their inclusion. But there is no evidence that Johnson wanted to include them; the evidence goes to show that his acquaintance with them was very limited, and that he was perfectly content to edit a library of poetry which began with Cowley and Milton. The very fine Preface to Shakespeare is a separate work, and shows no evidence of awareness of the need to estimate any poet in relation to his predecessors and contemporaries. Yet this very innocence of the historical and comparative methods which modern criticism takes for granted, contributes to the singular merit of this Preface; and the virtues of Shakespeare to which he calls attention, are mostly those in which Shakespeare was unique, which he did not share, even in degree, with the other dramatists.

This limitation of the area of English poetry is a positive characteristic of importance. It would be a capital error to attribute the narrow range of Johnson's interests solely to ignorance, or solely to lack of appreciation, or even to both. To say that his ignorance was due to lack of understanding, would probably be truer than to say that his lack of understanding was due to ignorance: but it is not so simple as that. If we censure an eighteenth-century critic for not having a modern, historical and comprehensive appreciation, we must ourselves adopt towards him, the attitude the lack of which we reprehend; we must not be narrow in accusing him of narrowness, or prejudiced in accusing him of prejudice. Johnson had a positive point of view which is not ours; a point of view which needs a vigorous effort of imagination to understand; but if we can grasp it, we shall see his ignorance or his insensibility in a different light. Walter Raleigh says of Johnson that 'he had read immensely for the *Dictionary*, but the knowledge of English literature which he had thus acquired was not always serviceable for a different purpose. In some respects it was even a hindrance. Johnson's *Dictionary* was intended primarily to furnish a standard of polite usage, suitable for the classic ideals of the new age. He was therefore obliged to forego the use of the lesser Elizabethans, whose authority no one acknowledged, and whose freedom and extravagance were enemies to his purpose.'

To the poet and critic of the eighteenth century, the values of language and literature were more closely allied than they seem to the writers and to the reading public of to-day. Eccentricity or uncouthness was reprehensible: a poet was prized, not for his invention of an original form of speech, but by his contribution to a common language. It was observed by Johnson and by men of his time, that there had been progress in refinement and precision of language, as of refinement and decorum of manners; and both these attainments, being recent, were highly esteemed. Johnson is able to censure Dryden, for his bad manners and bad taste in controversy. Now it is generally observable of mankind, that in the elation of success in some course which we have set ourselves, we can be oblivious of many things which we have been obliged to resign in the accomplishment of it. We do not take kindly to the thought that, in order to gain one thing, we may have to give up something else of value. With these lost values the path of history is strewn and always will be: and perhaps a purblindness to such values is a necessary qualification, for anyone who aspires to be a political and social reformer. The improvement of language, which the eighteenth century had achieved, was a genuine improvement: of the inevitable losses only a later generation could become aware.

Johnson, certainly, saw the body of English poetry from a point of view which took for granted a progress, a refinement of language and versification along definite lines; and which implied a confidence in the rightness and permanence of the style which had been achieved — a confidence so much stronger than any we can place in the style, or styles, of our own age that we can hardly see it as anything but a blemish upon his critical ability. The emphasis upon, the care for, the common style and the common rules, which Johnson exhibits, and which make him sometimes appear to measure great genius by the standards suitable only to smaller minds, may lead to an exaggeration of the value of pedestrian poetry which conforms, over that of work of individual genius which is less law-abiding. Yet the obtuseness which we are apt to attribute to Johnson is seldom apparent in his positive affirmations, but chiefly by silence; and this silence is evidence, not of individual insensibility, but of an attitude which is difficult for us to assume. From Johnson's point of view, the English language of the previous age was not sufficiently advanced, it was still 'in its infancy'; the language with which earlier poets worked was too rough, for those poets to be treated on the same footing with those of a more polished age. Their work, when they were not of the very highest rank, was a subject of study more suitable for the antiquary than for the cultivated reading public. The sensibility of any period in the past is always likely to appear to be more limited than our own; for we are naturally much more aware of our ancestors' lack of awareness to those things of which we are aware, than we are of any lack in ourselves, of awareness to what they perceived and we do not. We may ask then whether there is not a capital distinction to be drawn between a limited sensibility — remembering that the longer extent of *history* of which we have knowledge, makes all minds of the past seem to us limited — and a defective sensibility; and accordingly ask whether Johnson, within his proper limits, is not a sensitive as well as judicial critic; whether the virtues he commended in poetry do not always remain virtues, and whether the kinds of fault that he censured do not always remain faults and to be avoided.

Even if I have not yet succeeded in making my meaning very clear, I hope that I have done something to unsettle your minds, and to prepare for an investigation of the charge against Johnson of being insensitive to the music of verse. A modern reader remembers nothing more clearly, from a reading of *The Lives of the Poets*, than Johnson's remarks on the versification of Donne and of Milton's *Lycidas*. If we recall no other opinion of Johnson, we recall the following:

'The metaphysical poets were men of learning, and to show their learning was their whole endeavour: but unluckily resolving to show it in rhyme, instead of writing poetry they only wrote verses, and very often such verses as stood the trial of the finger better than of the ear: for the modulation was so imperfect that they were only found to be verses by counting the syllables.'

Of the work of Cleveland, and some of the other minor metaphysicals, this judgment would be sound enough; but that Johnson included Donne in this censure, we can be sure from his observation that Ben Jonson resembled Donne 'more in the ruggedness of his lines than in the cast of his sentiments'. Nowadays we regard Donne as a very accomplished craftsman indeed, as a versifier of signal virtuosity, and what Johnson denotes as 'ruggedness' strikes our ear as a very subtle music. But the judgment on *Lycidas*, as well known as the judgment on the metaphysical poets, equally outrages our sensibility. Johnson declares that in this poem 'the diction is harsh, the rhymes uncertain, and the numbers unpleasing'. With some other of Johnson's remarks about *Lycidas* we may find it possible to agree. If we think that an elegy requires the justification of unfeigned and cordial regret, we may find the poem frigid. The conjunction of Christian and classical imagery is in accord with a baroque taste which did not please the eighteenth century: and I must admit for myself that I have never felt happy in the spectacle of Fr. Camus and St. Peter marching in the same procession, like a couple of professors strolling down King's Parade on their way to hear the university sermon. But surely it is the musical virtue of the verse which clothes the absurdities in grandeur, and makes all acceptable. So we ask, was Johnson insensible to the music of verse? Had he, had the whole of his generation, defective hearing?

There is perhaps no more stubborn cause of extreme differences of opinion, between respectable critics of poetry, than a difference of ear: and by 'ear' for poetry I mean an immediate apprehension of two things which can be considered in abstraction from each other, but which produce their effect in unity: rhythm and diction. They imply each other: for the diction — the vocabulary and construction — will determine the rhythm, and the rhythms which a poet finds congenial will determine his diction. It is the immediate favourable impression of rhythm and diction which disposes us to accept a poem, encourages us to give it further attention and to discover other reasons for liking it. This immediacy may be lacking, in the reading of the poetry of one generation by another. Not until a literature has arrived at maturity — not, perhaps, until it has passed the moment of maturity and advanced far into later age, can critics perceive that rhythm and diction do not simply improve, or deteriorate, from one generation to another, but that there is also pure change, such that something is always being lost, as well as something being gained. In the perfection of any style it can be observed, as in the maturing of an individual, that some potentialities have been brought to fruition only by the surrender of others; indeed, part of our pleasure in early literature, as of the delight which we take in children, is in our consciousness of many potentialities not all of which can be realized. In this respect, primitive literature can be richer than that which follows. A literature is different from a human life, in that it can return upon its own past, and develop some capacity which has been abandoned. We have seen in our own time, a renewed interest in Donne; and, after Donne, in earlier poets such as Skelton. A literature can also renew itself from the literature of another language. But the age in which Johnson lived, was not old enough to feel the need for such renewal: it had just arrived at its own maturity. Johnson could think of the literature of his age, as having attained the standard from which literature of the past could be judged. In a time like ours, in which novelty is often assumed to be the first requisite of poetry if it is to attract our attention, and in which the names of *pioneer* and *innovator* are among the titles most honoured, it is hard to apprehend this point of view. We easily see its absurdities, and marvel at the assurance with which Johnson could reprehend *Lycidas* for the absence of the merit which we find most conspicuous in it, and could dismiss Donne for the roughness of his diction. And when

Johnson writes of Shakespeare, we are puzzled by Johnson's silence about the mastery of versification. Here there was no prejudice against a particular fashion of writing, as when he discusses the metaphysicals; no personal dislike of the man, as when he treats of Milton; but only the acutest observation, the highest esteem, the most just and generous praise: but he assigns to Shakespeare the very highest rank among poets, on every other ground than that of the beauty of rhythm and diction.

My point is that we should not consider this obtuseness, which to us is very strange, as a personal defect of Johnson which diminishes his stature as a critic. What is lacking is an historical sense which was not yet due to appear. Here is something which Johnson can teach us: for if we have arrived at this historical sense ourselves, our only course is to develop it further; and one of the ways in which we can develop it in ourselves is through an understanding of a critic in whom it is not apparent. Johnson fails to understand rhythm and diction which to him were archaic, not through lack of sensibility but through specialization of sensibility. If the eighteenth century had admired the poetry of earlier times in the way in which we can admire it, the result would have been chaos: there would have been no eighteenth century as we know it. That age would not have had the conviction necessary for perfecting the kinds of poetry that it did perfect. The deafness of Johnson's ear to some kinds of melody was the necessary condition for his sharpness of sensibility to verbal beauty of another kind. Within his range, within his time, Johnson had as fine an ear as anybody. Again and again, when he calls attention to beauties or to blemishes in the work of the poets of whom he writes, we must acknowledge that he is right, and that he is pointing out something that we might not have noticed independently. It may prove that his criteria are permanently relevant.

There is another consideration, in the problem of the differ-

ence between the sensibilities of one century and another,
which is worth mention. That is the problem of the emphasis
on sound or on sense. The greatest poetry, I think we may
agree, passes the most severe examination in both subjects. But
there is a great deal of good poetry, which establishes itself by
a one-sided excellence. The modern inclination is to put up
with some degree of incoherence of sense, to be tolerant of
poets who do not know themselves exactly what they are trying
to say, so long as the verse sounds well and presents striking
and unusual imagery. There is, in fact, a certain merit in melodious raving, which can be a genuine contribution to literature, when it responds effectually to that permanent appetite
of humanity for an occasional feast of drums and cymbals. We
all want to get drunk now and again, whether we do or not:
though an exclusive addiction to some kinds of poetry has dangers analogous to those of a steady reliance upon alcohol. Besides the poetry of sound — and, from one point of view,
occupying an intermediate position between the poetry of
sound and the poetry of sense — there is poetry which represents an attempt to extend the confines of the human consciousness and to report of things unknown, to express the
inexpressible. But with this poetry I am not here concerned.
Between the two extremes of *incantation* and *meaning* we are
I think to-day more easily seduced by the music of the exhila-
ratingly meaningless, than contented with intelligence and wisdom set forth in pedestrian measures. The age of Johson, and
Johnson himself, were more inclined to the latter choice.
Johnson could accept much as poetry, which seems to us
merely competent and correct; we, on the other hand, are too
ready to accept as poetry what is neither competent nor correct. We forgive much to sound and to image, he forgave
much to sense. And to exceed in one direction or the other
is to risk mistaking the ephemeral for the permanent. Johnson
sometimes made mistakes. I referred, a little earlier, to Sir
Richard Blackmore.

Impressed by Johnson's assertion that Blackmore's *Creation*
alone was a poem which 'would have transmitted him to
posterity among the first favourites of the English Muse', and
his statement that it was by his own recommendation that
Blackmore was included in the library which he introduced, I
read the poem with some curiosity. I came to the conclusion
that Johnson's praise of this poem shows a grievous lapse in
two directions. In the first place, the poem almost at once
violates some excellent rules which Johnson himself, in treat-
ing of a greater poet, had laid down for the use of triplet and
alexandrine in the rhymed couplet form. Instead of reserving
the triplet [three lines rhyming together and alexandrine as
the third line] for the conclusion of a period, where this termination can be very effective, Blackmore introduces a triplet almost at the start; and presently offers us an alexandrine as the
second line of a couplet. What is much worse, the versification
is sometimes no better than that of a schoolboy's exercise. But
Johnson, like all good churchmen and all good Tories, abomi-
nated Hobbes — a notable atheist and totalitarian. He must
have been blinded to defects which he would have reproved
in Dryden or Pope, by the satisfaction he got from the following lines alluding to that philosopher:

> *At length Britannia's soil, immortal dame!*
> *Brought forth a sage of celebrated name,*
> *Who with contempt on blest Religion trod,*
> *Mocked all her precepts, and renounced her God.*

To apply the kind of minute criticism in which Johnson excelled, we may remark that the first line is bad grammar, because *dame* is grammatically in apposition to *soil* instead of
to *Britannia*; and we may censure the second line by remarking
that Hobbes's name was not celebrated until a long time after
his birth. We should expect also, that the personification of
Religion, as a helpless female stamped upon by Hobbes, would
be too inelegant for Johnson's taste. I think that this is the
kind of lapse which can most severely be censured in a critic —

the lapse from his own standards of taste. And secondly, my reading of the poem led me to suspect that even on grounds of content Johnson should have rejected it. For Johnson — and it is a very important thing about him — was one of the most orthodox churchmen, as well as one of the most devout Christians, of his day: and Blackmore seems to me to be expressing pure deism. I can only suppose that deism so permeated the atmosphere of the century that Johnson's nose failed to respond to its smell.

I want however to distinguish this species of error — the critic's failure to apply his own standards — from those apparent errors which spring from the principles of a particular mind at a particular time, and which no longer seem to us errors in the same sense, once we succeed in apprehending the point of view. Such will be found, and they will at first bewilder us, in Johnson's various remarks about writers of blank verse. For this kind of verse, he appears to give the highest place to Akenside, of whom he says, that 'in the general fabrication of his lines he is perhaps superior to any other writer of blank verse'. Even leaving out of account the blank verse of the great dramatic poets of a previous age — or the dramatic verse of Otway at his best — this seems at first an extravagant assertion.

Nowadays we use words so loosely that a writer's meaning may sometimes be concealed from us, simply because he has said exactly what he meant. To extract the meaning from Johnson's assertion about Akenside, we must first compare Akenside's versification with that of other blank verse writers of his century; we have also to compare what Johnson has said about the others, and with what he said about Milton's verse. In his essay on Milton, you will remember that Johnson confirms the words of Addison who said of Milton *the language sunk under him*. Johnson goes on to say that Milton 'had formed his style by a perverse and pedantic principle' and that 'he was desirous to use English words with a foreign

idiom'. But, having made this criticism, he goes on to utter
the highest praise: Milton 'was master of his language to its
full extent'. And in mentioning the weaknesses of 'heroic'
blank verse; particularly the difficulty, in speaking it, of preserving the metrical identity of each line; and finally, after saying everything that can be said against blank verse, he makes
the handsome admission: 'I cannot prevail upon myself to
wish that Milton had been a rhymer; for I cannot wish his
work to be other than it is; yet, like other heroes, he is to be
admired rather than imitated.' The acknowledgment of Milton's greatness as a versifier is unequivocal. But there are laws,
for the use of words and the construction of sentences, which
Milton defies. The lawbreaker should not be praised for his
lawlessness; and a second-rate poet may be more law-abiding
than a poet of great genius. So, Akenside, 'in the general fabrication of his lines,' may be more correct than Milton; and if
we value correctness, in that respect superior.

I do not think that the history of blank verse since Milton's
time altogether gives him the lie. 'The music of the English
heroic lines strikes the ear so faintly,' says Johnson, 'that it is
easily lost.' That is true: the alternative danger is a monotonous thumping, which ceases to have any music at all. What
Johnson failed to remark is, that Milton made blank verse a
successful medium for the heroic poem, by that very eccentricity which Johnson reproves.

Johnson did, however, see the verse of Milton as an exception. He admits that there are purposes for which blank verse
remains the proper medium; though he does not trouble to
define and particularize those purposes. Of Young's *Night
Thoughts* he says:

'This is one of the few poems in which blank verse could
not be changed for rhyme but with disadvantage. The wild
diffusion of the sentiments, and the digressive sallies of imagination would have been compressed and restrained by confine-
ment to rhyme.'

His approval of the use of blank verse by Thomson in his *Seasons* expresses a similar approval:

'His is one of the works in which blank verse is properly used. Thomson's wide expansion of general views, and his enumeration of circumstantial varieties, would have been obstructed and embarrassed by the frequent intersections of the sense, which are necessary effects of rhyme.'

Let us return to Akenside, the author upon whose blank verse Johnson has bestowed such high commendation:

'In the general fabrication of his lines, he is perhaps superior to any other author of blank verse; his flow is smooth, and his pauses are musical; but the concatenation of his verse is too long continued, and the full close does not occur with sufficient frequency. The sense is carried on through a long intertexture of complicated clauses, and, as nothing is distinguished, nothing is remembered.

'The exemption [Johnson continues, generalizing from his criticism of Akenside] which blank verse affords from the necessity of closing the sense with the couplet betrays luxuriant and active minds into such self-indulgence, that they pile image upon image, ornament upon ornament, and are not easily persuaded to close the sense at all. Blank verse will therefore, I fear, be too often found in description exuberant, in argument loquacious, and in narration tiresome.'

To say that the concatenation of Akenside's verse is too long continued, and that the sense is carried on through a long intertexture of complicated clauses, is a censure which is fully justified by our examination of Akenside's lines; though it is only fair to remark that this concatenation, these complicated clauses, were exactly what Milton was able to manipulate with conspicuous and solitary success. But the general observations on the dangers of blank verse are such as later writers in this form would have done well to ponder. And Johnson could not foresee that later poets would also be able to exhibit in the rhymed couplet, through their desire to extend the resources

of this form beyond the rigid limits imposed by the best eighteenth-century verse, the same exuberance, the same loquacity,
and the same tiresomeness that Johnson lists as the vices of
blank verse. We have only to look at William Morris for
examples.

Amongst all the poets whose works Johnson introduced, we
can I think agree that Thomson and Young are the only ones
who have left blank verse poems which are still more or less
readable, and which are still of importance for the student of
English poetry to read. In praising their versification, therefore, Johnson shows himself to be not unaware of how blank
verse should be written. In qualification of his approval of
Akenside's versification, it must be added that his praise of the
poem which shows Akenside's moderate gifts at their best,
The Pleasures of Imagination [or, *Pleasures of the Imagination*] is very faint indeed.

'The words are multiplied till the sense is hardly perceived;
attention deserts the mind, and settles in the ear. The reader
wanders through the gay diffusion, sometimes amazed, and
sometimes delighted; but, after many turnings in the flowery
labyrinth, comes out as he went in. He remarked little, and
laid hold on nothing.'

Which is as direct an intimation that the poetry is not worth
reading, as Johnson cared to give. I have put myself to the
mechanical operation of reading this poem through, yet I cannot say that I have read it; for, as Johnson foretold, 'attention
deserted the mind.' So in effect I have read only passages. Yet
I retain the impression that the sound is more melodious than
that of the verses of either Thomson or Young, though these
are much more substantial poets. His syllables are well dis-
posed; his pauses, his sentence structures, are generally such as
to give perpetual variety, without breaking down the metre
altogether; and though he is always dull, he is seldom absurd.
If you dip into Thomson's *Seasons*, you will constantly find
delightful landscapes; but you will find also a frequent en-

deavour to elevate the humble, and embellish the matter-of-fact, which invites ridicule. Take for instance his humane exhortation to the angler:

> But let not on thy hook the tortur'd worm
> Convulsive, twist in agonising fold.

Akenside never says anything worth saying, but what is not worth saying he says well. The close of the third book of his poem [which is left unfinished in the middle of the fourth book] is good enough to quote:

> When at last
> The Sun and Nature's face again appear'd,
> Not far I found me; where the public path,
> Winding through cypress groves and swelling meads,
> From Cnossus to the cave of Jove ascends.
> Heedless I followed on; till soon the skirts
> Of Ida rose before me, and the vault
> Wide-opening pierced the mountain's rocky side.
> Entering within the threshold, on the ground
> I flung me, sad, faint, overworn with toil.

If you did not know who wrote these lines, you might attribute them to some better poet. But, as Johnson observes of the same writer's odes: 'to what use can the work be criticized that will not be read?' Yet I think we can now understand, and within limits accept, the assertion that 'in the general fabrication of his lines, [Akenside] is perhaps superior to any other writer of blank verse'.

I cannot help wondering how many blank verse poems of the nineteenth century will be perused by posterity with any greater excitement, than we now derive from those of Thomson, Young, or Cowper. There will remain *Hyperion*, *The Prelude* [which, however tedious in many places, has to be read entire], a few fine short pieces of Tennyson, some dramatic monologues of Browning. But in general, I think that the nineteenth-century poems which promise to remain permanently pleasurable, are poems in rhyme.

That Johnson regarded blank verse as more suitable for the theatre than rhyme, we may infer from his preference for *All for Love* among Dryden's heroic plays, and from his having chosen blank verse as the medium for his own tragedy *Irene*. That Johnson failed to understand the peculiarities of *dramatic* blank verse is evident from this play: for we find the blank verse to be that of a writer who thought and felt in terms of the rhymed couplet. I have already observed, that in all of Johnson's high and just praise of Shakespeare as a dramatic poet, he speaks as if Shakespeare had written in a language of which the sense had been preserved, but of which the sound meant nothing to us: for there is not a word about the music of Shakespeare's verse. Johnson holds that blank verse is more suitable to the stage, simply because it is nearer to prose: in other words, people conversing do occasionally produce an unconscious iambic pentameter, but almost never fall into rhyme. I do not think that this judgment is altogether valid. If Johnson failed, on the one hand, to appreciate the special music of dramatic blank verse, he was also deceived in thinking that blank verse is necessarily the more conversational form. I remarked long ago, that Dryden seems to me to approximate more closely to the tones of conversation in his rhymed plays than he does in *All for Love*. Johnson's *Irene* has all the virtues which verse by Johnson should be expected to have; and for Johnson, who did not ordinarily labour at his writing, it appears a very painstaking piece of work. His verse has none of the dramatic qualities; it is correct, but correctness in such isolation becomes itself a fault. The play would be more readable to-day, if he had written it in rhyme; the whole would be more easily declaimed, and the good things more easily remembered; it would lose none of its excellence of structure, thought, vocabulary and figures of speech. What would be mellifluous in rhyme, is merely monotonous without it.

I have been occupied so far, primarily with the task of trying to reduce some of the obstacles to the appreciation of Johnson as a critic. Before closing, there remain two incidental opinions of Johnson which I must face, because otherwise I should expose myself to the charge of evading them. The first is Johnson's opinion of choral drama, which was unfavourable; the second is his attitude towards religious or devotional verse, which was condescending. I must therefore direct the jury on these two points.

'If *Paradise Regained* has been too much depreciated, *Samson Agonistes* has in requital been too much admired. It could only be by long prejudice, and the bigotry of learning, that Milton preferred the ancient tragedies, with their encumbrance of a chorus, to the exhibitions of the French and English stages, and it is only by a blind confidence in the reputation of Milton, that a drama can be praised in which the intermediate parts have neither cause nor consequence, neither hasten nor retard the catastrophe.'

I may have occasion to remind you again, how emphatically Johnson was *modern* in his time: his preference of the French and English theatre to the Greek is only one example of this. I should wish to qualify his reproof of Milton, in the passage I have just quoted, by saying that I do not believe it was primarily long prejudice, or the bigotry of learning, which led Milton to write his play on the Greek model. I think that it was first of all a knowledge, conscious or unconscious, of what were his own gifts. He chose, in *Samson*, the one subject most suitable for him; and he took the Greek model because he was a poet, and not a dramatist, and in this form he could best exhibit his mastery and conceal his weaknesses. What is more odd, however, since Johnson holds up French as well as English drama for imitation, is that he makes no reference to the case, inconvenient for his thesis, of Racine's *Athalie*. Racine was a poet of the theatre, if there ever was one; in *Athalie* he employs the chorus; and *Athalie*, I think, is a very great play indeed. But, with this exception, Johnson was judging choral drama according to dramatic standards which I do not think that most of us apply to *Samson*. For many people, *Samson* is the most readable of Milton's major works: certainly, more readable than *Paradise Regained*. We can even enjoy *Samson*, as we can enjoy *Comus*, when it is performed. But I do not believe that anyone could enjoy them directly as drama: we need either to be pretty familiar with the text, or else have a very quick ear for the appreciation of verbal beauty. Otherwise, I do not think that the plot or the characterization of either piece would long hold our attention.

I am inclined to believe that on the whole Johnson, if he is allowed to criticize *Samson* as drama, is right. I do not believe that he appreciated the dramatic force of the Greek conventions in their own place and time. Indeed, I doubt whether it was possible for anyone to do so in the undeveloped state of archaeological knowledge in his time: certainly, our own understanding of the Greek plays as plays has been immensely extended by recent study and research. But the real question is whether the form of Greek drama can be naturalized for the modern world. And I suspect that the chief justification for Milton, as for some later poets, in imitating the Greek form of drama, is that the use of a chorus enables poets with no skill in the theatre, to make the most of their accomplishments, and thereby conceal some of their defects.

Johnson's opinions on religious verse are most fully stated in his Life of Waller. It is there that he observes

'Let no pious ear be offended, if I advance, in opposition to many authorities, that poetical devotion cannot often please. . . .

'Contemplative piety, of the intercourse between God and the human soul, cannot be poetical. . . .'

These and other words might have been transposed into his Life of Watts, and are confirmed there by the following:

'His devotional poetry is, like that of others, unsatisfactory. The paucity of its topics enforces perpetual repetition, and the sanctity of the matter rejects the ornaments of figurative diction.'

As a criticism of Watts, this is just enough. To a generation which has learned to admire the religious sonnets of Donne, the lyrics of George Herbert, Crashaw and Vaughan, it seems narrowly perverse. I think that we have to take account, not only of the limitations of the literary taste of his time, but of its religious limitations also. The two support each other here: for as it did not occur to the mind of Johnson that there were poetic values, in earlier periods, which had vanished during the perfecting of those of his own, so I do not think that it could occur to him that there was a religious sensibility which had disappeared also. Johnson's strictures are applicable to *most* of the religious verse that has been written since, as well as to that of his own time. What vitiates his condemnation, is the absence of any discrimination between the religious poetry of public worship, and the religious poetry of personal experience. In the hymn, the anthem, the sequence, the intrusion of personal experience would be impertinent; and perhaps for this reason the poetry of public worship is at its best in the impersonal eloquence of the Latin language. It is true that some devotional religious verse appears to be equally valid in both contexts. Some of George Herbert's poems are found in hymnals: yet I always feel them to be less satisfactory as hymns than those of Watts; for I am always aware of the personality of Herbert, and never conscious of any personality of Watts. But most of the devotional poetry of the eighteenth century has the merit neither of the one kind nor of the other. The reasons why good poetry in this kind was not written, and the reasons why Johnson could not recognize its possibility, have to do with the limitations of religious sensibility in that century. I say limitations, rather than lack of sensibility, for no one can read Johnson's *Prayers and Meditations* or Law's *Seri-*

ous Call without acknowledging that this age also has its monuments of religious devotion.

II

I do not propose to discuss the poetry of the eighteenth century in general; or even to discuss Johnson's Lives of Dryden and Pope, except to extract from them some statements indicating Johnson's critical theory. I must say something of Johnson's poetry, on the principle which I have already affirmed, that we can only understand a poet's criticism of poetry in relation to the poetry which he writes. Of his shorter poems, we can only say of the most of them that they possess those two qualities which Johnson believed to be all that can be asked of short poems: neatness and elegance. One of them, *Long expected one-and-twenty*, might provide an interesting comparison, not to Johnson's disadvantage, with *The Shropshire Lad:* Housman's verse is also neat and elegant, but on the point of poetic diction, and on that of edification — two of Johnson's criteria, as we shall see—we might grant that Johnson's poem is superior. The only one, I think, of Johnson's short poems which is more than neat and elegant, the only one which does what no one before him could have done and which no successor could emulate, is the poem on the death of Dr. Levett, the man 'obscurely wise and coarsely kind' — a poem unique in tenderness, piety and wisdom. The two poems on which Johnson's title as a poet must rest are *The Vanity of Human Wishes* and *London*. *London* has 364 lines, *The Vanity of Human Wishes* 263. Johnson was a meditative poet: he could not have expressed himself fully in a poem of less length; and being only a meditative poet, he did not have the resources for a poem of more ample scope.

London has fine lines and passages, but it does not seem to me successful as a whole. The setting, or prologue to the poem, is artificial. It is wearisome to have the invective against the metropolis presented as the speech of 'injur'd Thales' to a friend who is seeing him off at Greenwich, as he enters a wherry for the ship which will take him into voluntary exile in Pembrokeshire. There is, as elsewhere in the poem, a suspicion of falsity. Johnson wished to write a satire in the manner of Juvenal, in order to denounce the wickedness of London; but that Johnson should ever have contemplated leaving London for the remote promontory of St. David's is so inconsistent with his character, and his confessed sentiments in later life, that we cannot believe he ever meant it. He was the last man to have domiciled himself at St. David's, or to have appreciated the beauties of that romantic spot when he got there.

> For who would leave, unbribed, Hibernia's land,
> Or change the rocks of Scotland for the Strand?

The answer is, Samuel Johnson, if anybody. These may seem carping objections. But they reinforce my doubt, whether Johnson was the right man for satire. Johnson was a moralist, and he lacked a certain divine levity which makes sparkle the lines of the two great English verse satirists. Indignation may make poetry, but it must be indignation recollected in tranquillity; in London I feel that a feigned indignation is presented, instead of a real indignation being recalled. In the satire of Dryden, as in a different way in that of Pope, the object satirized disappears in the poetry, is hardly more than the pretext for poetry. With Dryden, the man ridiculed becomes absurdly gigantic; and Pope's noxious insect becomes something beautiful and strange. In London the total effect is one of querulousness. The indictment of a whole city fails: it is incredible, even in the eighteenth century, that you could never go out at night without being set upon by boisterous drunkards, or sleep in your own house without danger of being killed by burglars. Johnson utters generalizations, and the generalizations are not true: what keeps the poem alive is the undercurrent of personal feeling, the bitterness of the hard-

ships, slights, injuries and privations, really experienced by
Johnson in his youth.

Johnson's mind tended towards the general reflection supported by instances. In a well known passage, Imlac, the pre-
ceptor of Rasselas, is made to observe that

'The business of a poet is to examine, not the individual,
but the species; to remark general properties and large appearances; he does not number the streaks of the tulip, or describe
the different shades in the verdure of the forest. He is to exhibit in his portraits of nature such prominent and striking fea-
tures, as recall the original to every mind; and must neglect
the minuter discriminations, which one may have remarked,
and another have neglected, for those characteristics which are
alike obvious to vigilance and carelessness.'

This disposition to the general affects even Johnson's regula-
tions of poetic diction. 'It is a general rule of poetry,' he says
in his Life of Dryden, 'that all appropriated terms of art should
be sunk in general impressions, because poetry is to speak an
universal language. This rule is still stronger with regard to
arts not liberal, and therefore far removed from common
knowledge;' and he proceeds to reprimand Dryden for using
technical terms of seamanship, most of which — such as *seam,
mallet, tarpauling* — we should now consider unexceptionable.
But with Johnson's ideas of poetic diction I am not yet concerned: I only wish to suggest that Johnson's rules for poetry
were to some degree limited by the kind of poetry which he
himself was able to write.

In *The Vanity of Human Wishes* Johnson found the perfect
theme for his abilities. The idea, which is indicated by the
title, was not new, and never had been. That is not necessary
or even desirable for a poem of this sort: what is essential is
that it should be an idea which the reader will not for a moment question. In this respect, as a meditative poem, *The
Vanity of Human Wishes* is superior to Gray's *Elegy*; for the
latter poem contains one or two ideas which are perhaps not

very sound: the likelihood that the village churchyard, or any churchyard, contained the body of a potential Hampden, Milton or Cromwell is exceedingly small. Gray, of course, in this poem, is by no means purely meditative: what the *Elegy* gains by its description, by its evocation of the rural landscape of England, is all important. On the other hand, if Johnson had confined himself to the general, and not supported it with instances, there would be little left of *The Vanity of Human Wishes*. Of these, the passage on Charles of Sweden is the most quoted and the best sustained. These thirty-two lines compose a paragraph which is, in itself, quite perfect in form: the rising curve of ambition, the sudden calamity, and the slow decline and degradation through which we see the conqueror

> *Compelled a needy supplicant to wait*
> *While ladies interpose and slaves debate,*

culminating in

> *a barren strand,*
> *A petty Fortress, and a dubious hand.*

But this passage is not one which preserves its full value when extracted: it requires both what precedes and what follows, and takes only its proper place in the complete poem.

Great poetry of the type of *The Vanity of Human Wishes* is rare; and we cannot reproach Johnson for not writing more of it, when we consider how little of such poetry there is. Yet this type of poetry cannot rise to the highest rank. It is, by its nature, of rather loose construction; the idea is given at the start, and as it is one universally accepted, there can be but little development, only variations on the one theme. Johnson did not have the gift of structure. For a more elaborate construction — and structure I hold to be an important element of poetic composition — a variety of talents — descriptive, narrative and dramatic — are required. We do not ordinarily expect a very close structure of a poem in rhymed couplets, which often looks as if, but for what the author has to say, it might begin or end anywhere. But there is a poem, by a contemporary and friend of Johnson, which has a high degree of organisation. I place *The Deserted Village* higher than any poem by Johnson or by Gray. In Goldsmith's poem, the art of transition is exemplified in perfection. If you examine it paragraph by paragraph, you will find always a shift just at the right moment, from the descriptive to the meditative, to the personal, to the meditative again, to the landscape with figures, to the delineation of individuals [the clergyman and the schoolmaster] with a skill and concision seldom equalled since Chaucer. These parts are properly proportioned. Finally, the idea is one which, while as acceptable as Johnson's, is more original and also prophetic:

> *Ill fares the land, to hastening ills a prey,*
> *Where wealth accumulates, and men decay.*

I have made this digression, because I do not think that Johnson shows great power of construction in his own poems, and because I do not think that he recognizes the importance of considering structure in the valuation of a poem. I pass now to review those properties of a good poem, which Johnson both illustrates in his own verse and especially commends in the work of others.

Johnson attached importance to *originality*. Originality is one of those numerous terms the meaning of which may alter from generation to generation, and we must be careful to examine what it meant to Johnson. His use of the word is illustrated by the following passage from his Life of Thomson:

'As a writer, Thomson is entitled to one praise of the highest kind: his mode of thinking, and of expressing his thought, is original. His blank verse is no more the blank verse of Milton, or of any other poet, than the rhymes of Prior are the rhymes of Cowley. His numbers, his pauses, his diction, are of his own growth, without transcription, without imitation. He thinks in a peculiar train, and he thinks always as a man of genius; he looks round on Nature and on Life with the eye which Nature bestows only upon a poet; the eye that distinguishes in everything presented to its view, whatever there is on which imagination can delight to be detained, and with a mind that at once comprehends the vast, and attends to the minute. The reader of *The Seasons* wonders that he never saw before what Thomson shows him, and that he never yet has felt what Thomson impresses.'

Originality is found, here, in a 'mode of thinking and of expression'. But the thought itself does not have to be novel or difficult of apprehension and acceptance; it may be, and for Johnson most often is, the commonplace, or a thought which, when grasped, is so quickly admitted that the reader wonders that he never thought of it for himself. Originality does not require the rejection of convention. We have grown accustomed, during the last century and more, to such a riot of individual styles that we may forget that originality is as significant in a settled period as it is in one of constant change; we have become so accustomed to differences of poetic style recognizable by anybody, that we may be less sensitive to the finer variations within a form, which the mind and ear habituated to that form may perceive. But originality, when it becomes the only, or the most prized virtue of poetry, may cease to be a virtue at all; and when several poets, and their respective groups of admirers, cease to have in common any standards of versification, any identity of taste or of tenets of belief, criticism may decline to an advertisement of preference. The originality which Johnson approves, is an originality limited by the other qualities which he demands.

Johnson attached importance to *edification*. This term has become the object of derision, though what the term means may be something from which we can never escape. That poetry should teach wisdom or inculcate virtue, seems to most people a quite secondary, even an extraneous value; to some it even seems incompatible with the true function of poetry. But we must first observe, that Johnson, when his critical sense is alert, is never given to overrating a poem on the sole ground of its teaching a pure morality. He held that a poem should be interesting, and that it should give immediate pleasure. Indeed, I think he overstates this requirement, when he says, in his Life of Cowley:

'Whatever professes to benefit by pleasing, must please at once. The pleasures of the mind imply something sudden and unexpected; that which elevates must also surprise. What is perceived by slow degrees may gratify us with the consciousness of improvement, but will never strike with the sense of pleasure.'

I agree that a poem which makes no immediate impression, which in no way compels our attention, is not likely to arouse a thrill later. But Johnson does not seem to me to allow for the possibility of any development or expansion of enjoyment, and the gradual awareness to new beauties, to follow from better acquaintance; nor does he allow for the ripening of the reader and the development of his sensibility through deeper experience and more extensive knowledge. I did not, however, quote his sentence for the purpose of disagreement, but to indicate the strictness with which pleasure and edification are associated in Johnson's mind. He speaks of 'whatever professes to benefit by pleasing'; he says, 'that which elevates must always surprise.' The edification is not a separable addition to a poem, it is organically essential to it. We do not have *two* experiences, one of pleasure and one of edification: it is one experience which we analyse into constituents.

In judging the permanence of the principles of a critic belonging to an age very different from our own, we must constantly reinterpret his language according to our own situation. In the most generalized sense, I suppose that 'edification' means only that from good poetry, certainly from great poetry, we must derive some benefit as well as pleasure. If we identify 'edification' with the propagation of the moral ideas of Johnson's time — ideas which Christians may hold to be tainted with deism, and which others may find too Christian — we fail to see that it is merely our notions of edification that have changed. When Matthew Arnold said that poetry was a criticism of life, he was maintaining the standard of edification. Even the doctrine of 'art for art's sake' is only a variation under the guise of a protest; and in our time, the defence of poetry as a substitute for religion, and the attempt, not always successful or beneficial to poetry, to express or impose a social philosophy in verse, indicate that it is only the content of 'edification' that changes.

If, therefore, we allow to 'edification' all the elasticity of which the term is capable, it seems to come to no more than the assertion that poetry should have some serious value for the reader: a proposition which will not be denied and which is therefore hardly worth affirming. Our only disagreement will be about the kind of content which we consider edifying. Our real difficulty with Johnson's view is rather different. We distinguish more clearly between the conscious intention of the writer, and the effect of the work. We distrust verse in which the author is deliberately aiming to instruct or to persuade. This distinction does not form one of the commonplaces of Johnson's thinking. He is, however, I believe, really concerned with the morality of the poem, and not with the moral designs of the poet.

'Bossu is of opinion [says Johnson in his Life of Milton] that the poet's first work is to find a *moral*, which his fable is afterwards to illustrate and establish. This seems to have been the process only of Milton; the moral of other poems is incidental and consequent; in Milton's only it is essential and intrinsic.'

I think that this statement is true of Milton, though if Johnson had been better acquainted with Dante he might not have taken Milton as an unique example. It appears to show, however, that what interests Johnson is the edifying power of the poem, rather than the deliberate intention of the poet.

We are all, of course, influenced in our degree of attraction to any particular work of art, by our sympathy with, or antipathy towards, the ideas, as well as the personality of the author. We endeavour, and in our time must endeavour, to discount this attraction or repulsion, in order to arrive at a just valuation of the artistic merit. If we lived, like Johnson, in an age of relative unity and of generally accepted assumptions, we should probably be less concerned to make this effort. If we were agreed upon the nature of the world we live in, on the place of man in it and on his destiny; if we were agreed as to what we meant by wisdom, by the good life for the individual and for society, we should apply moral judgments to poetry as confidently as did Johnson. But in an age in which no two writers need agree about anything, an age in which we must constantly admit that a poet with a view of life which we believe to be mistaken, may write much better poetry than another whose view is the same as our own, we are forced to make this abstraction; and in making it, we are tempted to ignore, with unfortunate results, the moral value of poetry altogether. So that, of a poet's view of life, we incline to ask, not 'is it true?' but 'is it original?' And it is one of the theses maintained in this discussion of Johnson's criticism, that Johnson was in a position, as no critic of equal stature has been since, to write purely *literary* criticism, just because he was able to assume that there was a general attitude towards life, and a common opinion as to the place of poetry in it.

I come next to Johnson's use of the term *poetic diction*. To most people nowadays, I imagine, 'poetic diction' means an idiom and a choice of words which are out of date, and which perhaps were never very good at their best. If we are temperate, we mean the use of idiom and vocabulary borrowed from poets of a different generation, idiom and vocabulary no longer suitable for poetry. If we are extreme, we mean that this idiom and vocabulary were always bad, even when they were fresh. Wordsworth, in his Preface, says: 'there will also be found in these volumes little of what is usually called poetic diction.' Johnson uses the term in a eulogistic sense. In the Life of Dryden he remarks:

'There was, therefore, before the time of Dryden no poetical diction, no system of words at once refined from the grossness of domestic use, and free from the harshness of terms appropriate to particular arts. Words too familiar, or too remote, defeat the purpose of a poet. From those sounds which we hear on small or on coarse occasions, we do not easily receive strong impressions, or delightful images; and words to which we are nearly strangers, whenever they occur, draw that attention to themselves which they should transmit to things.'

We must bear in mind, with regard to vocabulary and construction, what I tried to put before more generally: that the notion of the language as perpetually in change is not one which had impressed itself upon the age of Johnson. He looked back some two centuries and marked in language, as in manners, a continuous improvement. As for the improvement which he noted, he was not deceived: but he had neither the awareness of anything lost, nor the apprehension of inevitable changes to come. Nor does Wordsworth himself evince any more consciousness of the constancy with which language must change, than does Johnson: what he thought he had established was a return to a diction of popular simplicity and rural purity. In his perception that the language of literature must not lose its connexion with the language of speech, Wordsworth was right; but his standard of the right poetic diction was no more relative than Johnson's. We, on the contrary, should be able to recognize that there should be, for every period, some standard of correct poetic diction, neither identical with, nor too remote from, current speech; and must concede that the right poetic diction, fifty years hence, will not be the same as that for to-day. I mean that the vocabulary, the idiom, and the grammatical rules for poetry cannot be identical with those of prose. In the choice of words, Johnson's restriction remains true: that 'those sounds which we hear on small or on coarse occasions' are to be avoided — except, I must add, when it is the purpose of the poet to present something small or coarse; and that 'words to which we are nearly strangers, whenever they occur, draw that attention to themselves which they should transmit to things' — except I should add, when the word is the only word for that thing, or when it is the poet's purpose to draw attention to the word.

To criticize the poetic diction of eighteenth-century poetry is one thing, to criticize an eighteenth-century theory of poetic diction is another. We must remember that if there is no 'poetic diction' admitted, we have no standard for criticizing good and bad writing in poetry: to deny that there is any right common style, is as dangerous as to insist that the poetic style of our time should be the same as that of the nineteenth century. Our modern vocabulary accommodates many comparatively new words which to Johnson would have sounded barbarous. We have been inventing, discovering, fashioning and theorizing at a rate unknown to any earlier time, and a new word establishes itself much more quickly. No word is too new, if it is the only word for the purpose; no word is too archaic, if it is the only word for the purpose. And many occasions, which to Johnson would have seemed 'small' or 'coarse', seem to us fit occasions to be celebrated in verse. Johnson's view of poetic diction remains sound; but we have to use our own wits in the application of it.

That Johnson was alert to the vice of *mannerism*, appears from another passage in his Life of Dryden, a passage which should be taken to heart by everyone who aspires to write good verse:

'He who writes much will not easily escape a manner, such a recurrence of particular modes as may easily be noted. Dryden is always *another and the same*; he does not exhibit a

second time the same elegancies in the same form, nor appears to have any art other than that of expressing with clear-
ness what he thinks with vigour. His style could not easily be
imitated, either seriously or ludicrously; for, being always
equable and always varied, it has no prominent or discrimina-
tive characters.'

I wished to draw particular attention to this point of poetic
diction, because it is an essential standard of Johnson's criticism, and because I think that the absence of any common
standard of poetic diction is a weakness both of modern verse
and of our criticism of it. And I deliberately took this up
directly after touching upon his standard of *edification*. That
poetry, when it illustrates some moral truth or inculcates some
virtuous practice, is more to be commended than when it does
not; and that poetry which recommends or insinuates bad
principles, or leads into error, is to be condemned, is shown
throughout in Johnson's treatment of his authors. Yet Johnson said, in praising Akenside's *Pleasures of Imagination*: 'with
the philosophical or religious tenets of the author I have
nothing to do; my business is with his poetry.' Johnson did not
confuse his judgment of what an author was saying, with his
judgment about the way in which he said it. Now I observe
sometimes in contemporary criticism of poetry, and in the
more ambitious reviewing of poetry, a confusion of these
judgments. The standard of edification has been fractured into
a variety of prejudices: with no common opinion as to what
poetry ought to teach, the critic is not necessarily liberated
from moral judgment, but will frequently declare a poem good
or bad, according to his sympathy with, or antipathy from, the
author's point of view. Not infrequently too, the critic's knowledge of the author's views will be derived from other sources
than the particular poem presented for his criticism, and will
influence his judgment upon that poem. And with the question whether a poem is well or ill written, whether it could be
improved, whether the cadences are musical, whether the

choice of words is fastidious and literate, whether the imagery
is happily found and properly distributed, whether the syntax
is correct and whether the violations of normal construction
are justified: such questions are avoided as if they laid the
questioner under suspicion of pedantry. The result is too often
comment which is of no value to the author, except when, if
favourable, it may be good advertisement; a criticism of the
hustings, by which reviewers range themselves for or against
a particular poet.

That there is to-day no definite standard of taste in poetry,
is partly the result of conditions of society and historical
origins, beyond our control and beyond our responsibility. The
most, perhaps, that we can do, and that is worth the doing, is
to learn to recognize the benefits to the writer and to his critic
of *common style* in poetry. It is in fact only when a common
style is recognized, from which the poet may not depart too
far without censure, that the term 'poetic diction', in any but a
derogatory sense, has meaning. When such standards for a
common style exist, the author who would achieve originality
is compelled to attend to the finer shades of distinction. To be
original within definite limits of propriety may require greater
talent and labour, than when every man may write as he
pleases, and when the first thing expected of him is to be
different. To be obliged to work upon the finer shades is to be
compelled to strive for precision and clarity: a good deal of
what is blamed as wilful obscurity on the part of modern
writers is the result of the lack of any common style, and the
consequent difficulty of communication. Those conditions also
favour the flowering of something for which Johnson's own
verse, at its best, is eminent: *eloquence*. Eloquence is a virtue
associated with great oratory: it should be distinguished from
the baser, and far commoner type of political oratory, by the
test of its appeal to the reason and to the sensibility, and its
avoidances of appeal to the coarser and more inflammable
passions. Eloquence is that which can stir the emotions of the

intelligent and judicious. But, in poetry, not all poetry which does this is, in my use of the word, eloquent; poetry is eloquent, only if the poet is appealing to emotions which the intelligent and judicious can experience together — in other words, not to a single reader but to an audience. It is not an universal virtue in poetry; it is effective of some results and incompatible with the attainment of others; but most of the great poets have displayed it on occasion. It is related to that peculiar force in the poetry of Johnson and Goldsmith, as in the poetry of Dryden and Pope before them, which I may indicate by saying that every word and epithet goes straight to its mark. In comparison, much of later poetry has employed words rather for the sake of overtones, associations, and indefinite suggestiveness. The greatest poets have done this too; we must admit that we can err by exclusive attention to the one kind of use of words or to the other.

In the Life of Pope, Johnson defines, as illustrated in Pope's poetry, the three qualities which constitute poetic genius. He says significantly that Pope has these three qualities 'in proportions very nicely adjusted to each other'; which is a wholesome reminder that it is not separate qualities, but qualities in relation to each other, by which we must judge a poet — that, in fact, the perfection of their proportion is itself the final quality. He writes as follows:

'He had *invention*, by which new trains of events are formed, and new scenes of imagery displayed, as in *The Rape of the Lock*, and by which extrinsic and adventitious embellishments and illustrations are connected with a known subject, as in the *Essay on Criticism*. He had *imagination*, which strongly impresses on the writer's mind, and enables him to convey to the reader, the various forms of nature, incidents of life, and energies of passion, as in his *Eloisa*, *Windsor Forest*, and *Ethic Epistles*. He had *judgment*, which selects from life or nature what the present purpose requires, and by separating the essence of things from its concomitants, often makes the representation more powerful than the reality; and he had colours of language always before him, ready to decorate his matter with every grace of elegant expression, as when he accommodates his diction to the wonderful multiplicity of Homer's sentiments and descriptions.'

The dangers of attempting to catalogue the faculties of the poet are of two kinds. These denominations may separate, in the mind of the reader, faculties which are only found together; and they may be taken too seriously, as final psychological or philosophical truth, when they are merely analyses of pragmatic validity, to be tested by their usefulness in helping us to weigh the merits of particular poets. It is prudent, not simply to choose the set of definitions which we find most congenial, or to assume that that one is most exact which is most recent; but to collate all those of respectable authority of different ages. We find that these have a great deal in common. Johnson follows Dryden in the use of the term *invention*, but puts it beside *imagination*, whereas Dryden had made *invention* a species of *imagination*, together with *fancy* and *elocution*; Johnson does not employ *elocution*, but introduces *judgment*. Coleridge concentrates upon *imagination*, in which he finds depths of meaning unsuspected by either Dryden or Johnson; and belittles *fancy* — with a sharpness of distinction between *fancy* and *imagination* which I find difficult to apply in practice. The changes in the meaning of words, and these changes of emphasis, are part of the history of our civilization. A contemporary critic, engaged in the same task of analysis, would produce another, and more complicated account, which would probably be influenced by the study of sciences of more recent growth. The modern account would fit in better with our mental furniture, but would not necessarily be more true for this reason; because of the unsettled state of the sciences upon which it might draw, it might even be more inclined to stray from what is the true purpose of such discriminations, the help they afford in discerning the merits and defects of

particular pieces of poetry. The accounts of Dryden and Johnson, because these critics were concerned with literature as
literature, and not with psychology or sociology, and because
of their very simplicity, have enduring usefulness. The particular interest of Johnson's variation, I think, lies in his use of
the term *judgment* — a reminder of the great importance of
the critical faculty in creative composition.

'In the present age the poet — [I would wish to be understood as speaking generally, and without allusion to individual
names] — seems to propose to himself as his main object, and
as that which is the most characteristic of his art, new and
striking images; with incidents that interest the affections or
excite the curiosity. Both his characters and his descriptions,
as much as possible, are specific and individual, even to a degree of portraiture. In his diction and metre, on the other
hand, he is comparatively careless.'

These words are not mine, but Coleridge's. They could well
enough be applied to the present time; and on the other hand
the principle maintained is one which I am sure Johnson
would have approved. Similarly, Coleridge's observations on
poetic diction, when compared with Johnson's, show a fundamental agreement on the difference between the use of language in verse and its use in prose. In an age like ours, lacking
common standards, poets need to remind themselves that it
is not sufficient to rely upon those gifts which are native to
them, and which they exercise with ease, but that good poetry
must exhibit several qualities in proportion, of which one is
good sense. Their judgment should also be employed, in discovering for themselves the sources of their own strength and
weakness; in curbing the exuberance of their force, and avoiding occasions on which they would display only their weakness. I remember once being told that a famous tennis player
had said, that she was all the better for being naturally weak
in certain strokes; for the effort to overcome her deficiency,
and manoeuvre so that it should be least exposed, had greatly

increased her resourcefulness. There is something here which
poets might ponder.

A thorough examination of Johnson's criticism would require, first, a study of the eighteenth-century background; second, a study of Johnson himself, not as the subject of anec-
dote, but in his other works, and in his religious and political
opinions; and, finally, a much more detailed study of his criticism of the greater of the poets who came under his observation: Shakespeare, Milton, Dryden, Pope, Gray. Such would
be a work of more scholarship than I profess. I only want to
suggest to the student of English poetry and of the criticism
of poetry that here is a subject which deserves much more serious investigation than it has yet received. And, in closing, I
wish to sum up those points which seem to me to have particular relevance to the criticism of poetry in our own time.

In the first place, it is remarkable that Johnson's *Lives of the
Poets* is the only monumental collection of critical studies of
English poets in the language, with a coherence, as well as an
amplitude, which no other English criticism can claim. It is
worth while asking ourselves why no later work of criticism is of
the same kind. Nineteenth century criticism, when it has not belonged primarily to the category of scholarly research, the pres-
entation of the ascertainable facts about one author or another,
has tended to be something less purely *literary*. With Coleridge,
criticism merges into philosophy and a theory of aesthetics;
with Arnold, it merges into ethics and propaedeutics, and
literature becomes a means towards the formation of character;
in some critics, of whom Pater is a specimen, the subject-matter of criticism becomes a pretext of another kind. In our own
day, the influence of psychology and of sociology upon literary
criticism has been very noticeable. On the one hand, these influences of social discipline have enlarged the field of the
critic, and have affirmed, in a world which otherwise is inclined
to depreciate the importance of literature, the relations of literature to life. But from another point of view this enrichment

has also been an impoverishment, for the purely literary values, the appreciation of good writing for its own sake, have become submerged when literature is judged in the light of other considerations. That this has happened, must not be attributed either for approval or disparagement to individual critics. It is simply that the conditions under which literature is judged simply and naturally as literature and not another thing, no longer prevail. For such judgment of literature to be the normal and natural task of the critic, a settled society is necessary; a definite and limited public, in the midst of which there would be a smaller number of persons of taste and discrimination, with the same background of education and manners. It must be a society which believes in itself, a society in which the differences of religious and political views are not extreme. Only in such a society can the standard of a *common style* of good writing become established and unquestioned. That is the kind of society for which Johnson wrote. It is evidence of the change of society, accelerated in our own time, a change which brings inevitably a change in the consciousness of the literary critic himself, that in attempting to explain, to myself and to my audience, the peculiar interest of Johnson's criticism, I am forced to put myself at a point of view so very different from his own, and intrude the suggestion of social background which has become the necessary concern of criticism.

The conclusion that no work comparable to *The Lives of the Poets* could be written to-day, should not lead us either to elevate Johnson to a pinnacle, and lament the decline of civility which makes such criticism impossible; nor should it on the other hand tempt us to treat these essays merely as a curiosity of no bearing upon our actual problems. Their first value is a value which all study of the past should have for us: that it should make us more conscious of what we are, and of our own limitations, and give us more understanding of the world in which we now live. Their secondary value is, that by studying them, and in so doing attempting to put ourselves at their author's point of view, we may recover some of the criteria of judgment which have been disappearing from the criticism of poetry. We do not need to accept all of Johnson's judgments, or agree with all his opinions, to extract this lesson. Nor do we need to overrate the poetry of that period of which the names of Dryden and Johnson may serve as boundaries. But amongst the varieties of chaos in which we find our ourselves immersed to-day, one is a chaos of language, in which there are discoverable no standards of writing, and an increasing indifference to etymology and the history of the use of words. And of the responsibility of our poets and our critics, for the preservation of the language, we need to be repeatedly reminded.

Byron *

T<small>HE</small> facts of a large part of Byron's life have been well set forth, in the last few years, by Sir Harold Nicolson and Mr. Quennell, who have also provided interpretations which accord with each other and which make the character of Byron more intelligible to the present generation. No such interpretation has yet been offered in our time for Byron's verse. In and out of universities, Wordsworth, Coleridge, Shelley and Keats have been discussed from various points of view: Byron and Scott have been left in peace. Yet Byron, at least, would seem the most nearly remote from the sympathies of every living critic: it would be interesting, therefore, if we could have half a dozen essays about him, to see what agreement could be reached. The present article is an attempt to start that ball rolling.

There are several initial difficulties. It is difficult to return critically to a poet whose poetry was — I suppose it was for many of our contemporaries, except those who are too young to have read any of the poetry of that period — the first boyhood enthusiasm. To be told anecdotes of one's own childhood by an elderly relative is usually tedious; and a return, after many years, to the poetry of Byron is accompanied by a similar gloom: images come before the mind, and the recollection of some verses in the manner of Don Juan, tinged with that disillusion and cynicism only possible at the age of sixteen, which

* Contributed to From Anne to Victoria, a collection of essays edited by Bonamy Dobrée. Published by Cassell & Co., 1937.

appeared in a school periodical. There are more impersonal
obstacles to overcome. The bulk of Byron's poetry is distressing, in proportion to its quality; one would suppose that he
never destroyed anything. Yet bulk is inevitable in a poet of
Byron's type; and the absence of the destructive element in his
composition indicates the kind of interest, and the kind of lack
of interest, that he took in poetry. We have come to expect
poetry to be something very concentrated, something distilled;
but if Byron had distilled his verse, there would have been
nothing whatever left. When we see exactly what he was
doing, we can see that he did it as well as it can be done.
With most of his shorter poems, one feels that he was doing
something that Tom Moore could do as well or better; in his
longer poems, he did something that no one else has ever
equalled.

It is sometimes desirable to approach the work of a poet
completely out of favour, by an unfamiliar avenue. If my
avenue to Byron is a road that exists only for my own mind, I
shall be corrected by other critics; it may at all events upset
prejudice and encourage opinion to form itself anew. I therefore suggest considering Byron as a Scottish poet — I say
'Scottish', not 'Scots', since he wrote in English. The one poet
of his time with whom he could be considered to be in competition, a poet of whom he spoke invariably with the highest
respect, was Sir Walter Scott. I have always seen, or imagined
that I saw, in busts of the two poets, a certain resemblance in
the shape of the head. The comparison does honour to Byron,
and when you examine the two faces, there is no further resemblance. Were one a person who liked to have busts about,
a bust of Scott would be something one could live with. There
is an air of nobility about that head, an air of magnanimity,
and of that inner and perhaps unconscious serenity that belongs to great writers who are also great men. But Byron —
that pudgy face suggesting a tendency to corpulence, that
weakly sensual mouth, that restless triviality of expression, and

worst of all that blind look of the self-conscious beauty; the bust of Byron is that of a man who was every inch the touring tragedian. Yet it was by being so thorough-going an actor that Byron arrived at a kind of knowledge: of the world outside, which he had to learn something about in order to play his role in it, and of that part of himself which was his role. Superficial knowledge, of course: but accurate so far as it went.

Of a Scottish quality in Byron's poetry, I shall speak when I come to *Don Juan*. But there is a very important part of the Byronic make-up which may appropriately be mentioned before considering his poetry, for which I think his Scottish antecedence provided the material. That is his peculiar diabolism, his delight in posing as a damned creature — and in providing evidence for his damnation in a rather horrifying way. Now, the diabolism of Byron is very different from anything that the Romantic Agony [as Mr. Praz calls it] produced in Catholic countries. And I do not think it is easily derived from the comfortable compromise between Christianity and paganism arrived at in England and characteristically English. It could come only from the religious background of a people steeped in Calvinistic theology.

Byron's diabolism, if indeed it deserves the name, was of a mixed type. He shared, to some extent, Shelley's Promethean attitude, and the Romantic passion for Liberty; and this passion, which inspired his more political outbursts, combined with the image of himself as a man of action to bring about the Greek adventure. And his Promethean attitude merges into a Satanic [Miltonic] attitude. The romanic conception of Milton's Satan is semi-Promethean, and also contemplates Pride as a *virtue*. It would be difficult to say whether Byron was a proud man, or a man who liked to pose as a proud man — the possibility of the two attitudes being combined in the same person does not make them any less dissimilar in the abstract. Byron was certainly a vain man, in quite simple ways:

> I can't complain, whose ancestors are there,
>   Erneis, Radulphus — eight-and-forty manors
> [If that my memory doth not greatly err]
>   Were their reward for following Billy's banners....

His sense of damnation was also mitigated by a touch of unreality: to a man so occupied with himself and with the figure he was cutting nothing outside could be altogether real. It is therefore impossible to make out of his diabolism anything coherent or rational. He was able to have it both ways, it seems; and to think of himself both as an individual isolated and superior to other men because of his own crimes and as a naturally good and generous nature distorted by the crimes committed against it by others. It is this inconsistent creature that turns up as the Giaour, the Corsair, Lara, Manfred and Cain; only as Don Juan does he get nearer to the truth about himself. But in this strange composition of attitudes and beliefs the element that seems to me most real and deep is that of a perversion of the Calvinist faith of his mother's ancestors.

One reason for the neglect of Byron is, I think, that he has been admired for what are his most ambitious attempts to be poetic; and these attempts turn out, on examination, to be fake: nothing but sonorous affirmations of the commonplace with no depth of significance. A good specimen of such imposture is the well-known stanza at the end of Canto XV of Don Juan:

> Between two worlds life hovers like a star,
>   'Twixt night and morn, upon the horizon's verge.
> How little do we know that which we are!
>   How less what we may be! The eternal surge
> Of time and tide rolls on, and bears afar
>   Our bubbles; as the old burst, new emerge,
> Lashed from the foam of ages; while the graves
> Of empire heave but like some passing waves.

verses which are not too good for the school magazine. Byron's
real excellence is on a different level from this.

   The qualities of narrative verse which are found in *Don
Juan* are no less remarkable in the earlier tales. Before under-
taking this essay I had not read these tales since the days of
my schoolboy infatuation, and I approached them with apprehension. They are readable. However absurd we find their
view of life, they are, as tales, very well told. As a *tale-teller* we
must rate Byron very high indeed: I can think of none other
since Chaucer who has a greater readability, with the exception
of Coleridge whom Byron abused and from whom Byron
learned a great deal. And Coleridge never achieved a narrative
of such length. Byron's plots, if they deserve that name, are
extremely simple. What makes the tales interesting is first a
torrential fluency of verse and a skill in varying it from time to
time to avoid monotony; and second a genius for divagation.
Digression, indeed, is one of the valuable arts of the story-
teller. The effect of Byron's digressions is to keep us interested
in the story-teller himself, and through this interest to interest
us more in the story. On contemporary readers this interest
must have been strong to the point of enchantment; for even
still, once we submit ourselves to the point of reading a poem
through, the attraction of the personality is powerful. Any few
lines, if quoted in almost any company, will probably provide
a momentary twitch of merriment:

> *Her eye's dark charm 'twere vain to tell,*
> *But gaze on that of the Gazelle,*
> *It will assist thy fancy well;*
> *As large, as languishingly dark,*
> *But Soul beam'd forth in every spark. . . .*

but the poem as a whole can keep one's attention. *The Giaour*
is a long poem, and the plot is very simple, though not always
easy to follow. A Christian, presumably a Greek, has managed,
by some means of which we are not told, to scrape acquaint-

ance with a young woman who belonged to the harem, or was perhaps the favourite wife of a Moslem named Hassan. In the endeavour to escape with her Christian lover Leila is recaptured and killed; in due course the Christian with some of his friends ambushes and kills Hassan. We subsequently discover that the story of this vendetta — or part of it — is being told by the Giaour himself to an elderly priest, by way of making his confession. It is a singular kind of confession, because the Giaour seems anything but penitent, and makes quite clear that although he has sinned, it is not really by his own fault. He seems impelled rather by the same motive as the Ancient Mariner, than by any desire for absolution — which could hardly have been given: but the device has its use in providing a small complication to the story. As I have said, it is not altogether easy to discover what happened. The beginning is a long apostrophe to the vanished glory of Greece, a theme which Byron could vary with great skill. The Giaour makes a dramatic entrance:

> Who thundering comes on blackest steed,
> With slackened bit and hoof of speed?

and we are given a glimpse of him through a Moslem eye:

> Though young and pale, that sallow front
> Is scathed by fiery passion's brunt . . .

which is enough to tell us, that the Giaour is an interesting person, because he is Lord Byron himself, perhaps. Then there is a long passage about the desolation of Hassan's house, inhabited only by the spider, the bat, the owl, the wild dog and weeds; we infer that the poet has skipped on to the conclusion of the tale, and that we are to expect the Giaour to kill Hassan — which is of course what happens. Not Joseph Conrad could be more roundabout. Then a bundle is privily dropped into the water, and we suspect it to be the body of Leila. Then follows a reflective passage meditating in succession on Beauty, the

Mind, and Remorse. Leila turns up again, alive, for a moment, but this is another dislocation of the order of events. Then we witness the surprise of Hassan and his train — this may have been months or even years after Leila's death — by the Giaour and his banditti, and there is no doubt but that Hassan is killed:

> Fall'n Hassan lies — his unclosed eye
> Yet lowering on his enemy. . . .

Then comes a delightful change of metre, as well as a sudden transition, just at the moment when it is needed:

> The browsing camels' bells are tinkling:
> His mother look'd from her lattice high—
> She saw the dews of eve besprinkling
> The pasture green beneath her eye,
> She saw the planets faintly twinkling:
> ' 'Tis twilight — sure his train is nigh.'

Then follows a sort of exequy for Hassan, evidently spoken by another Moslem. Now the Giaour reappears, nine years later, in a monastery, as we hear one of the monks answering an inquiry about the visitor's identity. In what capacity the Giaour has attached himself to the monastery is not clear; the monks seem to have accepted him without investigation, and his behaviour among them is very odd; but we are told that he has given the monastery a considerable sum of money for the privilege of staying there. The conclusion of the poem consists of the Giaour's confession to one of the monks. Why a Greek of that period should have been so oppressed with remorse [although wholly impenitent] for killing a Moslem in what he would have considered a fair fight, or why Leila should have been guilty in leaving a husband or master to whom she was presumably united without her consent, are questions that we cannot answer.

I have considered the Giaour in some detail in order to exhibit Byron's extraordinary ingenuity in story-telling. There is nothing straight-forward about the telling of the simple tale; we are not told everything that we should like to know; and the behaviour of the protagonists is sometimes as unaccountable as their motives and feelings are confused. Yet the author not only gets away with it, but gets away with it *as narrative*. It is the same gift that Byron was to turn to better account in *Don Juan*; and the first reason why *Don Juan* is still readable is that it has the same narrative quality as the earlier tales.

It is, I think, worth noting, that Byron developed the verse *conte* considerably beyond Moore and Scott, if we are to see his popularity as anything more than public caprice or the attraction of a cleverly exploited personality. These elements enter into it, certainly. But first of all, Byron's verse tales represent a more mature stage of this transient form than Scott's, as Scott's represent a more mature stage than Moore's. Moore's *Lalla Rookh* is a mere sequence of tales joined together by a ponderous prose account of the circumstances of their narration [modelled upon the *Arabian Nights*]. Scott perfected a straightforward story with the type of plot which he was to employ in his novels. Byron combined exoticism with actuality, and developed most effectively the use of *suspense*. I think also that the versification of Byron is the ablest: but in this kind of verse it is necessary to read at length if one is to form an impression, and relative merit cannot be shown by quotation. To identify every passage taken at random as being by Byron or by Moore would be connoisseurship beyond my powers; but I think that anyone who had recently read Byron's tales would agree that the following passage could not be by him:

> And oh! to see the unburied heaps
> On which the lonely moonlight sleeps —
> The very vultures turn away,
> And sicken at so foul a prey!
> Only the fierce hyaena stalks

Throughout the city's desolate walks
At midnight, and his carnage plies —
  Woe to the half-dead wretch, who meets
The glaring of those large blue eyes
  Amid the darkness of the streets!

This is from *Lalla Rookh,* and was marked as if with approval by some reader of the London Library.

Childe Harold seems to me inferior to this group of poems [*The Giaour, The Bride of Abydos, The Corsair, Lara,* etc.]. Time and time again, to be sure, Byron awakens fading interest by a purple passage, but Byron's purple passages are never good enough to do the work that is expected of them in *Childe Harold:*

> *Stop! for thy tread is on an Empire's dust!*

is just what is wanted to revive interest, at that point; but the stanza that follows, on the Battle of Waterloo, seems to me quite false; and quite representative of the falsity in which Byron takes refuge whenever he *tries* to write poetry:

> *Stop! for thy tread is on an Empire's dust!*
> *An Earthquake's spoil is sepulchred below!*
> *Is the spot mark'd with no colossal bust?*
> *Nor column trophied for triumphal show?*
> *None; but the moral's truth tells simpler so,*
> *As the ground was before, so let it be;—*
> *How that red rain hath made the harvest grow!*
> *And is this all the world has gained by thee,*
> *Thou first and last of fields! king-making victory?*

It is all the more difficult, in a period which has rather lost the appreciation of the kind of virtues to be found in Byron's poetry, to analyse accurately his faults and vices. Hence we fail to give credit to Byron for the instinctive art by which, in a poem like *Childe Harold,* and still more efficiently in *Beppo* or

Don Juan, he avoids monotony by a dexterous turn from one subject to another. He has the cardinal virtue of being never dull. But, when we have admitted the existence of forgotten virtues, we still recognize a falsity in most of those passages which were formerly most admired. To what is this falsity due?

Whatever it is, in Byron's poetry, that is 'wrong', we should be mistaken in calling it rhetoric. Too many things have been collected under that name; and if we are going to think that we have accounted for Byron's verse by calling it 'rhetorical', then we are bound to avoid using that adjective about Milton and Dryden, about both of whom [in their very different kinds] we seem to be saying something that has meaning, when we speak of their 'rhetoric'. Their failures, when they fail, are of a higher kind than Byron's success, when he succeeds. Each had a strongly individual idiom, and a sense of language; at their worst, they have an interest in the *word*. You can recognize them in the single line, and can say: here is a particular way of using the language. There is no such individuality in the line of Byron. If one looks at the few single lines, from the Waterloo passage in *Childe Harold*, which may pass for 'familiar quotations', you cannot say that any of them is great poetry:

> *And all went merry as a marriage bell . . .*
> *On with the dance! let joy be unconfined. . . .*

Of Byron one can say, as of no other English poet of his eminence, that he added nothing to the language, that he discovered nothing in the sounds, and developed nothing in the meaning, of individual words. I cannot think of any other poet of his distinction who might so easily have been an accomplished foreigner writing English. The ordinary person talks English, but only a few people in every generation can write it; and upon this undeliberate collaboration between a great many people talking a living language and a very few people writing it, the continuance and maintenance of a language depends.

Just as an artisan who can talk English beautifully while about his work or in a public bar, may compose a letter painfully written in a dead language bearing some resemblance to a newspaper leader, and decorated with words like 'maelstrom' and 'pandemonium': so does Byron write a dead or dying language.

This imperceptiveness of Byron to the English word — so that he has to use a great many words before we become aware of him — indicates for practical purposes a defective sensibility. I say 'for practical purposes' because I am concerned with the sensibility in his poetry, not with his private life; for if a writer has not the language in which to express feelings they might as well not exist. We do not even need to compare his account of Waterloo with that of Stendhal to feel the lack of minute particulars; but it is worth remarking that the prose sensibility of Stendhal, being sensibility, has some values of poetry that Byron completely misses. Byron did for the language very much what the leader writers of our journals are doing day by day. I think that this failure is much more important than the platitude of his intermittent philosophizing. Every poet has uttered platitudes, every poet has said things that have been said before. It is not the weakness of the ideas, but the schoolboy command of the language, that makes his lines seem trite and his thought shallow:

Mais que Hugo aussi était dans tout ce peuple. The words of Péguy have kept drifting through my mind while I have been thinking of Byron:

'Non pas vers qui chantent dans la mémoire, mais vers qui dans la mémoire sonnent et retentissent comme une fanfare, vibrants, trépidants, sonnant comme une fanfare, sonnant comme une charge, tambour éternel, et qui battra dans les mémoires françaises longtemps après que les réglementaires tambours auront cessé de battre au front des régiments.'

But Byron was not 'in *this* people', either of London or of

England, but in his mother's people, and the most stirring
stanza of his Waterloo is this:

> And wild and high the 'Cameron's gathering' rose!
> The war-note of Lochiel, which Albyn's hills
> Have heard, and heard, too, have her Saxon foes; —
> How in the noon of night that pibroch thrills,
> Savage and shrill! But with the breath which fills
> Their mountain-pipe, so fill the mountaineers
> With the fierce native daring which instils
> The stirring memory of a thousand years,
> And Evan's, Donald's fame rings in each clansman's ears!

All things worked together to make *Don Juan* the greatest of
Byron's poems. The stanza that he borrowed from the Italian
was admirably suited to enhance his merits and conceal his
defects, just as on a horse or in the water he was more at ease
than on foot. His ear was imperfect, and capable only of crude
effects; and in this easy-going stanza, with its habitually femi-
nine and occasionally triple endings, he seems always to be reminding us that he is not really trying very hard and yet producing something as good or better than that of the solemn
poets who takes their verse-making more seriously. And Byron
really is at his best when he is not trying too hard to be poetic; when he tries to be poetic in a few lines he produces
things like the stanza I have already quoted, beginning:

> Between two worlds life hovers like a star.

But at a lower intensity he gets a surprising range of effect.
His genius for digression, for wandering away from his subject
(usually to talk about himself) and suddenly returning to it, is,
in *Don Juan*, at the height of its power. The continual banter
and mockery, which his stanza and his Italian model serve to
keep constantly in his mind, serve as an admirable antacid to
the high-falutin which in the earlier romances tends to upset
the reader's stomach; and his social satire helps to keep him to

the objective and has a sincerity that is at least plausible if not profound. The portrait of himself comes much nearer to honesty than any that appears in his earlier work. This is worth examining in some detail.

Charles Du Bos, in his admirable *Byron et le besoin de la fatalité*, quotes a long passage of self-portraiture from *Lara*. Du Bos deserves full credit for recognizing its importance; and Byron deserves all the credit that Du Bos gives him for having written it. This passage strikes me also as a masterpiece of self-analysis, but of a self that is largely a deliberate fabrication — a fabrication that is only completed in the actual writing of the lines. The reason why Byron understood this self so well, is that it is largely his own invention; and it is only the self that he invented that he understood perfectly. If I am correct, one cannot help feeling pity and horror at the spectacle of a man devoting such gigantic energy and persistence to such a useless and petty purpose: though at the same time we must feel sympathy and humility in reflecting that it is a vice to which most of us are addicted in a fitful and less persevering way; that is to say, Byron made a vocation out of what for most of us is an irregular weakness, and deserves a certain sad admiration for his degree of success. But in *Don Juan*, we get something much nearer to genuine self-revelation. For Juan, in spite of the brilliant qualities with which Byron invests him — so that he may hold his own among the English aristocracy — is not an heroic figure. There is nothing absurd about his presence of mind and courage during the shipwreck, or about his prowess in the Turkish wars: he exhibits a kind of physical courage and capacity for heroism which we are quite willing to attribute to Byron himself. But in the accounts of his relations with women, he is not made to appear heroic or even dignified; and these impress us as having an ingredient of the genuine as well as of the make-believe.

It is noticeable — and this confirms, I think, the view of Byron held by Mr. Peter Quennell — that in these love-epi-

sodes Juan always take the passive role. Even Haidee, in spite
of the innocence and ignorance of that child of nature, appears
rather as the seducer than the seduced. This episode is the
longest and most carefully elaborate of all the amorous passages, and I think it deserves pretty high marks. It is true that
after Juan's earlier initiation by Donna Julia, we are hardly so
credulous as to believe in the innocence attributed to him with
Haidee; but this should not lead us to dismiss the description
as false. The *innocence* of Juan is merely a substitute for the
passivity of Byron; and if we restore the latter we can recognize
in the account some authentic understanding of the human
heart, and accept such lines as

> *Alas! They were so young, so beautiful,*
>   *So lonely, loving, helpless, and the hour*
> *Was that in which the heart is always full,*
>   *And having o'er itself no further power,*
> *Prompts deeds eternity cannot annul. . . .*

The lover of Donna Julia and of Haidee is just the man, we
feel, to become subsequently the favourite of Catherine the
Great — to introduce whom, one suspects, Byron had prepared
himself by his eight months with the Countess of Oxford. And
there remains, if not innocence, that strange passivity that has
a curious resemblance to innocence.

Between the first and the second part of the poem, between
Juan's adventures abroad and his adventures in England, there
is a noticeable difference. In the first part the satire is incidental; the action is picaresque, and of the best kind. Byron's
invention never fails. The shipwreck, an episode too well-
known to quote, is something quite new and quite successful,
even if it be somewhat overdone by the act of cannibalism in
which it culminates. The last wild adventure occurs directly
after Juan's arrival in England, when he is held up by footpads
on the way to London; and here again, I think, in the obituary
of the dead highwayman, is something new in English verse:

He from the world had cut off a great man,
  Who in his time had made heroic bustle.
Who in a row like Tom could lead the van,
  Booze in the ken, or at the spellken hustle?
Who queer a flat? Who [spite of Bow-street's ban]
  On the high toby-spice so flash the muzzle?
Who on a lark, with black-eyed Sal [his blowing]
So prime, so swell, so nutty, and so knowing?

That is first-rate. It is not a bit like Crabbe, but it is rather suggestive of Burns.

The last four cantos are, unless I am greatly mistaken, the most substantial of the poem. To satirize humanity in general requires either a more genial talent than Byron's, such as that of Rabelais, or else a more profoundly tortured one, such as Swift's. But in the latter part of *Don Juan* Byron is concerned with an English scene, in which there was for him nothing romantic left; he is concerned with a restricted field that he had known well, and for the satirizing of which an acute animosity sharpened his powers of observation. His understanding may remain superficial, but it is precise. Quite possibly he undertook something that he would have been unable to carry to a successful conclusion; possibly there was needed, to complete the story of that monstrous house-party, some high spirits, some capacity for laughter, with which Byron was not endowed. He might have found it impossible to deal with that remarkable personage Aurora Raby, the most serious character of his invention, within the frame of his satire. Having invented a character too serious, in a way too real for the world he knew, he might have been compelled to reduce her to the size of one of his ordinary romantic heroines. But Lord Henry and Lady Adeline Amundeville are persons exactly on the level of Byron's capacity for understanding and they have a reality for which their author has perhaps not received due credit.

What puts the last cantos of *Don Juan* at the head of

Byron's works is, I think, that the subject matter gave him at
last an adequate object for a genuine emotion. The emotion is
hatred of hypocrisy; and if it was reinforced by more personal
and petty feelings, the feelings of the man who as a boy had
know the humiliation of shabby lodgings with an eccentric
mother, who at fifteen had been clumsy and unattractive and
unable to dance with Mary Chaworth, who remained oddly
alien among the society that he knew so well — this mixture
of the origin of his attitude towards English society only gives
it greater intensity. And the hypocrisy of the world that he
satirized was at the opposite extreme from his own. Hypocrite,
indeed, except in the original sense of the word, is hardly the
term for Byron. He was an actor who devoted immense trouble
to *becoming* a role that he adopted; his superficiality was
something that he created for himself. It is difficult, in considering Byron's poetry, not to be drawn into an analysis of the
man: but much more attention has already been devoted to
the man than to the poetry, and I prefer, within the limits of
such an essay as this, to keep the latter in the foreground. My
point is that Byron's satire upon English society, in the latter
part of *Don Juan,* is something for which I can find no parallel in English literature. He was right in making the hero of
his house-party a Spaniard, for what Byron understands and
dislikes about English society is very much what an intelligent
foreigner in the same position would understand and dislike.

One cannot leave *Don Juan* without calling attention to another part of it which emphasizes the difference between this
poem and any other satire in English: the Dedicatory Verses.
The Dedication to Southey seems to me one of the most ex-
hilarating pieces of abuse in the language:

> Bob Southey! You're a poet — Poet Laureate,
> And representative of all the race;
> Although 'tis true that you turn'd out a Tory at

Last, yours has lately been a common case;
And now, my Epic Renegade! what are ye at? . . .

kept up without remission to the end of seventeen stanzas.
This is not the satire of Dryden, still less of Pope; it is perhaps
more like Hall or Marston, but they are bunglers in comparison. This is not indeed English satire at all; it is really a *flyting*,
and closer in feeling and intention to the satire of Dunbar:

Lene larbar, loungeour, baith lowsy in lisk and lonye;
  Fy! skolderit skyn, thow art both skyre and skrumple;
For he that rostit Lawrance had thy grunye,
  And he that hid Sanct Johnis ene with ane womple,
  And he that dang Sanct Augustine with ane rumple,
Thy fowll front had, and he that Bartilmo flaid;
  The gallowis gaipis eftit thy graceles gruntill,
As thow wald for ane haggeis, hungry gled.

To some this parallel may seem questionable, but to me it
has brought a keener enjoyment, and I think a juster appreciation of Byron than I had before. I do not pretend that Byron
is Villon [nor, for other reasons, does Dunbar or Burns equal
the French poet], but I have come to find in him certain qualities, besides his abundance, that are too uncommon in English
poetry, as well as the absence of some vices that are too common. And his own vices seem to have twin virtues that closely
resemble them. With his charlatanism, he has also an unusual
frankness; with his pose, he is also a *poète contumace* in a solemn country; with his humbug and self-deception he has also
a reckless raffish honesty; he is at once a vulgar patrician and a
dignified toss-pot; with all his bogus diabolism and his vanity
of pretending to disreputability, he is genuinely superstitious
and disreputable. I am speaking of the qualities and defects
visible in his work, and important in estimating his work: not
of the private life, with which I am not concerned.

Goethe as the Sage*

O N THE mantelpiece of my office room there has stood for some fifteen years and more, among portraits of literary friends, the facsimile of a drawing of Goethe in old age. The drawing is full of life — the work, one feels, not only of a gifted draughtsman but of an artist inspired by his subject.[1] Goethe stands with his hands clasped behind his back; the shoulders are bent and the posture stooping; but although the body may be weakened by infirmities, it is obviously still ruled by a vigorous mind. The eyes are large and luminous, the expression mischievous, both benign and mephistophelian: we are in the presence of a man who combines the vitality of youth with the wisdom of age. There was a moment, some years ago, when the picture was violently dislodged, together with its mantelpiece companions; but, as one would expect of Goethe, this portrait, serene, alert and critical, survived and ignored the incidents of that disturbed time.

This is the Goethe of the days of the conversations with Eckermann. It is Goethe the Sage: and as what I have to say here might almost be called a Discourse in Praise of Wisdom, this picture would form an appropriate frontispiece to my text. If one employs this word 'sage' with all the care and scruple it deserves, then one has in mind one of the rarest achievements of the human spirit. Poetic inspiration is none too common,

*An address delivered at Hamburg University on the occasion of the award of the Hanseatic Goethe Prize for 1954, in May 1955.
[1] The artist, I am informed, was Maclise, then a young man on a visit to Weimar.

but the true sage is rarer than the true poet; and when the two gifts, that of wisdom and that of poetic speech, are found in the same man, you have the great poet. It is poets of this kind who belong, not merely to their own people but to the world; it is only poets of this kind of whom one can think, not primarily as limited by their own language and nation, but as great Europeans.

At first, I had wondered whether there remained anything to say about Goethe which had not been better said already. When I came, however, to the point at which I had to choose a topic and outline my mode of treatment, I found myself bewildered by excess of possibilities — by the numberless aspects of Goethe, and the numberless contexts in which Goethe could be considered. In the end I was able to reduce my possible topics to two, but on further meditation, I discovered that the two were so closely connected in my mind as to form one problem which I must treat as a whole. The first problem was: what are the common characteristics of that select number of authors, of whom Goethe is one, who are Great Europeans? And the second was: what is the process by which one becomes reconciled to those great authors to whom in one's youth one was indifferent or antipathetic — not only why it takes place, but why it ought to take place; not only the process but the moral necessity of the process. In the course of this essay I shall be considering these two problems in turn; I hope that the reader may come to agree that the sub-title I have had in mind — a Discourse in Praise of Wisdom — is not wholly unjustified.

In the development of taste and critical judgment in literature — a part or an aspect of the total process of coming to maturity — there are, according to my own experience, three important phases. In adolescence, I was swept with enthusiasm for one author after another, to whichever responded to the instinctive needs at my stage of development. At this enthusiastic stage the critical faculty is hardly awake, for there is no comparison of one author with another, no full awareness of the basis of the relationship between oneself and the author in whose work one is engrossed. Not only is there but little awareness of rank: there is no true understanding of greatness. This is a standard inaccessible to the immature mind: at that stage, there are only the writers by whom one is carried away and those who leave one cold. As one's reading is extended, and one becomes acquainted with an increasing variety of the best writers of prose and verse, at the same time acquiring greater experience of the world and stronger powers of reflection, one's taste becomes more comprehensive, one's passions calmer and one's understanding more profound. At this stage, we begin to develop that critical ability, that power of self-criticism, without which the poet will do no more than repeat himself to the end of his life. Yet, though we may at this stage enjoy, understand and appreciate an indefinite variety of artistic and philosophic genius, there will remain obstinate cases of authors of high rank whom we continue to find antipathetic. So the third stage of development — of maturation so far as that process can be represented by the history of our reading and study — is that at which we begin to enquire into the reasons for our failure to enjoy what has been found delightful by men, perhaps many generations of men, as well qualified or better qualified for appreciation than ourselves. In trying to understand why one has failed to appreciate rightly a particular author, one is seeking for light, not only about that author, but about oneself. The study of authors whose work one fails to enjoy can thus be a very valuable exercise, though it is one to which common sense imposes limits: for nobody has the time to study the work of all the great authors in whose work he takes no pleasure. This process of examination is not an effort to enjoy what one has failed to enjoy: it is an effort to understand that work, and to understand oneself in relation to it. The enjoyment will come, if it does come, only as a consequence of the understanding.

There are obvious reasons, in my own case, for difficulty with Goethe. For anyone like myself, who combines a Catholic cast of mind, a Calvinistic heritage, and a Puritanical temperament, Goethe does indeed present some obstacles to be surmounted. But my experience is, that recognition of the obstacles — a recognition requiring self-examination still more than examination of the author — while it does not make these obstacles disappear, can render them less important. Differences which are unexamined never emerge from the obscurity of prejudice: the better we understand our failure to appreciate an author, the nearer we come to appreciation — since understanding and sympathy are closely related. Without ever having denied Goethe's genius, without remaining unmoved by that part of his poetry most easily assimilated by a foreigner, I had, I fear, been irritated by him. In time, I came to understand that my quarrel with Goethe was — apart from some personal traits which now seem to me of diminished importance — primarily a quarrel with his age; for I had, over the years, found myself alienated from the major English poets of the nineteenth century, both of the Romantic Movement and of the Victorian period. I still enjoy particular poems; but with the exception of Coleridge — and Coleridge rather as philosopher and theologian and social thinker than as poet — I have more and more lost touch with their authors. Tennyson, Browning, Arnold, Meredith: their philosophy of life came to seem to me flimsy, their religious foundations insecure. But I had had the experience of living through that poetry in my boyhood: that remained to me. I had been, for a time, very much moved by these poets: I felt, and feel, that I had learned from them what I was capable of learning and what they were capable of teaching me. With Goethe it is a different matter. As for the English poets to whom I have just alluded, I can imagine them as greater poets if they had held a different view of life. But with Goethe, on the other hand, it seems right and necessary that he should have believed what he did, and behaved as he did. And antipathy overcome, when it is antipathy to any figure so great as that of Goethe, is an important liberation from a limitation of one's own mind.

It may seem egotistic frivolity for me to spend so much time on the mutations of my own attitude towards Goethe. I do so for two reasons. First, because the few scattered references to Goethe in my earlier critical essays are mostly grudging and denigratory; so that if I am to justify my present attitude, and avert all suspicion of insincerity, I must give some account of the evolution of my own mind. Second, because I think that the situation can be generalized in such a way as to be of value. I have said that, so far as my own development is typical, one's self-education begins, in adolescence, by being enraptured, invaded, carried away by one writer after another [I am thinking of course of one's education in poetry]. Subsequently, one acquires a knowledge and enjoyment of a variety of work; one is influenced by minds of increasingly different character; one becomes more self-possessed; critical judgment develops; one is more conscious of what one is doing and of what is happening in one's explorations of the masterpieces of thought and imagination. After middle age, again, two further changes have come upon me. On the one hand, my literary predilections shrink: I wish to return more and more often to the work of fewer and fewer poets. And on the other hand, I find that there may be a few authors whom I have never really known, in the sense of intimacy and ease, with whom I must settle my account before I die.

I began, some years ago, to think that I must eventually make the effort to reconcile myself to Goethe: not primarily to repair an injustice done, for one has committed many such literary injustices without compunction, but because I should otherwise have neglected some opportunity of self-development, which it would be culpable to neglect. To entertain this feeling, is already an important admission: it is, surely, the admission that Goethe is one of the Great Europeans. The reader will now see, I hope, how it is that the two subjects — the problem of reconciliation and the definition of the Great European — become so closely entangled in my mind that I could not consider one without touching on the other.

It seems to me that the safest approach to this definition, is to take a few men whose right to this title is universally admitted, and consider what they have in common. I shall first, however, lay down the limits within which my selection is made. In the first place, I shall limit myself to poets, because poetry is the department in which I am best qualified to appreciate greatness. In the second place, I shall exclude all Latin and Greek poets. My reason for doing this is indicated by the title which Theodor Haecker gave to his essay on Virgil: *Vergil, Vater des Abendlandes*. The great poets of Greece and Rome, as well as the prophets of Israel, are ancestors of Europe, rather than Europeans in the mediaeval and modern sense. It is because of our common background, in the literatures of Greece, Rome and Israel, that we can speak of 'European literature' at all: and the survival of European literature, I may mention in passing, depends on our continued veneration of our ancestors. As such, they are set apart from my present investigation. There are also modern poets, whose influence has been very important in countries and languages not their own, who are unsuitable for my purpose. In Byron we have a poet who was the poet of an Age, and for that Age the poet of all Europe. In Edgar Poe, America produced a poet who, largely through his influence on three French poets of three successive generations, may be considered European; but the exact place and rank of these two men is still, and perhaps will always be, the subject of controversy; and I wish to limit myself to men whose qualifications are undisputed.

What, to begin with, are our criteria? Two, surely, are *Permanence* and *Universality*. The European poet must not only be one who holds a certain position in history: his work must continue to give delight and benefit to successive generations.

His influence is not a matter of historical record only; he will
continue to be of value to every Age, and every Age will
understand him differently and be compelled to assess his work
afresh. And he must be as important to readers of his own race
and language as to others: those of his own race and language
will feel that he is wholly one of them, and indeed their representative abroad. To readers of different nations and different
ages he may mean many different things: but his importance
no nation or generation will question. The history of what has
been written about the work of such a man will be a part of
the history of the European mind.

Obviously, one cannot draw up two lists, one of great poets
who are great Europeans, the other of those who fail to qualify
for this distinction. All we can do, I think, is to agree upon a
minimal number, consider what common characteristics they
have, and endeavour to approximate to a definition, by which
we then proceed to measure other poets. Of three I do not
think that there can be any doubt: they are Dante, Shakespeare and Goethe.

Here I must introduce a word of caution I doubt whether
we should call a poet a 'great European' unless he is also a
great poet; but I think that we have to admit that there are
great poets who are not Great Europeans. Indeed, I suspect
that when we call any Man of Letters a Great European, we
are exceeding the limits of purely literary judgment — we are
making an historical, a social, and an ethical valuation as well.
Compare Goethe with a somewhat younger English contemporary, William Wordsworth. Wordsworth was surely a great
poet, if the term has any meaning at all; at his best, his flight
was much higher than that of Byron, and as high as that of
Goethe. His influence was, moreover, decisive for English poetry at a certain moment: his name marks an epoch. Yet he
will never mean to Europeans of other nationality, what he
means to his own compatriots; nor can he mean to his own
compatriots what Goethe means to them. Similarly — but here

I speak with becoming diffidence — it seems to me possible to maintain that Hölderlin was at moments more inspired than Goethe: yet he also, can never be to the same degree a European figure. Into the possible account of the differences between the two kinds of poet, I do not propose to enter: I wish only, in this context, to remind you that if Dante, Shakespeare, and Goethe are incontestably European men, it is not merely because they are the greatest poets of their languages. They would not be great Europeans unless they were great poets, but their greatness as Europeans is something more complex, more comprehensive, than their superiority over other poets of their own language.

There is also the temptation, with Shakespeare and Goethe though not with Dante, to think of the two great mythical figures whom they created: Hamlet and Faust. Now, Hamlet and Faust have become European symbols. They have this in common with Odysseus and Don Quixote, that each is very much of his own country, and yet the fellow-countryman of all of us. Who could be more Greek than Odysseus, more Spanish than Don Quixote, more English than Hamlet, or more German than Faust? Yet they have all entered into the composition of all of us, they have all helped — as is the function of such figures — to explain European man to himself. So we may be tempted to classify Shakespeare and Goethe as European men, simply because they have each created a European myth-hero. Yet the play of *Hamlet* and the drama of *Faust* are only parts of the structures built by Shakespeare and Goethe: parts which would be very much diminished if each were the only work of its author. What gives Shakespeare and Goethe their status is not any one masterpiece, but the total work of a lifetime. And on the other hand Cervantes is, for those of us who are not learned in Spanish literature, the man of one book: however great the book, this is not enough to give Cervantes a place with Dante, Shakespeare and Goethe. *Don Quixote* is unquestionably among that select number of books that satisfy the test of 'European literature': that is to say, books without a knowledge of which — in the sense of having not only read, but assimilated — no man of European race can be truly educated. But we cannot say that it is necessary for the educated European to know Cervantes, in the sense in which we can say that the educated European must know Dante, Shakespeare and Goethe. As a man of one book, Cervantes is for us entirely in that book; he is, so to speak, Don Quixote understanding himself. What part of the work of Dante, Shakespeare or Goethe can we isolate and say that it gives us the essential Dante, Shakespeare or Goethe? It is not to belittle Cervantes simply to say that we cannot know him, as we can know these three other men. And I am not committing the error of separating the men from their writings, and idolizing the men, though that, especially in the case of Goethe, where we have so much documentation about the man, as well as the immense body of his own work, is dangerously easy to do. I am speaking of the men as they exist in their writings, in the three worlds which they have created to remain forever part of the European experience.

I would say first, as something immediately obvious, that in the work of these three men we find three common characteristics: *Abundance, Amplitude* and *Unity*. Abundance: they all wrote a good deal, and nothing that any of them wrote is negligible. By Amplitude, I mean that each had a very wide range of interest, sympathy and understanding. There is a variety of interests, there is universal curiosity and a more comprehensive capacity than that of most men. Other men have had versatile talent, other men have had restless curiosity: what characterizes the variety of interests and the curiosity of men like Dante, Shakespeare and Goethe is the fundamental Unity. This unity is hard to define, except by saying that what each of them gives us is Life itself, the World seen from a particular point of view of a particular European age and a particular man in that age.

I have no need to dilate upon the diversity of the interests and activities of Dante and Goethe. Shakespeare, it is true, confined himself, or was confined by circumstance, to the medium of the theatre; but when we consider the immense range of theme and character within that framework, the immense variety and development of his technique, his continuous attack on new problems, we must acknowledge at least that in this amplitude and abundance Shakespeare stands apart even from those few writers for the theatre who as dramatists and poets are his equals. As to Unity, I think that the unity of Dante's political, theological, moral and poetic aims is too evident to need demonstration. I would assert, from my own experience, that the unity of Shakespeare's work is such that you not only cannot understand the later plays unless you know the early plays: you cannot understand the early plays without knowing the late ones. It is not so easy to detect the unity in Goethe's work. For one thing, it is more bewilderingly miscellaneous than that of either of the other men; for another thing, I must confess that there is so much of this vast work that I do not know, or know only superficially, that I am far from being the advocate best qualified to plead the case. I will say only then, that I believe sincerely that the better I knew his work — every volume of the most voluminous edition — the more certain I should be of its unity. The test is this: does every part of a man's work help us to understand the rest?

I shall risk affirming this belief at the point at which it is most likely to be questioned. For most of my life I had taken it for granted that Goethe's scientific theories — his speculations about the plant-type, about mineralogy and about colour — were no more than the amiable eccentricities of a man of abounding curiosity who had strayed into regions for which he was not equipped. Even now, I have made no attempt to read his writings on these subjects. It was, first, that the unanimity of ridicule and the ease with which the learned in these matters appear to dismiss Goethe's views, impelled me to wonder whether Goethe may not have been right, or at least whether his critics might not be wrong. Then, only a few years ago, I came on a book in which Goethe's views were actually defended: *Man or Matter*, by Dr. Ernst Lehrs. It is true that Dr. Lehrs is a disciple of Rudolf Steiner, and I believe that Rudolf Steiner's science is considered very unorthodox; but that is not my affair. What Dr. Lehrs did for me was to suggest that Goethe's scientic views somehow fitted with his imaginative work, that the same insight was struggling for expression in both, and that it is not reasonable to dismiss as utter nonsense in the field of scientific enquiry, what we accept as inspired wisdom in poetry. I shall return to this point presently in another context: but, at the risk of exposing myself to ridicule, I will say that in consequence of what Dr. Lehrs has written about Goethe's science, I think I understand parts of *Faust*, such as the opening scene of Part II, better than before; and now I believe that Part II is a greater work than Part I — the contrary of what I had always been told by those more learned than myself.

It is at least certain that we must, in endeavouring to understand such men as the three I am talking about, try to enter into all of their interests. Literary criticism is an activity which must constantly define its own boundaries; also, it must constantly be going beyond them: the one invariable rule is, that when the literary critic exceeds his frontiers, he should do so in full consciousness of what he is doing. We cannot get very far with Dante, or Shakespeare, or Goethe, without touching upon theology, and philosophy, and ethics, and politics; and in the case of Goethe penetrating, in a clandestine way and without 'legitimation papers', into the forbidden territory of science.

My argument or pleading up to this point has been purely negative. I have merely affirmed that in the work of Dante, Shakespeare and Goethe you find Abundance, Amplitude and Unity. Abundance and Amplitude patently, and Unity if you take the trouble to look for it. Having postulated that Dante,

Shakespeare and Goethe were three great Europeans, it seems to follow that these characteristics must be found together in any other author before we can award him the same rank. It is possible, however, that an author might illustrate Abundance, Amplitude and Unity and yet fail to be a great European. I think there is a further positive character to be considered. But before approaching the final problem, there is another term to be discussed: *Universality*.

So far as we can judge from our three exemplars, the European writer is no less emphatically a man of his own country, race and language than any of those lesser authors whose appeal is exclusively, or with few exceptions, to their own compatriots. One may even say that Dante, Shakespeare and Goethe are not only very Italian, very English, very German, but are also representative each of the particular region in which he was born. It is obvious, of course, that the sense in which they are local is no limitation of their appeal, though there is much about each to which only his fellow-countrymen can respond. They are local because of their concreteness: to be human is to belong to a particular region of the earth, and men of such genius are more conscious than other human beings. The European who belonged to no one country would be an abstract man — a blank face speaking every language with neither a native nor a foreign accent. And the poet is the least abstract of men, because he is the most bound by his own language: he cannot even afford to know another language equally well, because it is, for the poet, a lifetime's work to explore the resources of his own. The way in which he is attached to, dependent upon, and representative of his own people, is not, I should add, to be identified with patriotism [a conscious response to particular circumstances] though it be the kind of attachment out of which the noblest patriotism may spring. It is a kind of attachment which may even be in sharp contrast with the patriotic sentiment of many of the poet's compatriots.

Next, the European poet is not necessarily a poet whose

work is easier to translate into another language than that of
poets whose work has significance only to their fellow-countrymen. His work is more translatable, only in this way: that
whereas in the translating of such a poet as Shakespeare, into
another language, just as much of the original significance is
lost, as is lost when we translate a lesser English poet, there is
also more saved — for more was there. What can be translated?
A story, a dramatic plot, the impressions of a living character
in action, an image, a proposition. What cannot be translated
is the incantation, the music of the words, and that part of the
meaning which is in the music. But here again, we have not
got to the bottom of the matter; we have only attempted to
indicate what makes a poet translatable, and not put our
finger on the reason why Dante, Shakespeare and Goethe can
be said to belong, as we cannot with equal confidence say of
any other poets, not only to their fellow-countrymen but to
all Europeans.

We can, I think, accept without much difficulty the apparent paradox that the European poet is at the same time no less,
but in a way rather more positively a man of his particular
race, country and local culture than is the poet appreciable
only by his compatriots. We can at one and the same time feel
that such a poet, to whatever nation he belongs, is our com-
patriot, and yet that he is a representative, one of the greatest
representatives, of his own people. Such a man can help his
fellow-countrymen to understand themselves, and help other
people to understand, and to accept them. But the question of
the way in which he is representative of his own age is somewhat more difficult. In what way is a man representative of his
own age, and yet of permanent importance — not because of
his 'representative' character, but in himself alone — for all
subsequent ages?

As we should expect from the foregoing, just as a man can
be a great poet, without being a 'European' poet, just as he can
be representative of his people, and have interest for other peo-

ples only in that capacity, so a man can be representative of his own time and be of importance to other times only as a help towards the understanding of his own time. But, as I tried to say earlier, we are interested in Dante, Shakespeare and Goethe not only in relation to their own country, language and race, but timelessly and directly: every educated European must ask the question, irrespective of his language, his citizenship, his heredity, and the age into which he was born, 'what have Dante and Shakespeare and Goethe to say directly to me — and how shall I answer them?' It is this direct confrontation that is of ultimate importance. Now, if we take the word literally, the really 'representative' man of a period, like the representative man of a nation, is a man who is neither too big nor too small. I do not mean that he is *l'homme moyen sensuel*. But a man who was insignificant could only represent an insignificant period — and no period in history is so negligible as that; whereas the very exceptionality of a truly great man must make us suspect that he is not altogether 'representative'. I think that if we could take our three poets as wholly representative of their ages, we should find that they were each limited by his age in a way in which they are not limited. In short, we take these men as representative, only to find them unrepresentative. For a man can be unrepresentative, not only by being behind or ahead of his age, but by being above it. Certainly, we must not assume that such men as these share all the ideas of their age. They share the problems, they share the language in which the problems are discussed — but they may repudiate all the current solutions. And even when they lead a social or a public life, they have also more solitude than the majority of men. Their representative character, if representative they be, must be something that we feel but cannot altogether formulate.

There is a great deal we do not know about Dante the man, there is very little we do know about Shakespeare. About the life of Goethe a great deal is known. I am, I confess, not one

of those who know very much. But the more I have learnt
about Goethe, from his own work and from commentaries on
it, the less I find it possible to identify him with his age. I
find him sometimes in complete opposition to his age, so complete perhaps as to have been greatly misunderstood. He seems
to me to have lived more fully and consciously on several levels
than most other men. The Privy Councillor, the lion of a
small court, the collector of prints, drawings, and intaglios,
was also the man who lay awake in anguish in Weimar, because an earthquake was taking place in Messina. After reading
Dr. Lehrs's book, to which I have alluded, and then re-reading
certain passages of *Faust*, it came to me that 'Nature' to
Wordsworth and to Goethe meant much the same thing, that
it meant something which they had experienced — and which
I had not experienced — and that they were both trying to
express something that, even for men so exceptionally endowed
with the gift of speech, was ultimately ineffable. Not so very
long ago I was sent a postcard reproduction of a portrait of
William Blake: it was a well-known drawing, with which I was
quite familiar. But I happened to set it for a moment on my
mantelpiece, beside the portrait of Goethe, and I thought I
noticed a similar expression in their eyes. Only, Blake looked
other-worldly: Goethe looked, at the moment when the
artist had caught him, equally at home in both worlds. Blake
also rejected some of the dominant opinions of his age. You
see that I cannot get away from the Farbenlehre and the
Ur-Pflanze. Is it simply a question of who was right. Goethe
or the scientists? Or is it possible that Goethe was wrong only
in thinking the scientists wrong, and the scientists wrong only
in thinking Goethe wrong? Is it not possible that Goethe,
without wholly knowing what he was doing, was to assert the
claims of a different type of consciousness from that which
was to dominate the nineteenth and twentieth centuries? If
so, then Goethe is about as unrepresentative of his Age as a
man of genius can be. And perhaps the time has come when

we can say that there is something in favour of being able to see the universe as Goethe saw it, rather than as the scientists have seen it: now that the 'living garment of God' has become somewhat tattered from the results of scientific manipulation.

Certainly Goethe was of his age. We can hardly ignore or treat as accidental, the fact that Dante, Shakespeare and Goethe should have come to stand, each for a period in modern European history, in so far as a poet can occupy that role; and we remember Goethe's own words about the man and the moment. But we must remember, for one thing, that we tend to think of an Age in terms of the man whom we take as representative of it, and forget that equally a part of the man's significance may be his battle with his Age. I have merely been trying to introduce some cautious reservations into our use of the term 'representative', dangerous when applied to such men. The man who is a 'representative' of his people may be the severest critic of his people and an outcast from it; the man who is 'representative' of his time may be in opposition to the most widely-accepted beliefs of his time.

So far I have been engaged, first in recognizing certain qualities in default of which we cannot admit a poet to this select company; and then in defining the sense in which 'representativeness', either of a place and a language, or of an age, may be considered characteristic. But we have yet to ask: what is the quality which survives translation? which transcends place and time, and is capable of arousing a direct response as of man to man, in readers of any place and any time? It must be also something which can be present in varying degrees — for obviously Dante, Shakespeare and Goethe are not the only 'European' poets. But it must be something capable of recognition by a great diversity of men: for the ultimate test of such a poet, as I have said at the beginning, is that no European who is quite ignorant of his work can be called educated — whether the poet's language is his own, or whether he has learnt that language by painful study, or whether he can only read a translation. For while complete ignorance of the language very narrowly limits one's appreciation of such a poet, it is no excuse whatever for complete ignorance of his work.

I am afraid that the word I am about to pronounce will strike many an ear as an anticlimax to this exordium, for it is simply the word *Wisdom*. There is no word, however, more impossible to define, and no word more difficult to understand. To understand what Wisdom is, is to be wise oneself: and I have only the degree of understanding of Wisdom, that can be attained by a man who knows that he is not wise, yet has reason to believe that he is wiser than he was twenty years ago. I say twenty years ago, because I am under the distressing necessity of quoting a sentence I printed in 1933. It is this:

'Of Goethe perhaps it is truer to say that he dabbled in both philosophy and poetry and made no great success of either; his true role was that of the man of the world and sage, a La Rochefoucauld, a La Bruyère, a Vauvenargues.'

I have never re-read the passage in which this sentence is buried: I have always found the re-reading of my own prose writings too painful a task. I discovered this quotation not so very long ago in Mr. Michael Hamburger's introduction to his edition and translation of the text of Hölderlin's poems: Mr. Hamburger is my authority for attributing this sentence to myself. He quoted it, I need hardly say, with disapproval. It is an interesting sentence: interesting because it enunciates so many errors in so few words together with one truth: that Goethe was a sage. But the error to which I particularly wish to call attention, is the identification of wisdom with worldly wisdom. It does not diminish my admiration for La Rochefoucauld, to say that the wisdom of a 'man of the world' is a very limited wisdom indeed; but now, at least, I can no longer confound the two wisdoms. There is worldly wisdom, and there is spiritual wisdom. Wisdom which is merely the former may turn out in the end to be folly, if it ignores, or aspires to judge, those things which are beyond its understanding; wisdom which is purely spiritual wisdom may be of no help in affairs of this world. So I think that generally we mean, when we speak of a man as 'wise' and where the context does not show that we mean one kind of wisdom rather than another, that such a man has wisdom of a greater range than other men. And this we can say of Goethe. It may be that there are areas of wisdom that he did not penetrate: but I am more interested in trying to understand the wisdom he possessed, than in defining its limitations. When a man is a good deal wiser than oneself, one does not complain that he is no wiser than he is.

There may be observed another error in the sentence which I quoted against myself, beyond the one I have just pointed out. It seems to suggest that wisdom is something expressible in wise sayings, aphorisms and maxims; and that the sum of such maxims and sayings, including those which a man has thought but never communicated, constitute his 'wisdom'. These may be tokens of wisdom, certainly; and to study the sayings of a sage can contribute towards the development of any wisdom of which the reader is capable. But wisdom is greater than any sum of wise sayings, and Wisdom herself is greater than the actualization of wisdom in any human soul.

Wisdom shall praise herself,
And shall glory in the midst of her people.
In the congregation of the Most High shall she open her mouth,
And triumph before His power.

Ecclus. xxiii.

The wisdom of a human being resides as much in silence as in speech; and, says Philotheus of Sinai, 'men with a silent mind are very rarely found.' [1] Wisdom is a native gift of intuition, ripened and given application by experience, for understanding the nature of things, certainly of living things, most

---

[1] It is relevant to mention an essay by Josef Pieper: *Ueber das Schweigen Goethes* (Kösel-Verlag, München).

certainly of the human heart. In some men it may appear fit-
fully and occasionally, or once in a lifetime, in the rapture of
a single experience beatific or awful: in a man like Goethe it
appears to have been constant, steady and serene. But the wise
man, in contrast to the merely worldly-wise on the one hand,
and the man of some intense vision of the heights or the
depths on the other, is one whose wisdom springs from spiritual sources, who has profited by experience to arrive at understanding, and who has acquired the charity that comes from
understanding human beings in all their variety of temperament, character and circumstance. Such men hold the most
diverse beliefs; they may even hold some tenets which we find
abhorrent; but it is part of our own pursuit of wisdom, to try
to understand them.

I believe then, that it is finally by virtue of the wisdom in-
forming his work, that a European enters this category of 'great
Europeans'; by virtue of his wisdom that he is the common
countryman of all of us. He is not necessarily easy to understand; as I have said, he may present as many difficulties of interpretation as any other. But the foreigner who has been reading Dante or Shakespeare or Goethe in translation, or who has
been handicapped by imperfect knowledge of the language in
reading the original, does not ask, as he may ask about many of
our great poets, 'what is it that Italians, or Englishmen, or Ger-
mans, find to admire in this author?' I am far from suggesting
that the wisdom of these poets is something distinct from the
poetry, and that what the foreigner enjoys is the former without the latter. The wisdom is an essential element in making
the poetry, and it is necessary to apprehend it as poetry in
order to profit by it as wisdom. The foreign reader, in absorb-
ing the wisdom, is being affected by the poetry as well. For it is
the wisdom of poetry, which would not be communicated at
all, if it were not experienced by the reader as poetry.

There arises, at this point, a question which cannot be left
unanswered: partly because I have raised it myself, in a some-

what different form, many years ago, and am no longer satisfied with my own account of it; and partly because it has recently been raised by a philosophical critic for whose opinions
I have great respect, Professor Erich Heller of Cardiff. I refer
to a recent book, *The Disinherited Mind*,[2] and particularly to
a chapter on Rilke and Nietzsche. Professor Heller criticizes,
severely but without asperity, certain pronouncements of my
own on *Thought and Belief in Poetry*, made many years ago.
Some of what I said then I would not now defend, and some
I should now be inclined to qualify or put differently: but with
regard to other of my assertions, I am not too downcast by
Professor Heller's censure, inasmuch as, by Dr. Heller's own
admission, I share these errors with Goethe himself. The question is as to the place of 'ideas' in poetry, and as to any 'philosophy' or system of beliefs held by the poet. Does the poet
hold an 'idea' in the same way that a philosopher holds it; and
when he expresses a particular 'philosophy' in his poetry,
should he be expected to believe this philosophy, or may he
legitimately treat it merely as suitable material for a poem?
And furthermore, is the reader's acceptance of the same philosophy a necessary condition for his full appreciation of the
poem?

Now in so far as anything I have written on the subject in
the past says or suggests that the poet need not believe a philosophical idea which he has chosen to embody in his verse, Professor Heller is, no doubt, quite right in contradicting me. For
such a suggestion would appear to be a justification of insincerity, and would annihilate all poetic values except those of
technical accomplishment. To suggest that Lucretius deliberately chose to exploit for poetic purposes a cosmology which
he thought to be false, or that Dante did not believe the philosophy drawn from Aristotle and the scholastics, which gave
him the material for several fine cantos in the *Purgatorio*,

[2] Published by Bowes & Bowes, Cambridge. A German edition has been published under the title of *Enterbter Geist* (Suhrkamp-Verlag).

would be to condemn the poems they wrote. But I think that
Professor Heller oversimplifies the problem by generalizing
from the particular case that he is arguing: he is in this essay
concerned to show that Rilke was not only deeply influenced
by Nietzsche in his youth, but that the view of life revealed in
Rilke's most mature poems is a kind of poetic equivalent of the
philosophy of Nietzsche. And I am quite prepared to admit
that in the case of the relation of Rilke to Nietzsche, Dr.
Heller makes out a very good case.

To explore the problem of poetic belief versus philosophic
belief, and the nature of the attitude [whether of belief or of
Annahme] of the poet towards a philosophic system, would
not only take us very far but would take us a long way from
my subject: what is however pertinent to our investigation is
the question of the belief called for from the reader of a poem.
Dr. Heller seems to me to imply that the reader himself must
accept the philosophy of the poet, if he is to appreciate the
poetry. It is, apparently, on this ground that Dr. Heller censures the judgment of a brilliant critic, Hans Egon Holthusen,
about Rilke. 'If the ideas [of Rilke] were all humbug,' says
Dr. Heller, 'or if, as Herr Holthusen says in his book about
Rilke,[3] they were all wrong, in the sense of contradicting that

---

[1] Rilke: by H. E. Holthusen. Bowes & Bowes, Cambridge, in an excellent
series (*Studies in Modern European Literature and Thought*) edited by Dr.
Heller himself. Dr. Heller does not quote, but the following paragraph from
Herr Holthusen's essay must be the origin of his comment:
'Once abstracted from the concrete liveliness of their metaphorical language,
from their aesthetic context, and regarded as philosophical doctrine, Rilke's
"ideas" are wrong. And this assertion is valid if we assume that there is an
objectively valid criterion of distinction between "right" and "wrong" ideas,
that there is a kind of intuitive logic governing groups of ideas in their agreement with the being of man, that, in brief, there exists an intellectual equilibrium enabling us to distinguish right ideas from wrong ones. The idea of "my
own death" is wrong because death cannot be conquered by monistic feeling;
for death must always remain wholly other than ourselves, a conquest through
that which is alien to us, an invasion of human reality by a reality that is more
than human. The idea of love that abdicates from Possession is wrong: so is
the idea of a glorification of the world: of creation without a creator, of im-
manence without transcendence: the metamorphosis of all transcendent reali-

"intuitive logic" which tells us what is a true and what is a false picture of man, then the poetry would have little chance of being what he believes it to be: great poetry.'

Dr. Heller goes so far as to say: 'there is no poetry left if we feel that the "ideas" are false to the point of being a distortion of the true image of man.' We are led, it seems to this strange conclusion: that Herr Holthusen is suffering from a delusion when he imagines that he enjoys the poetry of Rilke, because for him there can be no poetry left. And on the other hand, Dr. Heller himself is driven to accept an intolerable situation: that of a 'rift which has made it possible for most Christians not to feel, or at least not to feel also as true many "truths" which are incompatible with the truth of their faith'. Which not only *appear* incompatible, mind you, but which *are* incompatible! But if we feel the truth of 'incompatible truths', is not the feeling of truth wholly illusory? I find myself in agreement with Herr Holthusen: and indeed, if he is wrong and Dr. Heller is right, then I can only enjoy the poetry of Rilke under a misunderstanding.

What I am aiming at, by a devious route, is the establishment of a distinction between the *philosophy* of a poet and his *wisdom*. Unless it is possible to draw such a distinction, then I am condemned to remain blind to the merits of some of the greatest poets. But first I must venture a theory of the relation between acceptance of the philosophy and enjoyment of the poetry.

It is best, I think, to keep in mind not the philosophy of a poet — for that may vary with his development — but the philosophy of what can be called a philosophical poem. There are three obvious examples: the *Bhagavadgita, De rerum na-*

---

ties into an imminent all-and-one: the dissolving of God into inwardness: the dissolving of His person into the most intense feeling: the naming of the Divine in terms of feeling — indeed the whole vocabulary of the "unsayable" and "invisible". All these ideas are as wrong as the prophetic theses, of Nietzsche — the doctrine of the Eternal Recurrence, of the Superman — or "satanism" of Baudelaire.'

tura of Lucretius, and the *Divine Comedy* of Dante. And the third of these has peculiar advantages for our purposes in that it is based upon theological doctrine which belongs to the Western World and which is still believed by a great many people. These three poems represent three views of the world in as sharp contradiction of each other as possible. Ignoring the other differentiæ — the fact that the *Bhagavadgita* is the most remote from me in language and in culture, and that Dante is nearer to me in time than Lucretius, am I called upon to admit that as a Christian I can understand Dante's poem better than the others, though I ought to be able to understand it still better if I was a Roman Catholic? It seems to me that what I do, when I approach a great poem such as the *Holy Song* of the Indian epic, or the poem of Lucretius, is not only, in Coleridge's words, to suspend my disbelief, but to try to put myself in the position of a believer. But this is only one of the two movements of my critical activity: the second movement is to detach myself again and to regard the poem from outside the belief. If the poem is remote from my own beliefs, then the effort of which I am the more conscious is the effort of identification: if the poem is very close to my own beliefs, the effort of which I am more conscious is the effort of detachment. With the *Divine Comedy*, I find a kind of equilibrium: it is rather with the poetic parts of the Bible, the prophets and most of all the Gospels, that I find the effort of detachment — that is, the effort to appreciate 'the Bible as literature' — and in the translations of our Authorized Version and of Martin Luther the Bible is a part of both our literatures — there, is the effort of detachment most difficult. With the *Duinese Elegies*, I admit, I find myself at the opposite extreme: I could be content to enjoy the verbal beauty, to be moved by the music of the verse; and I have to force myself to try to enter into thought which is for me both difficult and uncongenial.

You will observe that in this systole and diastole, this movement to and fro, of approach and withdrawal, or identi-

fication and distinction, I have been careful to avoid the terms
form and *content*. The notion of appreciation of form without
content, or of content ignoring form, is an illusion: if we ignore the content of a poem, we fail to appreciate the form; if
we ignore the form, we have not grasped the content — for the
meaning of a poem exists in the words of the poem and in those
words only. Nor does what I have been talking about exhaust
the content. We have not, in what I have just been saying,
been concerned with the whole of the content: only with the
content as philosophical system, as 'ideas' which can be formu-
lated in other words, as a system of ideas to which there is always some possible alternative system for the reason to accept.
This philosophical system must be tenable: a poem arising out
of a religion which struck us as wholly vile, or out of a philosophy which seemed to us pure nonsense, simply would not
appear to be a poem at all. Otherwise, when two readers of
equal intelligence and sensibility approach in a great poem,
the one from the starting point of belief in the philosophy of
the author, and the other from the starting point of some different philosophy, they should tend towards a point, which
they may never quite reach, at which the two appreciations
correspond. Thus it is conceivable that Professor Heller and
Herr Holthusen might almost arrive at the point of sharing
their appreciation of Rilke.

I entered upon this analysis not for its own sake, but in
order to reach the conclusion that there is something more in
the greatest poetry than 'ideas' of a kind that we must either
accept or reject, expressed in a form which makes the whole a
work of art. Whether the 'philosophy' or the religious faith of
Dante or Shakespeare or Goethe is acceptable to us or not [and
indeed, with Shakespeare, the question of what his beliefs were
has never been finally settled] there is the Wisdom that we can
all accept. It is precisely for the sake of learning Wisdom that
we must take the trouble to frequent these men; it is because
they are wise men that we should try, if we find one of them

uncongenial, to overcome our aversion or indifference. Of revealed religions, and of philosophical systems, we must believe
that one is right and the others wrong. But wisdom is λόγος
ξυνός, the same for all men everywhere. If it were not so, what
profit could a European gain from the Upanishads, or the
Buddhist Nikayas? Only some intellectual exercise, the satisfaction of a curiosity, or an interesting sensation like that of tast-
ing some exotic oriental dish. I have said that Wisdom cannot
really be defined. What is the Wisdom of Goethe? As I have
suggested, Goethe's sayings, in prose or in verse, are merely
illustrations of his wisdom. The best evidence of the wisdom
of a great writer, is the testimony of those who can say, after a
long acquaintance with his works, 'I feel a wiser man because
of the time that I have spent with him.' For wisdom is communicated on a deeper level than that of logical propositions;
all language is inadequate, but probably the language of poetry
is the language most capable of communicating wisdom. The
wisdom of a great poet is concealed in his work; but in becoming aware of it we become ourselves more wise. That Goethe
was one of the wisest of men I have long admitted; that he was
a great lyric poet I have long since come to recognize; but that
the wisdom and the poetry are inseparable, in poets of the
highest rank, is something I have only come to perceive in becoming a little wiser myself. Thus I return to gaze at the fea-
tures of the Goethe on my mantelpiece. I have named him
and two others as the three poets who are incontestably great
Europeans. But I should not like to close without reminding
you that I think of these men as set apart, not in kind, but in
degree; that there have been others, even within living memory,
who though of lower rank are of the same company; and that
one measure of the survival of our European culture in the future, will be the ability of European peoples to continue to
produce such poets. And if the time comes when the term
'European literature' ceases to have any meaning, then the
literature of each of our nations and languages will wither
away and perish also.

Rudyard Kipling*

THERE are several reasons for our not knowing Kipling's poems so well as we think we do. When a man is primarily known as a writer of prose fiction we are inclined — and usually, I think, justly — to regard his verse as a by-product. I am, I confess, always doubtful whether any man can so divide himself as to be able to make the most of two such very different forms of expression as poetry and imaginative prose. If I make an exception in the case of Kipling, it is not because I think he succeeded in making the division successfully, but because I think that, for reasons which it will be partly the purpose of this essay to put forward, his verse and his prose are inseparable; that we must finally judge him, not separately as a poet and as a writer of prose fiction, but as the inventor of a mixed form. So a knowledge of his prose is essential to the understanding of his verse, and a knowledge of his verse is essential to the understanding of his prose. In so far therefore as I concern myself here with his verse by itself, it is only with the aim of restoring it to its place afterwards and seeing the total work more clearly. In most studies of Kipling that I have read, the writers seem to me to have treated the verse as secondary, and in so doing to have evaded the question — which is, nevertheless, a question that everyone asks — whether Kipling's verse really is poetry; and, if not, what it is.

* The introduction to A Choice of Kipling's Verse, published in 1941 in England by Faber & Faber in association with Methuen and Macmillan, and in America by Charles Scribner's Sons.

The starting point for Kipling's verse is the motive of the ballad-maker; and the modern ballad is a type of verse for the appreciation of which we are not provided with the proper critical tools. We are therefore inclined to dismiss the poems, by reference to poetic criteria which do not apply. It must therefore be our task to understand the type to which they belong, before attempting to value them: we must consider what Kipling was trying to do and what he was not trying to do. The task is the opposite of that with which we are ordinarily faced when attempting to defend contemporary verse. We expect to have to defend a poet against the charge of obscurity; we have to defend Kipling against the charge of excessive lucidity. We expect a poet to be reproached for lack of respect for the intelligence of the common man, or even for deliberately flouting the intelligence of the common man: we have to defend Kipling against the charge of being a 'journalist' appealing only to the commonest collective emotions. We expect a poet to be ridiculed because his verse does not appear to scan: we must defend Kipling against the charge of writing jingles. In short, people are exasperated by poetry which they do not understand, and contemptuous of poetry which they understand without effort; just as an audience is offended by a speaker who talks over its head, and by a speaker whom it suspects of talking down to it.

A further obstacle to the appreciation of many of Kipling's poems is their topicality, their occasional character, and their political associations. People are often inclined to disparage poetry which appears to have no bearing on the situation of to-day; but they are always inclined to ignore that which appears to bear only on the situation of yesterday. A political association may help to give poetry immediate attention: it is in spite of this association that the poetry will be read, if it is read, to-morrow. Poetry is condemned as 'political' when we disagree with the politics; and the majority of readers do not want either imperialism or socialism in verse. But the question is not what is ephemeral, but what is permanent: a poet who appears to be wholly out of touch with his age may still have something very important to say to it; and a poet who has treated problems of his time will not necessarily go out of date. Arnold's *Stanzas from the Grande Chartreuse* voice a moment of historic doubt, recorded by its most representative mind, a moment which has passed, which most of us have gone beyond in one direction or another; but it represents that moment forever.

We have therefore to try to find the permanent in Kipling's verse: but this is not simply to dissociate form from content. We must consider the content itself, the social and political attitude in its development; and, making an effort to detach ourselves from the assumptions of our own generation, enquire whether there is something more in Kipling than is expressed by Beerbohm's caricature of the Bank Holiday cornet virtuoso on a spree.

I

In my selection of Kipling's verse I have found no place for the earliest published: to be precise, the selection begins from page 81 of the Collected Edition. The earlier work is juvenilia, yet it is work which, having been published in its time and had a success in its time, is essential reading for a full understanding of Kipling's progress. Most of it is what it was intended to be, light reading in an English newspaper in India: it exhibits that same precocious knowingness about the more superficial level of human weakness that is both effective and irritating in some of his early stories of India. It is obviously the work of a clever young man who might go far in journalism, but neither in feeling nor in rhythm does most of it give any hint that the author would ever write a memorable poem. It is unnecessary to say that it is not poetry: what is surprising and interesting is that it does not pretend to be poetry, that it is not the work of a youth whom anyone would suspect of any aspiration to write poetry. That he is gifted, that he is worth watching, is obvious when you know how young he is: but the gift appears to be only for the ephemeral, and the writer appears to aim at nothing higher.

There were, however, literary influences in the background. We have among his verse a pastiche of *Atalanta in Calydon* made for his own immediate purposes; we remember also that McIntosh Jellaluddin [who is introduced as falling over a camel foal while reciting *The Song of the Bower*] on one occasion recited the whole of *Atalanta* beating time with a bedstead leg. There was Kipling's family connection with Pre-Raphaelite society; and Kipling's debt to Swinburne is considerable. It is never an imitation: the vocabulary is different, the content is different, the rhythms are different. There is one early monologue which is much more closely imitated from Browning than anything is imitated from Swinburne: but it is in two poems extremely unlike Browning's in style — *McAndrew's Hymn* and *The 'Mary Gloster'* — that Browning's influence is most visible. Why is the influence of Swinburne and Browning so different from what you would expect? It is due, I think, to a difference of motive: what they wrote they intended to be poetry; Kipling was not trying to write poetry at all.

There have been many writers of verse who have not aimed at writing poetry: with the exception of the few writers of humorous verse, they are mostly quickly forgotten. The difference is that they never did write poetry. Kipling does write poetry, but that is not what he is setting out to do. It is this peculiarity of intention that I have in mind in calling Kipling a 'ballad-writer' and it will take some time to make clear what I mean by that. For I am extending and also somewhat limiting the meaning of the word 'ballad'. It is true that there is an unbroken thread of meaning connecting the various kinds of verse to which the term 'ballad' has been applied. In the narrative Border Ballad, the intention is to tell a story in what, at that stage of literature, is the natural form for a story which is intended to arouse emotion. The poetry of it is incidental and to some extent unconscious; the form is the short rhymed stanza. The attention of the reader is concentrated on the story and the characters; and the ballad must have a meaning immediately apprehensible by its auditors. Repeated hearings may confirm the first impressions, may repeat the effect, but full understanding should be conveyed at one hearing. The metrical form must be of a simple kind which will not call attention to itself, but repetitions and refrains may contribute an incantatory effect. There should be no metrical complications corresponding to subtleties of feeling that cannot be immediately responded to. At another stage of culture — as in Anglo-Saxon and in the elaborate forms of Welsh — poetry develops a conscious virtuosity, requiring a virtuosity of appreciation on the part of the audience: the forms impose upon the bard restrictions and obstacles in overcoming which he exhibits his skill. It must be remembered that this sophistication is not only present in what we call 'modern' literature or in the later stages of development of classical literatures such as those of Latin, Greek, Sanskrit, Persian, or Chinese: it is a stage sometimes reached in the poetry of peoples of lower cultures. And on the other hand, ballad verse is not simply a stage in historical development: the ballad persists and develops in its own way, and corresponds to a permanent level of enjoyment of literature. There is always a potential public for the ballad: but the social conditions of modern society make it difficult for the good ballad to be written. It is perhaps more difficult now than it was at the time when *Barrack Room Ballads* were written: for Kipling had at least the inspiration and refreshment of the living music-hall.

In order to produce the contemporary ballad, it is of no particular help to hold advanced social views, or to believe that the literature of the future must be a 'popular' literature. The ballad must be written for its own sake and for its own pur-

poses. It would be a mistake, also, and a supercilious kind of
mistake, to suppose that the audience for balladry consists of
factory workers, mill hands, miners and agricultural labourers.
It does contain people from these categories, but the composition of this audience has, I suspect, no relation to any social
and economic stratification of society. The audience for the
more highly developed, even for the more esoteric kinds of
poetry is recruited from every level: often the uneducated find
them easier to accept than do the half-educated. On the other
hand, the audience for the ballad includes many who are, according to the rules, highly educated; it includes many of the
powerful, the learned, the highly specialized, the inheritors of
prosperity. I do not mean to suggest that the two audiences
ought to be, or must be, two worlds: but that there will be one
audience capable only of what I may call ballad attention, and
a smaller audience capable of enjoying both the ballad and
the more difficult forms of poetry. Now it is to the ballad attention that Kipling addresses himself: but that does not mean
that all of his poems appeal only on that level.

What is unusual about Kipling's ballads is his singleness of
intention in attempting to convey no more to the simple
minded than can be taken in on one reading or hearing. They
are best when read aloud, and the ear requires no training to
follow them easily. With this simplicity of purpose goes a
consummate gift of word, phrase, and rhythm. There is no
poet who is less open to the charge of repeating himself. In the
ballad, the stanza must not be too long and the rhyme scheme
must not be too complicated;[1] the stanza must be immediately apprehensible as a whole; a refrain can help to insist upon
the identity within which a limited range of variation is possible. The variety of form which Kipling manages to devise for
his ballads is remarkable; each is distinct, and perfectly fitted
to the content and the mood which the poem has to convey.
Nor is the versification too regular: there is the monotonous

---

[1] Though Kipling could manage even so difficult a form as the sestina.

beat only when the monotonous is what is required; and the irregularities of scansion have a wide scope. One of the most interesting exercises in the combination of heavy beat and variation of pace is found in *Danny Deever*, a poem which is technically [as well as in content] remarkable. The regular recurrence of the same end-words, which gain immensely by imperfect rhyme [*parade* and *said*] gives the feeling of marching feet and the movement of men in disciplined formation — in a unity of movement which enhances the horror of the occasion and the sickness which seizes the men as individuals; and the slightly quickened pace of the final lines marks the change in movement and in music. There is no single word or phrase which calls too much attention to itself, or which is not there for the sake of the total effect; so that when the climax comes:

'What's that that whimpers over'ead?' said Files-on-Parade,
'It's Danny's soul that's passin' now,' the Colour Sergeant said.

[the word *whimper* being exactly right] the atmosphere has been prepared for a complete suspension of disbelief.

It would be misleading to imply that all of Kipling's poems, or at least all that matter, are 'ballads': there is a great variety of kinds. I mean only that the approach to the understanding of what he was trying to do, in all his varied verse, is through the ballad motive. The best introduction, for my present purpose, is to call attention to a dozen or so particular poems representing his different types. For the reader to whom the ballad approach to poetry is the most natural, there is no need to show that Kipling's verse reaches from time to time the intensity of 'poetry': for such readers it is more useful to discuss the content, the view of life, and to overcome the prejudices which they may entertain against any verse which has a different subject matter or a different point of view from that which they happen to accept: to detach it, furthermore, from irrelevant association with subsequent events and attitudes. That I shall

attempt in the next section. In choosing the examples which
follow here, I have in mind rather the reader who, if he believes that Kipling wrote 'political jingles', stresses the word
jingles rather than the word *political*.

The first impression we may take from inspection of a number of the poems chosen to show the variety, is that this variety
is suspiciously great. We may, that is, fail to see in it more
than the virtuosity of a writer who could turn his hand to any
form and matter at will: we may fail to discern any unity. We
may be brought to admit that one poem after another does, in
one way or another have its 'poetic' moment, and yet believe
that the moments are only accidental or illusory. It would be a
mistake to assume that a few poems can be chosen which are
'poetry', and that the rest, by implication, need not be read. A
selection made in this way would be arbitrary, because there is
no handful of poems which can be so isolated from the rest; it
would be misleading because the significance of the 'poems'
would be lost except with the background of the 'verse', just as
the significance of the verse is missed except in the context of
the prose. No part of Kipling's work, and no period of his
work, is wholly appreciable without taking into account the
others: and in the end, this work, which studied piecemeal appears to have no unity beyond the haphazard of external circumstances, comes to show a unity of a very complicated kind.

If, therefore, I call particular attention to *Danny Deever* as
a barrack-room ballad which somehow attains the intensity of
poetry, it is not with the purpose of isolating it from the other
ballads of the same type, but with the reminder that with
Kipling you cannot draw a line beyond which some of the
verse becomes 'poetry'; and that the poetry, when it comes,
owes the gravity of its impact to being something over and
above the bargain, something more than the writer undertook
to give you; and that the matter is never simply a pretext, an
occasion for poetry. There are other poems in which the element of poetry is more difficult to put one's finger on, than in

Danny Deever. Two poems which belong together are *McAndrew's Hymn* and *The 'Mary Gloster'.* They are dramatic monologues, obviously, as I have said, owing something to Browning's invention, though metrically and intrinsically ballads. The popular verdict has chosen the first as the more memorable: I think that the popular verdict is right, but just what it is that raises *McAndrew's Hymn* above *The 'Mary Gloster'* is not easy to say. The rapacious old ship owner of the latter is not easily dismissed, and the presence of the silent son gives a dramatic quality absent from McAndrew's soliloquy. One poem is no less successful than the other. If the McAndrew poem is the more memorable, it is not because Kipling is more inspired by the contemplation of the success of failure than by that of the failure of success, but because there is greater poetry in the subject matter. It is McAndrew who creates the poetry of Steam, and Kipling who creates the poetry of McAndrew.

We sometimes speak as if the writer who is most consciously and painstakingly the 'craftsman' were the most remote from the interests of the ordinary reader, and as if the popular writer were the artless writer. But no writer has ever cared more for the craft of words than Kipling: a passion which gives him a prodigious respect for the artist of any art, and the craftsman of any craft,[1] and which is perhaps involved in his respect for Free Masonry. The problems of the literary artist constantly recur in his stories:[2] in *Wireless*, for instance, where the poor consumptive chemist's assistant is for a night identified with Keats at the moment of writing *The Eve of St. Agnes*; in *The Finest Story in the World*, where Kipling

[1] *The Bull That Thought* in the bull-ring 'raged enormously; he feigned defeat; he despaired in statuesque abandon, and thence flashed into fresh paroxysms of wrath — but always with the detachment of the true artist who knows that he is but the vessel of an emotion whence others, not he, must drink'.
[2] In *Proofs of Holy Writ* [a story published in the *Sussex* edition only], Shakespeare and Jonson discuss a problem of choice of words put before them by one of the translators of the King James Bible.

takes the trouble to provide a very good poem, in rather free verse [the *Song of the Galley Slaves*] and a very bad poem in regular verse, to illustrate the difference between the poem which forces its way into the consciousness of the poet and the poem which the writer himself forces. The difference between the craft and the art of poetry is of course as difficult to determine as the difference between poetry and balladry. It will not help us to decide the place of Kipling in poetry: we can only say that Kipling's craftsmanship is more reliable than that of some greater poets, and that there is hardly any poem, even in the collected works, in which he fails to do what he has set out to do. The great poet's craft may sometimes fail him: but at his greatest moments he is doing what Kipling is usually doing on a lower plane — writing transparently, so that our attention is directed to the object and not to the medium. Such a result is not simply attained by absence of decoration — for even the absence of decoration may err in calling attention to itself — but by never using decoration for its own sake,[3] though, again, the apparently superfluous may be what is really important. Now one of the problems which arise concerning Kipling is related to that skill of craftsmanship which seems to enable him to pass from form to form, though always in an identifiable idiom, and from subject to subject, so that we are aware of no inner compulsion to write about this rather than that — a versatility which may make us supect him of being no more than a performer. We look, in a poet as well as in a novelist, for what Henry James called the Figure in the Carpet. With the greatest of modern poets this Figure is perfectly manifest [for we can be sure of the existence of the Figure without perfectly understanding it]: I mention Yeats at this point because of the contrast between his development, which is very apparent in the way he writes, and Kipling's development, which is only apparent in what he writes about. We ex-

---

[3] The great speech of Enobarbus in *Antony and Cleopatra* is highly decorated, but the decoration has a purpose beyond its own beauty.

pect to feel, with a great writer, that he *had* to write about the
subject he took, and in that way. With no writer of equal eminence to Kipling is this inner compulsion, this unity in variety,
more difficult to discern.

I pass from the earlier ballads to mention a second category
of Kipling's verse: those poems which arise out of, or comment upon topical events. Some of these, such as *The Truce of
the Bear*, in the form of an apologue, do not aim very high.[4]
But to be able to write good verse to occasion is a very rare
gift indeed: Kipling had the gift, and he took the obligation
to employ it very seriously. Of this type of poem I should put
Gehazi — a poem inspired by the Marconi scandals — very
high, as a passionate invective rising to real eloquence [and a
poem which illustrates, incidentally, the important influence
of Biblical imagery and the Authorized Version language upon
his writing]. The poems on Canada and Australia, and the
exequy on King Edward VII, are excellent in their kind,
though not very memorable individually. And the gift for occasional verse is allied to the gift for two other kinds of verse
in which Kipling excelled: the epigram and the hymn. Good
epigrams in English are very few; and the great hymn writer is
very rare. Both are extremely objective types of verse: they can
and should be charged with intense feeling, but it must be a
feeling that can be completely shared. They are possible to a
writer so impersonal as Kipling: and I should like the reader to
look attentively at the *Epitaphs of the War*. I call Kipling a
great hymn writer on the strength of *Recessional*. It is a poem
almost too well known to need to have the reader's attention
called to it, except to point out that it is one of the poems in
which something breaks through from a deeper level than that
of the mind of the conscious observer of political and social
affairs — something which has the true prophetic inspiration.
Kipling might have been one of the most notable of hymn

4 Though *The Truce of the Bear* should be cited among the poems which
evidence Kipling's political insight.

writers. The same gift of prophecy appears, on the political plane, in other poems, such as *The Storm Cone*, but nowhere with greater authority than in *Recessional*.

It is impossible, however, to fit all of Kipling's poems into one or another of several distinct classes. There is the poem *Gethsemane*, which I do not think I understand,[5] and which is the more mysterious because of the author's having chosen to place it so early in his collected edition, since it bears the sub-heading '1914–1918'. And there are the poems of the later period.

The verse of the later period shows an even greater diversity than the early poems. The word 'experimentation' may be applied, and honourably applied, to the work of many poets who develop and change in maturity. As a man grows older, he may turn to new subject-matter, or he may treat the same material in a different way; as we age we both live in a different world, and become different men in the same world. The changes may be expressed by a change of rhythm, of imagery, of form: the true experimenter is not impelled by restless curiosity, or by desire for novelty, or the wish to surprise and astonish, but by the compulsion to find, in every new poem as in his earliest, the right form for feelings over the development of which he has, as a poet, no control. But just as, with Kipling, the term 'development' does not seem quite right, so neither does the term 'experimentation'. There is great variety, and there are some very remarkable innovations indeed, as in *The Way Through the Woods* and in *The Harp Song of the Dane Women*:

> *What is a woman that you forsake her,*
> *And the hearth-fire and the home-acre,*
> *To go with the old gray Widow-maker?*

and in the very fine *Runes on Weland's Sword*. But there were equally original inventions earlier [*Danny Deever*]; and there

[5] Though the death of his son must be the cause of its intensity.

are too, among the later poems, some very fine ones cast in more conventional form, such as *Cold Iron*, *The Land*, *The Children's Song*.

I confess therefore that the critical tools which we are accustomed to use in analysing and criticizing poetry do not seem to work; I confess furthermore that introspection into my own processes affords no assistance — part of the fascination of this subject is in the exploration of a mind so different from one's own. I am accustomed to the search for form: but Kipling never seems to be searching for form, but only for a particular form for each poem. So we find in the poems an extraordinary variety, but no evident pattern — the connexion is to be established on some other level. Yet this is no display of empty virtuosity, and we can be sure that there is no ambition of either popular or esoteric success for its own sake. The writer is not only serious, he has a vocation. He is completely ambidexterous, that is to say completely able to express himself in verse or prose: but his necessity for often expressing the same thing in a story and in a poem is a much deeper necessity than that merely to exhibit skill. I know of no writer of such great gifts for whom poetry seems to have been more purely an instrument. Most of us are interested in the form for its own sake — not apart from the content, but because we aim at making something which shall first of all *be*, something which in consequence will have the capability of exciting, within a limited range, a considerable variety of responses from different readers. For Kipling the poem is something which is intended to *act* — and for the most part his poems are intended to elicit the same response from all readers, and only the response which they can make in common. For other poets — at least, for some other poets — the poem may begin to shape itself in fragments of musical rhythm, and its structure will first appear in terms of something analogous to musical form; and such poets find it expedient to occupy their conscious mind with the craftsman's problems, leaving the deeper meaning to emerge

from a lower level. It is a question then of what one chooses to
be conscious of, and of how much of the meaning, in a poem,
is conveyed direct to the intelligence and how much is conveyed indirectly by the musical impression upon the sensibility
— always remembering that the use of the word 'musical' and
of musical analogies, in discussing poetry, has its dangers if we
do not constantly check its limitations; for the music of verse
is inseparable from the meanings and associations of words. If
I say then, that this musical concern is secondary and infre-
quent with Kipling, I am not implying any inferiority of craftsmanship, but rather a different order of values from that which
we expect to determine the structure of poetry.

If we belong to the kind of critic who is accustomed to consider poems solely by the standards of the 'work of art' we may
tend to dismiss Kipling's verse by standards which are not
meant to apply. If, on the other hand, we are the biographical
critic, interested primarily in the work as a revelation of the
man, Kipling is the most elusive of subjects: no writer has been
more reticent about himself, or given fewer openings for curiosity, for personal adoration or dislike.

The purely hypothetical reader who came upon this essay
with no previous acquaintance with Kipling's verse, might perhaps imagine that I had been briefed in the cause of some
hopelessly second-rate writer, and that I was trying, as an exhibition of my ingenuity as an advocate, to secure some small
remission of the penalty of oblivion. One might expect that a
poet who appeared to communicate so little of his private ec-
stasies and despairs would be dull; one might expect that a
poet who had given so much of his time to the service of the
political imagination would be ephemeral; one might expect
that a poet so constantly occupied with the appearances of
things would be shallow. We know that he is not dull, because
we have all, at one time or another, by one poem or another,
been thrilled; we know that he is not ephemeral, because we
remember so much of what we have read. As for shallowness,

that is a charge which can only be brought by those who have continued to read him only with a boyish interest. At times Kipling is not merely possessed of penetration, but almost 'possessed' of a kind of second sight. It is a trifling curiosity in itself that he was reproved for having placed in defence of the Wall a Roman Legion which historians declared had never been near it, and which later discoveries proved to have indeed been stationed there: that is the sort of thing one comes to expect of Kipling. There are deeper and darker caverns into which he penetrated — whether through experience or through imagination does not matter: there are hints in *The End of the Passage*, and later in *The Woman in His Life* and *In the Same Boat*: oddly enough, these stories are foreshadowed by an early poem which I have not included, *La Nuit Blanche*, which introduces one image which reappears in *The End of the Passage*. Kipling knew something of the things which are underneath, and of the things which are beyond the frontier.[5]

I have not explained Kipling's verse or the permanent hold that it can have upon you. It will be enough if I can help to keep him out of the wrong pigeon-holes.[6] If the reader of this

[5] Compare the description of the agony in *In the Same Boat* [a story the end of which is truer to the experience than is the end of *The Brushwood Boy*]: 'Suppose you were a violin string — vibrating — and someone put his finger on you' with the image of the 'banjo string drawn tight' for the breaking wave in *The Finest Story in the World*. Compare also the story *A Matter of Fact* [of the submarine volcanic eruption which projects the sea-monster to the surface] with the opening passages of *Alice in Wonderland*: both depict external events which have exact nightmare correspondence to some spiritual terror. *A Matter of Fact* is a better story than *In the Same Boat*, for the psychological explanation in the latter comes as anti-climax to the experience.
[6] Dr. J. H. Oldham has drawn my attention to the relevance of the chapter on 'Art and Magic' in that very remarkable book, *The Principles of Art*, by Professor R. G. Collingwood. Collingwood takes Kipling as an example of 'the artist as magician', and defines a magical art as 'an art which is representative and therefore evocative of emotion, and evokes of set purpose some emotions rather than others in order to discharge them into the affairs of practical life'. Professor Collingwood's contribution here seems to me extremely valuable; but while Kipling is a very good example of what he calls 'the artist as magician', I do not feel that 'the artist as magician' is a complete description of Kipling as a writer of verse.

book denies that Kipling is a great writer of verse, I hope at
least that he will have found new reasons for his judgment, for
the ordinary charges brought against him are either untrue or
irrelevant. I have been using the term 'verse' with his own authority, for that is what he called it himself. There is poetry in
it; but when he writes verse that is not poetry it is not because
he has tried to write poetry and failed. He had another purpose, and one to which he adhered with integrity. It is expressed in the following poem [from A *Diversity of Creatures*]:

THE FABULISTS
1914–1918

When all the world would keep a matter hid,
   Since Truth is seldom friend to any crowd,
Men write in fable as old Æsop did,
   Jesting at that which none will name aloud.
And this they needs must do, or it will fall
Unless they please they are not heard at all.

When desperate Folly daily laboureth
   To work confusion upon all we have,
When diligent Sloth demandeth Freedom's death,
   And banded Fear commandeth Honour's grave
Even in that certain hour before the fall,
Unless men please they are not heard at all.

Needs must all please, yet some not all for need,
   Needs must all toil, yet some not all for gain,
But that men taking pleasure may take heed,
   Whom present toil shall snatch from later pain.
Thus some have toiled, but their reward was small
Since, though they pleased, they were not heard at all.

This was the lock that lay upon our lips,
   This was the yoke that we have undergone,

Denying us all pleasant fellowships
  As in our time and generation.
Our pleasures unpursued age past recall,
And for our pains — we are not heard at all.

What man hears aught except the groaning guns?
  What man heeds aught save what each instant brings?
When each man's life all imaged life outruns,
  What man shall pleasure in imaginings?
So it has fallen, as it was bound to fall,
We are not, nor we were not, heard it all.

II

I have expressed the view that the variety of Kipling's verse
and its mutations from one period to another, cannot be accounted for, and given a unified pattern, by tracing development as we might with most poets. His development cannot be
understood through his verse alone, because he was, as I said
at the beginning, an integral prose-and-verse writer; and to
understand changes we have to consider the prose and the
verse together. Kipling appears first to be a writer of different
phases and occupations, who in each phase is completely developed, who is never so committed to the pursuit of one verse
form as to be prevented from moving to another. He is so
different from other poets that the lazy critic is tempted merely
to assert that he is not a poet at all, and leave it at that. The
changes in his poetry, while they cannot be explained by any
usual scheme of poetic development, can to some extent be
explained by changes in his outward circumstances. I say 'to
some extent', because Kipling, apparently merely the reflection
of the world about him, is the most inscrutable of authors. An
immense gift for using words, an amazing curiosity and power
of observation with his mind and with all his senses, the mask
of the entertainer, and beyond that a queer gift of second
sight, of transmitting messages from elsewhere, a gift so discon-

certing when we are made aware of it that thenceforth we are
never sure when it is *not* present: all this makes Kipling a
writer impossible wholly to understand and quite impossible
to belittle.

Certainly an exceptional sensitiveness to environment is the
first characteristic of Kipling that we notice; so that on one
level, we may trace his course by external circumstances. What
life would have made of such a man, had his birth, growth,
maturity and age all taken place in one set of surroundings, is
beyond speculation: as life directed, the result was to give him
a peculiar detachment and remoteness from all environment,
a universal foreignness which is the reverse side of his strong
feeling for India, for the Empire, for England and for Sussex,
a remoteness as of an alarmingly intelligent visitor from another planet. He remains somehow alien and aloof from all
with which he identifies himself. The reader who can get a
little distance — but not deep enough — below the level of
Kipling's popularity as a teller of tales and reciter of ballads,
and who has a vague feeling of something further underneath,
is apt to give the wrong explanation of his own discomfort.
I have tried to disturb the belief that Kipling is a mere writer
of jingles: we must now consider whether these 'jingles' are,
in a denigratory sense, 'political.'

To have been born in India and to have spent the first remembered years there, is a circumstance of capital importance
for a child of such impressionability. To have spent the years
from seventeen to twenty-four earning his living there, is for a
very precocious and observant young man an important experience also. The result is, it seems to me, that there are two
strata in Kipling's appreciation of India, the stratum of the
child and that of the young man. It was the latter who observed the British in India and wrote the rather cocky and acid
tales of Delhi and Simla, but it was the former who loved the
country and its people. In his Indian tales it is on the whole
the Indian characters who have the greater reality, because

they are treated with the understanding of love. It is Purun Bhagat, it is the four great Indian characters in *Kim* who are real: the Lama, Mahbub Ali, Hurree Chunder Mookerjee, and the wealthy widow from the North. As for the Britons, those with whom he is most sympathetic are those who have suffered or fallen — McIntosh Jellaludin has learned more than Strickland.[7] Kipling is of India in a different way from any other Englishman who has written, and in a different way from that of any particular Indian, who has a race, a creed, a local habitation and, if a Hindu, a caste. He might almost be called the first citizen of India. And his relation to India determines that about him which is the most important thing about a man, his religious attitude. It is an attitude of comprehensive tolerance.[8] He is not an unbeliever — on the contrary, he can accept all faiths: that of the Moslem, that of the Hindu, that of the Buddhist, Parsee or Jain, even [through the historical imagination] that of Mithra: if his understanding of Christianity is less affectionate, that is due to his Anglo-Saxon background — and no doubt he saw enough in India of clergy such as Mr. Bennett in *Kim*.

To explain Kipling's feeling for the Empire, and his later feeling for Sussex, as merely the nostalgia of a man without a country, as the need for support felt by the man who does not belong, would be a mistake which would prevent us from understanding Kipling's peculiar contribution. To explain away his patriotic feeling in this way is only necessary for those who consider that such feeling is not a proper theme for verse. There are perhaps those who will admit to expression in poetry patriotism on the defensive: Shakespeare's *Henry V* is acceptable, in his otherwise embarrassing grandiloquence, because the French army was a good deal bigger than the English force, even though Henry's war could hardly be described as

[7] On the subject of Kipling's ethics, and the types of man which he holds up for respect, see a valuable essay by Mr. Bonamy Dobrée in *The Lamp and the Lute.*
[8] Not the tolerance of ignorance or indifference.

a defensive one. But if there is a prejudice against patriotic verse, there is a still stronger prejudice against imperial patriotism in verse. For too many people, an Empire has become something to apologize for, on the ground that it happened by accident, and with the addition that it is a temporary affair anyway and will eventually be absorbed into some universal world association: and patriotism itself is expected to be inarticulate. But we must accustom ourselves to recognizing that for Kipling the Empire was not merely an idea, a good idea or a bad one; it was something the reality of which he felt. And in his expression of his feeling he was certainly not aiming at flattery of national, racial or imperial vanity, or attempting to propagate a political programme: he was aiming to communicate the awareness of something in existence of which he felt that most people were very imperfectly aware. It was an awareness of grandeur, certainly, but it was much more an awareness of responsibility.

There is the question of whether 'political' poetry is admissible; there is the question of the way in which Kipling's political poetry is political; there is the question of what his politics were; and finally, there remains the question of what we are to say of that considerable part of his work which cannot, by any stretch of the term, be called political at all.

It is pertinent to call attention to one other great English writer who put politics into verse — Dryden. The question whether Kipling was a poet is not unrelated to the question whether Dryden was a poet. The author of *Absalom and Achitophel* was satirizing a lost cause in retrospect, and he was on the successful side; the author of *The Hind and the Panther* was arguing a case in ecclesiastical politics; and both of these purposes were very different from that which Kipling set himself. Both of Dryden's poems are more political in their appeal to the reason than any of Kipling's. But the two men had much in common. Both were masters of phrase, both employed rather simple rhythms with adroit variations; and by both the medium was employed to convey a simple forceful statement, rather than a musical pattern of emotional overtones. And [if it is possible to use these terms without confusion] they were both classical rather than romantic poets. They arrive at poetry through eloquence; for both, wisdom has the primacy over inspiration; and both are more concerned with the world about them than with their own joys and sorrows, and concerned with their own feelings in their likeness to those of other men rather than in their particularity. But I should not wish to press this likeness too far, or ignore the great differences: and if Kipling suffers in some respects by the comparison, it must be remembered that he has other qualities which do not enter into it at all.

Kipling certainly thought of verse as well as prose as a medium for a public purpose; if we are to pass judgment upon his purpose, we must try to set ourselves in the historical situations in which his various work was written; and whether our prejudice be favourable or antagonistic, we must not look at his observations of one historical situation from the point of view of a later period. Also, we must consider his work as a whole, and the earlier years in the light of the later, and not exaggerate the importance of particular pieces or phrases which we may not like. Even these may be misinterpreted. Mr. Edward Shanks, who has written the best book on Kipling that I have read [and whose chapter on 'The Prophet of Empire' resumes Kipling's political views admirably] says of the poem called *Loot* [a soldier ballad describing the ways of extorting hidden treasure from natives]: 'this is wholly detestable, and it makes the commentator on Kipling turn red when he endeavours to explain it.' This is to read an attitude into the poem which I had never suspected. I do not believe that in this poem he was commending the rapacity and greed of such irregularities, or condoning rapine. If we think this, we must also presume that *The Ladies* was written to glorify miscellaneous miscegenation on the part of professional soldiers quar-

tered in foreign lands. Kipling, at the period to which these
poems belong, undoubtedly felt that the professional ranker
and his officers too were unappreciated by their peaceful countrymen at home, and that in the treatment of the soldier and
the discharged soldier there was often less than social justice:
but his concern was to make the soldier known, not to idealize
him. He was exasperated by sentimentalism as well as by de-
preciation or neglect — and either attitude is liable to evoke
the other.

I have said that in Kipling as a poet there is no development,
but mutation; and that for the development we must look to
changes in the environment and in the man himself. The first
period is that of India; the second that of travel and of resi-
dence in America; the third is that of his settlement in Sussex.
These divisions are obvious: what is not so obvious is the development of his view of empire, a view which expands and
contracts at the same time. He had always been far from uncritical of the defects and wrongs of the British Empire, but
held a firm belief in what it should and might be. In his later
phase England and a particular corner of England became
the centre of his vision. He is more concerned with the problem of the soundness of the *core* of empire: this core is something older, more natural and more permanent. But at the
same time his vision takes a larger view, and he sees the
Roman Empire and the place of England in it. The vision is
almost that of an idea of empire laid up in heaven. And with
all his geographical and historical imagination, no one was
farther than he from interest in men in the mass, or the
manipulation of men in the mass: his symbol was always a
particular individual. The symbol had been, at one time, such
men as Mulvaney or Strickland: it became Parnesius and
Hobden. Technical mechanics do not lose their charm for
him; wireless and aviation succeed steam, and in one of his
most other-worldly stories — *They* — a considerable part is
played by an early, and not very reliable, model of a motor

car: but Parnesius and Hobden are more important than the machines. One is the defender of a civilization [of a civilization, not of civilization in the abstract] against barbarism; the other represents the essential contact of the civilization with the soil.

I have said that there is always something alien about Kipling, as of a visitor from another planet; and to some readers he may still seem alien in his identification of himself with Sussex. There is an element of *tour de force* in all his work, which makes some readers uncomfortable: we are always suspicious of people who are too clever. Kipling is apt to arouse some of the same distrust as another great man who was alien in a very different way, and on a more worldly level — though he too had his vision of empire and his flashes of profound insight. Even those who admire Disraeli most may find themselves more at ease with Gladstone, whether they like the man and his politics or not. But Disraeli's foreignness was a comparatively simple matter. And undoubtedly the difference of early environment to which Kipling's foreignness is due gave him an understanding of the English countryside different from the understanding of a man born and brought up in it, and provoked in him thoughts about it which the natives would do well to heed.

It may well be unfortunate for a man's reputation that he should have great success early in life, with one work or with one type of work: for then his early work is what he is remembered by, and people [critics, sometimes, most of all] do not bother to revise their opinions in accordance with his later work. With Kipling, furthermore, a prejudice against the content may combine with a lack of understanding of the form to produce an inconsistent condemnation. On the ground of content, he is called a Tory; and on the ground of style, he is called a journalist. Neither of these terms, to be sure, need be held in anything but honour: but the former has come to acquire popular odium by a vulgar identification with a nastier name: to many people a critical attitude towards 'democracy' has come to imply a friendly attitude towards fascism — which, from a truly Tory point of view, is merely the extreme degradation of democracy. Similarly the term 'journalist', when applied to anyone not on the staff of a newspaper, has come to connote truckling to the popular taste of the moment. Kipling was not even a Tory, in the sense of one giving unquestioning loyalty to a political party: he can be called a Tory in a sense in which only a handful of writers together with a number of mostly inarticulate, obscure and uninfluential people are ever Tories in one generation. And as for being a journalist [in the sense mentioned above] we must keep in mind that the causes he espoused were not popular causes when he voiced them; that he did not aim to idealize either border warfare or the professional soldier; that his reflections on the Boer War are more admonitory than laudatory. It may be proposed that, as he dwelt upon the glory of empire, in so doing he helped to conceal its more seamy side: the commercialism, exploitation and neglect. No attentive reader of Kipling can maintain, however, that he was unaware of the faults of British rule: it is simply that he believed the British Empire to be a good thing, that he wished to set before his readers an ideal of what it should be, but was acutely aware of the difficulty of even approximating to this ideal, and of the perpetual danger of falling away even from such standard as might be attained. I cannot find any justification for the charge that he held a doctrine of race superiority. He believed that the British have a greater aptitude for ruling than other people, and that they include a greater number of kindly, incorruptible and unselfseeking men capable of administration; and he knew that scepticism in this matter is less likely to lead to greater magnanimity than it is to lead to a relaxation of the sense of responsibility. But he cannot be accused of holding that any Briton, simply because of his British race, is necessarily in any way the superior or even the equal of an individual of another race. The types of men which he admires are unlimited by any prejudice; his maturest work on India, and his greatest book, is *Kim*.

The notion of Kipling as a popular entertainer is due to the fact that his works have been popular and that they entertain. However, it is permitted to express popular views of the moment in an unpopular style: it is not approved when a man holds unpopular views and expresses them in something very readable. I do not wish to argue longer over Kipling's early 'imperialism', because there is need to speak of the development of his views. It should be said at this point, before passing on, that Kipling is not a doctrinaire or a man with a programme. His opinions are not to be considered as the antithesis of those of H. G. Wells. Wells's imagination is one thing and his political opinions another: the latter changed but did not mature. But Kipling did not, even in the sense in which that activity can be ascribed to Wells, *think*: his aim, and his gift, is to make people see — for the first condition of right thought is right sensation: the first condition of understanding a foreign country is to smell it, as you smell India in *Kim*. If you have seen and felt truly, then if God has given you the power you may be able to think rightly.

The simplest summary of the change in Kipling, in his middle years, is 'the development of the imperial imagination into the historical imagination'. To this development his settling in Sussex must have contributed to no small degree: for he had the humility to subdue himself to his surroundings, and the freshness of vision of the stranger. My references here will be to stories rather than to poems: that is because the later unit is a poem and a story together — or a story and two poems — combining to make a form which no one has used in the same way and in which no one is ever likely to excel him. When I speak of 'historical imagination' I do not assume that there is only one kind. Two different kinds are exemplified by Victor Hugo and Stendhal in their accounts of the battle of Water-

loo. For the first it is the charge of the Old Guard, and the
sunken road of Ohain; for the latter it is Fabrice's sudden
awareness that the little pattering noise around him is caused
by bullets. The historian of one kind is he who gives life to
abstractions: the historian of another kind may imply a whole
civilization in the behaviour of a single individual. H. G. Wells
can give an epic grandeur to the accumulation of an American
fortune. Kipling's imagination dwells on the particular experience of the particular man, just as his India was realized in
particular men. In *The Finest Story in the World* there appears the same passion for the exact detail that is given scope
in his studies of machinery. The Greek galley is described
from the point of view of the galley slave. The ship was 'the
kind rowed with oars, and the sea spurts through the oar-holes,
and the men row sitting up to their knees in water. Then
there's a bench running down between the two lines of oars,
and an overseer with a whip walks up and down the bench
to make the men work. . . . There's a rope running overhead,
looped to the upper deck, for the overseer to catch hold of
when the ship rolls. When the overseer misses the rope once
and falls among the rowers, remember the hero laughs at him
and gets licked for it. He's chained to his oar, of course — the
hero . . . with an iron band round his waist fixed to the bench
he sits on, and a sort of handcuff on his left wrist chaining him
to the oar. He's on the lower deck where the worst men are
sent, and the only light comes from the hatchways and
through the oarholes. Can't you imagine the sunlight just
squeezing through between the handle and the hole and wob-
bling about as the ship moves?'

The historical imagination may give us an awful awareness
of the extent of time, or it may give us a dizzy sense of the
nearness of the past. It may do both. Kipling, especially in
Puck of Pook's Hill and *Rewards and Fairies*, aims I think to
give at once a sense of the antiquity of England, of the number
of generations and peoples who have laboured the soil and in

turn been buried beneath it, and of the contemporaneity of the past. Having previously exhibited an imaginative grasp of space, and England in it, he now proceeds to a similar achievement in time. The tales of English history need to be considered in relation to the later stories of contemporary Sussex, such as *An Habitation Enforced, My Son's Wife,* and *The Wish House,* together with *They* in one aspect of this curious story. Kipling's awareness and love of Sussex is a very different affair from the feeling of any other 'regional' writer of comparable fame, such as Thomas Hardy. It is not merely that he was highly conscious of what ought to be preserved, where Hardy is the chronicler of decay; or that he wrote of the Sussex which he found, where Hardy wrote of the Dorset that was already passing in his boyhood. It is, first, that the conscience of the 'fabulist' and the consciousness of the political and historical imagination are always at work. To think of Kipling as a writer who could turn his hand to any subject, who wrote of Sussex because he had exhausted his foreign and imperial material, or had satiated the public demand for it, or merely because he was a chameleon who took his colour from environment, would be to miss the mark completely: this later work is the continuation and consummation of the earlier. The second peculiarity of Kipling's Sussex stories I have already touched upon, the fact that he brings to his work the freshness of a mind and a sensibility developed and matured in quite different environment: he is discovering and reclaiming a lost inheritance. The American Chapins, in *A Habitation Enforced,* have a passive role: the protagonist in the story is the house and the life that it implies, with the profound implication that the countryman belongs to the land, the landlord to his tenants, the farmer to his labourers and not the other way about. This is a deliberate reversal of the values of industrial society. The Chapins, indeed [except for the point of their coming from a country of industrialized mentality] are a kind of mask for Kipling himself. He is also behind the hero of a less successful story in the same group, *My Son's Wife*. [I call this story less successful because he seems to point his moral a little too directly, and because the contrast between the garrulous society of London — or suburban — intellectuals and the speechless solicitor's daughter who likes hunting is hammered with too great insistence. The contrast between a bucolic world in which the second-rate still participates in the good, and an intellectual world in which the second-rate is usually sham and always tiresome, is not quite fair. The animus which he displays against the latter suggests that he did not have his eye on the object: for we can judge only what we understand, and must constantly dine with the opposition.] What is most important in these stories, and in *The Wish House*, and in *Friendly Brook*, is Kipling's vision of the people of the soil. It is not a Christian vision, but it is at least a pagan vision — a contradiction of the materialistic view: it is the insight into a harmony with nature which must be re-established if the truly Christian imagination is to be recovered by Christians. What he is trying to convey is, again, not a programme of agrarian reform, but a point of view unintelligible to the industrialized mind. Hence the artistic value of the *obviously* incredible element of the supernatural in *The Wish House*, which is exquisitely combined with the sordid realism of the women of the dialogue, the country bus, the suburban villa, and the cancer of the poor.

This hard and obscure story, *The Wish House*, has to be studied in relation to the two hard and obscure poems [not here included] which precede and follow it, and which would be still more hard and obscure without the story. We have gone a long way, at this stage, from the mere story-teller: a long way even from the man who felt it his duty to try to make certain things plain to his countrymen who would not see them. He could hardly have thought that many people in his own time or at any time would take the trouble to understand the parables, or even to appreciate the precision of observation, the calculating pains in selecting and combining elements, the choice of word and phrase, that were spent in their elaboration. He must have known that his own fame would get in the way, his reputation as a story-teller, his reputation as a 'Tory journalist', his reputation as a facile writer who could dash off something about what happened yesterday, his reputation even as a writer of books for children which children liked to read and hear read.

I return to the beginning. The late poems like the late stories with which they belong, are sometimes more obscure, because they are trying to express something more difficult than the early poems. They are the poems of a wiser and more mature writer. But they do not show any movement from 'verse' to 'poetry': they are just as instrumental as the early work, but now instruments for a matured purpose. Kipling could handle, from the beginning to the end, a considerable variety of metres and stanza forms with perfect competence; he introduces remarkable variations of his own; but as a poet he does not revolutionize. He is not one of those writers of whom one can say, that the *form* of English poetry will always be different from what it would have been if they had not written. What fundamentally differentiates his 'verse' from 'poetry' is the subordination of musical interest. Many of the poems give, indeed, judged by the ear, an impression of the mood, some are distinctly onomatopoeic: there is a harmonics of poetry which not merely is beyond their range but would interfere with the intention. It is possible to argue exceptions; but I am speaking of his work as a whole, and I maintain that without understanding the purpose which animates his verse as a whole, one is not prepared to understand the exceptions.

I make no apology for having used the terms 'verse' and 'poetry' in a loose way: so that while I speak of Kipling's work as verse and not as poetry, I am still able to speak of individual compositions as poems, and also to maintain that there is 'poetry' in the 'verse'. Where terminology is loose, where we have not the vocabulary for distinctions which we feel, our only precision is found in being aware of the imperfection of our tools, and of the different senses in which we are using the same words. It should be clear that when I contrast 'verse' with 'poetry' I am not, *in this context*, implying a value judgment. I do not mean, here, by verse, the work of a man who would write poetry if he could: I mean by it something which does what 'poetry' could not do. The difference which would turn Kipling's verse into poetry, does not represent a failure or deficiency: he knew perfectly well what he was doing; and from his point of view more 'poetry' would interfere with his purpose. And I make the claim, that in speaking of Kipling we are entitled to say '*great* verse'. What other famous poets should be put into the category of great verse writers is a question which I do not here attempt to answer. That question is complicated by the fact that we should be dealing with matters as imprecise as the shape and size of a cloud or the beginning and end of a wave. But the writer whose work is *always* clearly verse, is not a great verse writer: if a writer is to be that, there must be some of his work of which we cannot say whether it is verse or poetry. And the poet who could not write 'verse' when verse was needed, would be without that sense of structure which is required to make a poem of any length readable. I would suggest also that we too easily assume that what is most valuable is also most rare, and vice versa. I can think of a number of poets who have written great poetry, only of a very few whom I should call great verse writers. And unless I am mistaken, Kipling's position in this class is not only high, but unique.

Yeats *

T HE generations of poetry in our age seem to cover a span of about twenty years. I do not mean that the best work of any poet is limited to twenty years: I mean that it is about that length of time before a new school or style of poetry appears. By the time, that is to say, that a man is fifty, he has behind him a kind of poetry written by men of seventy, and before him another kind written by men of thirty. That is my position at present, and if I live another twenty years I shall expect to see still another younger school of poetry. One's relation to Yeats, however, does not fit into this scheme. When I was a young man at the university, in America, just beginning to write verse, Yeats was already a considerable figure in the world of poetry, and his early period was well defined. I cannot remember that his poetry at that stage made any deep impression upon me. A very young man, who is himself stirred to write, is not primarily critical or even widely appreciative. He is looking for masters who will elicit his consciousness of what he wants to say himself, of the kind of poetry that is in him to write. The taste of an adolescent writer is intense, but narrow: it is determined by personal needs. The kind of poetry that I needed, to teach me the use of my own voice, did not exist in English at all; it was only to be found in French. For this reason the poetry of the young Yeats hardly existed for

* The first annual Yeats Lecture, delivered to the Friends of the Irish Academy at the Abbey Theatre, Dublin, in 1940. Subsequently published in *Purpose*.

me until after my enthusiasm had been won by the poetry of
the older Yeats; and by that time — I mean, from 1919 on —
my own course of evolution was already determined. Hence,
I find myself regarding him, from one point of view, as a contemporary and not a predecessor; and from another point of
view, I can share the feelings of younger men, who came to
know and admire him by that work from 1919 on, which was
produced while they were adolescent.

Certainly, for the younger poets of England and America,
I am sure that their admiration for Yeats's poetry has been
wholly good. His idiom was too different for there to be any
danger of imitation, his opinions too different to flatter and
confirm their prejudices. It was good for them to have the
spectacle of an unquestionably great living poet, whose style
they were not tempted to echo and whose ideas opposed those
in vogue among them. You will not see, in their writing, more
than passing evidences of the impression he made, but the
work, and the man himself as poet, have been of the greatest
significance to them for all that. This may seem to contradict
what I have been saying about the kind of poetry that a young
poet chooses to admire. But I am really talking about something different. Yeats would not have this influence had he
not become a great poet; but the influence of which I speak
is due to the figure of the poet himself, to the integrity of his
passion for his art and his craft which provided such an impulse for his extraordinary development. When he visited London he liked to meet and talk to younger poets. People have
sometimes spoken of him as arrogant and overbearing. I never
found him so; in his conversations with a younger writer I
always felt that he offered terms of equality, as to a fellow
worker, a practitioner of the same mistery. It was, I think,
that, unlike many writers, he cared more for poetry than for
his own reputation as a poet or his picture of himself as a poet.
Art was greater than the artist: and this feeling he communi-

cated to others; which was why younger men were never ill at ease in his company.

This, I am sure, was part of the secret of his ability, after becoming unquestionably the master, to remain always a contemporary. Another is the continual development of which I have spoken. This has become almost a commonplace of criticism of his work. But while it is often mentioned, its causes and its nature have not been often analysed. One reason, of course, was simply concentration and hard work. And behind that is character: I mean the special character of the artist as artist — that is, the force of character by which Dickens, having exhausted his first inspiration, was able in middle age to proceed to such a masterpiece, so different from his early work, as *Bleak House*. It is difficult and unwise to generalize about ways of composition — so many men, so many ways — but it is my experience that towards middle age a man has three choices: to stop writing altogether, to repeat himself with perhaps an increasing skill of virtuosity, or by taking thought to adapt himself to middle age and find a different way of working. Why are the later long poems of Browning and Swinburne mostly unread? It is, I think, because one gets the essential Browning or Swinburne entire in earlier poems; and in the later, one is reminded of the early freshness which they lack without being made aware of any compensating new qualities. When a man is engaged in work of abstract thought — if there is such a thing as wholly abstract thought outside of the mathematical sciences — his mind can mature, while his emotions either remain the same or only atrophy, and it will not matter. But maturing as a poet means maturing as the whole man, experiencing new emotions appropriate to one's age, and with the same intensity as the emotions of youth.

One form, a perfect form, of development is that of Shakespeare, one of the few poets whose work of maturity is just as exciting as that of their early manhood. There is, I think, a difference between the development of Shakespeare and Yeats,

which makes the latter case still more curious. With Shakespeare, one sees a slow, continuous development of mastery
of his craft of verse, and the poetry of middle age seems implicit in that of early maturity. After the first few verbal exercises you say of each piece of work: 'This is the perfect expression of the sensibility of that stage of his development.' That
a poet should develop at all, that he should find something
new to say, and say it equally well, in middle age, has always
something miraculous about it. But in the case of Yeats the
kind of development seems to me different. I do not want to
give the impression that I regard his earlier and his later work
almost as if they had been written by two different men. Returning to his earlier poems after making a close acquaintance
with the later, one sees, to begin with, that in technique there
was a slow and continuous development of what is always the
same medium and idiom. And when I say development, I do
not mean that many of the early poems, for what they are,
are not as beautifully written as they could be. There are
some, such as *Who Goes with Fergus?*, which are as perfect
of their kind as anything in the language. But the best, and
the best known of them, have this limitation: that they are as
satisfactory in isolation, as 'anthology pieces', as they are in the
context of his other poems of the same period.

I am obviously using the term 'anthology piece' in a rather
special sense. In any anthology, you find some poems which
give you complete satisfaction and delight in themselves, such
that you are hardly curious who wrote them, hardly want to
look further into the work of that poet. There are others, not
necessarily so perfect or complete, which make you irresistibly
curious to know more of that poet through his other work.
Naturally, this distinction applies only to short poems, those
in which a man has been able to put only a part of his mind,
if it is a mind of any size. With some such you feel at once
that the man who wrote them must have had a great deal more
to say, in different contexts, of equal interest. Now among all

the poems in Yeats's earlier volumes I find only in a line here or there, that sense of a unique personality which makes one sit up in excitement and eagerness to learn more about the author's mind and feelings. The intensity of Yeats's own emotional experience hardly appears. We have sufficient evidence of the intensity of experience of his youth, but it is from the retrospections in some of his later work that we have our evidence.

I have, in early essays, extolled what I called impersonality in art, and it may seem that, in giving as a reason for the superiority of Yeats's later work the greater expression of personality in it, I am contradicting myself. It may be that I expressed myself badly, or that I had only an adolescent grasp of that idea — as I can never bear to re-read my own prose writings, I am willing to leave the point unsettled — but I think now, at least, that the truth of the matter is as follows. There are two forms of impersonality: that which is natural to the mere skilful craftsman, and that which is more and more achieved by the maturing artist. The first is that of what I have called the 'anthology piece', of a lyric by Lovelace or Suckling, or of Campion, a finer poet than either. The second impersonality is that of the poet who, out of intense and personal experience, is able to express a general truth; retaining all the particularity of his experience, to make of it a general symbol. And the strange thing is that Yeats, having been a great craftsman in the first kind, became a great poet in the second. It is not that he became a different man, for, as I have hinted, one feels sure that the intense experience of youth had been lived through — and indeed, without this early experience he could never have attained anything of the wisdom which appears in his later writing. But he had to wait for a later maturity to find expression of early experience; and this makes him, I think, a unique and especially interesting poet.

Consider the early poem which is in every anthology, *When you are old and grey and full of sleep*, or *A Dream of Death* in the same volume of 1893. They are beautiful poems, but only craftsman's work, because one does not feel present in them the particularity which must provide the material for the general truth. By the time of the volume of 1904 there is a development visible in a very lovely poem, *The Folly of Being Comforted*, and in *Adam's Curse*; something is coming through, and in beginning to speak as a particular man he is beginning to speak for man. This is clearer still in the poem *Peace*, in the 1910 volume. But it is not fully evinced until the volume of 1914, in the violent and terrible epistle dedicatory of *Responsibilities*, with the great lines

> *Pardon that for a barren passion's sake,*
> *Although I have come close on forty-nine. . . .*

And the naming of his age in the poem is significant. More than half a lifetime to arrive at this freedom of speech. It is a triumph.

There was much also for Yeats to work out of himself, even in technique. To be a younger member of a group of poets, none of them certainly of anything like his stature, but further developed in their limited path, may arrest for a time a man's development of idiom. Then again, the weight of the pre-Raphaelite prestige must have been tremendous. The Yeats of the Celtic twilight — who seems to me to have been more the Yeats of the pre-Raphaelite twilight — uses Celtic folklore almost as William Morris uses Scandinavian folklore. His longer narrative poems bear the mark of Morris. Indeed, in the pre-Raphaelite phase, Yeats is by no means the least of the pre-Raphaelites. I may be mistaken, but the play, *The Shadowy Waters*, seems to me one of the most perfect expressions of the vague enchanted beauty of that school: yet it strikes me — this may be an impertinence on my part — as the western seas descried through the back window of a house in Kensington, an Irish myth for the Kelmscott Press; and when I try to visualize the speakers in the play, they have the great dim, dreamy eyes of the knights and ladies of Burne-Jones. I think the phase in which he treated Irish legend in the manner of Rossetti or Morris is a phase of confusion. He did not master this legend until he made it a vehicle for his own creation of character — not, really, until he began to write the *Plays for Dancers*. The point is, that in becoming more Irish, not in subject-matter but in expression, he became at the same time universal.

The points that I particularly wish to make about Yeats's development are two. The first, on which I have already touched, is that to have accomplished what Yeats did in the middle and later years is a great and permanent example — which poets-to-come should study with reverence — of what I have called Character of the Artist: a kind of moral, as well as intellectual, excellence. The second point, which follows naturally after what I have said in criticism of the lack of complete emotional expression in his early work, is that Yeats is pre-eminently the poet of middle age. By this I am far from meaning that he is a poet only for middle-aged readers: the attitude towards him of younger poets who write in English, the world over, is enough evidence to the contrary. Now, in theory, there is no reason why a poet's inspiration or material should fail, in middle age or at any time before senility. For a man who is capable of experience finds himself in a different world in every decade of his life; as he sees it with different eyes, the material of his art is continually renewed. But in fact, very few poets have shown this capacity of adaptation to the years. It requires, indeed, an exceptional honesty and courage to face the change. Most men either cling to the experiences of youth, so that their writing becomes an insincere mimicry of their earlier work, or they leave their passion behind, and write only from the head, with a hollow and wasted virtuosity. There is another and even worse temptation: that of becoming dignified, of becoming public figures with only a public existence —

coat-racks hung with decorations and distinctions, doing, saying, and even thinking and feeling only what they believe the
public expects of them. Yeats was not that kind of poet: and
it is, perhaps, a reason why young men should find his later
poetry more acceptable than older men easily can. For the
young can see him as a poet who in his work remained in the
best sense always young, who even in one sense became young
as he aged. But the old, unless they are stirred to something of
the honesty with oneself expressed in the poetry, will be
shocked by such a revelation of what a man really is and remains. They will refuse to believe that *they* are like that.

> *You think it horrible that lust and rage*
> *Should dance attendance upon my old age;*
> *They were not such a plague when I was young:*
> *What else have I to spur me into song?*

These lines are very impressive and not very pleasant, and the
sentiment has recently been criticized by an English critic
whom I generally respect. But I think he misread them. I do
not read them as a personal confession of a man who differed
from other men, but of a man who was essentially the same as
most other men; the only difference is in the greater clarity,
honesty and vigour. To what honest man, old enough, can
these sentiments be entirely alien? They can be subdued and
disciplined by religion, but who can say that they are dead?
Only those to whom the maxim of La Rochefoucauld applies:
'Quand les vices nous quittent, nous nous flattons de la créance
que c'est nous qui les quittons.' The tragedy of Yeats's epigram
is all in the last line.

Similarly, the play *Purgatory* is not very pleasant, either.
There are aspects of it which I do not like myself. I wish he
had not given it this title, because I cannot accept a purgatory
in which there is no hint, or at least no emphasis upon Purga-
tion. But, apart from the extraordinary theatrical skill with
which he has put so much action within the compass of a very

short scene of but little movement, the play gives a masterly exposition of the emotions of an old man. I think that the epigram I have just quoted seems to me just as much to be taken in a dramatic sense as the play *Purgatory*. The lyric poet — and Yeats was always lyric, even when dramatic — can speak for every man, or for men very different from himself; but to do this he must for the moment be able to identify himself with every man or other men; and it is only his imaginative power of becoming this that deceives some readers into thinking that he is speaking for and of himself alone — especially when they prefer not to be implicated.

I do not wish to emphasize this aspect only of Yeats's poetry of age. I would call attention to the beautiful poem in *The Winding Stair*, in memory of Eva Gore-Booth and Con Markiewicz, in which the picture at the beginning, of:

> Two girls in silk kimonos, both
> Beautiful, one a gazelle,

gets great intensity from the shock of the later line;

> When withered, old and skeleton gaunt,

and also to *Coole Park*, beginning

> I meditate upon a swallow's flight,
> Upon an aged woman and her house.

In such poems one feels that the most lively and desirable emotions of youth have been preserved to receive their full and due expression in retrospect. For the interesting feelings of age are not just different feelings; they are feelings into which the feelings of youth are integrated.

Yeats's development in his dramatic poetry is as interesting as that in his lyrical poetry. I have spoken of him as having been a lyric poet — in a sense in which I should not think of myself, for instance, as lyric; and by this I mean rather a certain kind of selection of emotion rather than particular metrical forms. But there is no reason why a lyric poet should not also be a dramatic poet; and to me Yeats is the type of lyrical dramatist. It took him many years to evolve the dramatic form suited to his genius. When he first began to write plays, poetic drama meant plays written in blank verse. Now, blank verse has been a dead metre for a long time. It would be outside of my frame to go into all the reasons for that now: but it is obvious that a form which was handled so supremely well by Shakespeare has its disadvantages. If you are writing a play of the same type as Shakespeare's, the reminiscence is oppressive; if you are writing a play of a different type, it is distracting. Furthermore, as Shakespeare is so much greater than any dramatist who has followed him, blank verse can hardly be dissociated from the life of the sixteenth and seventeenth centuries: it can hardly catch the rhythms with which English is spoken nowadays. I think that if anything like regular blank verse is ever to be re-established, it can be after a long departure from it, during the course of which it will have liberated itself from period associations. At the time of Yeats's early plays it was not possible to use anything else for a poetry play: that is not a criticism of Yeats himself, but an assertion that changes in verse forms come at one moment and not at another. His early verse-plays, including the *Green Helmet*, which is written in a kind of irregular rhymed fourteener, have a good deal of beauty in them, and, at least, they are the best verse-plays written in their time. And even in these, one notices some development of irregularity in the metric. Yeats did not quite invent a new metre, but the blank verse of his later plays shows a great advance towards one; and what is most astonishing is the virtual abandonment of blank verse metre in *Purgatory*. One device used with great success in some of the later plays is the lyrical choral interlude. But another, and important, cause of improvement is the gradual purging out of poetical ornament. This, perhaps, is the most painful part of the labour, so far as the versification goes, of the modern poet

who tries to write a play in verse. The course of improvement
is towards a greater and greater starkness. The beautiful line
for its own sake is a luxury dangerous even for the poet who
has made himself a virtuoso of the technique of the theatre.
What is necessary is a beauty which shall not be in the line or
the isolable passage, but woven into the dramatic texture itself;
so that you can hardly say whether the lines give grandeur to
the drama, or whether it is the drama which turns the words
into poetry. [One of the most thrilling lines in *King Lear* is
the simple:

Never, never, never, never, never

but, apart from a knowledge of the context, how can you say
that it is poetry, or even competent verse?] Yeats's purification
of his verse becomes much more evident in the four *Plays for
Dancers* and in the two in the posthumous volume: those, in
fact, in which he had found his right and final dramatic form.

It is in the first three of the *Plays for Dancers*, also, that he
shows the internal, as contrasted with the external, way of
handling Irish myth of which I have spoken earlier. In the earlier plays, as in the earlier poems, about legendary heroes and
heroines, I feel that the characters are treated, with the respect
that we pay to legend, as creatures of a different world from
ours. In the later plays they are universal men and women. I
should, perhaps, not include *The Dreaming of the Bones* quite
in this category, because Dermot and Devorgilla are characters
from modern history, not figures of pre-history; but I would
remark in support of what I have been saying that in this play
these two lovers have something of the universality of Dante's
Paolo and Francesca, and this the younger Yeats could not
have given them. So with the Cuchulain of *The Hawk's Well*,
the Cuchulain, Emer and Eithne of *The Only Jealousy of
Emer*; the myth is not presented for its own sake, but as a
vehicle for a situation of universal meaning.

I see at this point that I may have given the impression, contrary to my desire and my belief, that the poetry and the plays of Yeats's earlier period can be ignored in favour of his later work. You cannot divide the work of a great poet so sharply as that. Where there is the continuity of such a positive personality and such a single purpose, the later work cannot be understood, or properly enjoyed, without a study and appreciation of the earlier; and the later work again reflects light upon the earlier, and shows us beauty and significance not before perceived. We have also to take account of the historical conditions. As I have said above, Yeats was born into the end of a literary movement, and an English movement at that: only those who have toiled with language know the labour and constancy required to free oneself from such influences — yet, on the other hand, once we are familiar with the older voice, we can hear its individual tones even in his earliest published verse. In my own time of youth there seemed to be no immediate great powers of poetry either to help or to hinder, either to learn from or to rebel against, yet I can understand the difficulty of the other situation, and the magnitude of the task. With the verse-play, on the other hand, the situation is reversed, because Yeats had nothing, and we have had Yeats. He started writing plays at a time when the prose-play of contemporary life seemed triumphant, with an indefinite future stretching before it, when the comedy of light farce dealt only with certain privileged strata of metropolitan life; and when the serious play tended to be an ephemeral tract on some transient social problem. We can begin to see now that even the imperfect early attempts he made are probably more permanent literature than the plays of Shaw; and that his dramatic work as a whole may prove a stronger defence against the successful urban Shaftesbury Avenue vulgarity which he opposed as stoutly as they. Just as, from the beginning, he made and thought his poetry in terms of speech and not in terms of print, so in the drama he always meant to write plays to be played and not merely to be read. He cared, I think, more for the theatre as an organ for the expression of the consciousness of a people, than as a means to his own fame or achievement; and I am convinced that it is only if you serve it in this spirit that you can hope to accomplish anything worth doing with it. Of course, he had some great advantages, the recital of which does not rob him of any of his glory: his colleagues, a people with a natural and unspoilt gift for speech and for acting. It is impossible to disentangle what he did for the Irish theatre from what the Irish theatre did for him. From this point of advantage, the idea of the poetic drama was kept alive when everywhere else it had been driven underground. I do not know where our debt to him as a dramatist ends — and in time, it will not end until that drama itself ends. In his occasional writings on dramatic topics he has asserted certain principles to which we must hold fast: such as the primacy of the poet over the actor, and of the actor over the scene-painter; and the principle that the theatre, while it need not be concerned only with 'the people' in the narrow Russian sense, must be for the people; that to be permanent it must concern itself with fundamental situations. Born into a world in which the doctrine of 'Art for Art's sake' was generally accepted, and living on into one in which art has been asked to be instrumental to social purposes, he held firmly to the right view which is between these, though not in any way a compromise between them, and showed that an artist, by serving his art with entire integrity, is at the same time rendering the greatest service he can to his own nation and to the whole world.

To be able to praise, it is not necessary to feel complete agreement; and I do not dissimulate the fact that there are aspects of Yeats's thought and feeling which to myself are unsympathetic. I say this only to indicate the limits which I have set to my criticism. The questions of difference, objection and protest arise in the field of doctrine, and these are vital questions. I have been concerned only with the poet and dramatist, so far as these can be isolated. In the long run they cannot be wholly isolated. A full and elaborate examination of the total work of Yeats must some day be undertaken; perhaps it will need a longer perspective. There are some poets whose poetry can be considered more or less in isolation, for experience and delight. There are others whose poetry, though giving equally experience and delight, has a larger historical importance. Yeats was one of the latter: he was one of those few whose history is the history of their own time, who are a part of the consciousness of an age which cannot be understood without them. This is a very high position to assign to him: but I believe that it is one which is secure.

Printed in the USA
CPSIA information can be obtained
at www.ICGtesting.com
LVHW090803150724
785511LV00004B/364